GW01081226

To Fred,

From Margaret,

With all my love
on your birthday.

15 Sept '03.

£22 £30
29/9/23
14/12/23
28/8/24

'OUR TREASURE OF ANTIQUITIES'

'OUR TREASURE OF ANTIQUITIES'

Beranger and Bigari's antiquarian sketching tour of Connacht in 1779

Based on material in the National Library of Ireland and the Royal Irish Academy

Peter Harbison

With photographs by Josephine Shields

in association with

The National Library of Ireland

First published 2002
Wordwell Ltd
 PO Box 69, Bray, Co. Wicklow
Copyright © The author

All rights reserved. No part of this book may be reprinted or reproduced or utilised in any electronic, mechanical or other means, now known or hereafter invented, including photocopying and recording, or otherwise without either the prior written consent of the publishers or a licence permitting restricted copying in Ireland issued by the Irish Copyright Licensing Agency Ltd, The Writers' Centre, 19 Parnell Square, Dublin 1.

Frontispiece Pastel on paper self-portrait of Gabriel Beranger (*c.* 1729/30–1817) in the National Gallery of Ireland (3292).

Cover design: Wordwell Ltd.

ISBN 1 869857 53 4

British Library Cataloguing-in-Publication Data.
A catalogue record for this book is available from the British Library.

This publication has received support from the Heritage Council under the 2002 Publications Grant Scheme.
The author also gratefully acknowledges tremendous assistance of various kinds from the National Library of Ireland.

Typeset in Ireland by Wordwell Ltd.
Repro: Niamh MacKenzie.
Duotones: Atomic Ltd
Editor: Emer Condit.

Book design: Nick Maxwell.

Printed in Spain by E.G: ZURE, E-48950 Erandio-Bizkaia

Published in association with the National Library of Ireland.

CONTENTS

FOREWORD

The National Library's Department of Prints and Drawings holds a rich and varied collection of about 100,000 works covering all aspects of Irish life and history, including an extensive collection of topographical prints and drawings. Among our most notable holdings are drawings by antiquarian artists Gabriel Beranger, Austin Cooper, and Francis and Daniel Grose, and their associates. These works are an invaluable record of Ireland and its buildings as they were in the late eighteenth and early nineteenth centuries.

The drawings by Gabriel Beranger and Angelo Maria Bigari which are the subject of this book are significant not only because they provide contemporary observations of abbeys, castles and other antiquities, many of which have since disappeared, but also because they show us a part of Ireland which was largely ignored by landscape painters of the period. Although depictions of Connemara appear more frequently through the nineteenth century, scenes from the provinces of Ulster and Connacht were not among the 'preferred landscapes' more popular among patrons of the arts a century earlier. The drawings which survive from Beranger and Bigari's 1779 tour are therefore a particularly valuable visual record of lesser-known sites and monuments.

Beranger and Bigari's journey is also represented among our other collections: our Department of Manuscripts holds material relating to both Beranger and Cooper, who acquired the pictorial material around 1810, while Sir William Wilde's published version of Beranger's diary of the tour is held in our printed books collection.

The Cooper Collection, which contains the 'Tour of Connacht' material, is not only the most extensive but also among the best-documented collections of surviving eighteenth-century antiquarian topographical drawings. Following the acquisition of the main collection by the Library in 1994, Dr Harbison prepared a full catalogue and this, together with records for the Cooper and Grose collections, can be consulted through the Prints and Drawings on-line catalogue, together with accompanying digitised images. These are among more than 7000 records of the holdings of the Department of Prints and Drawings currently listed in the on-line catalogue and accessible via the Library's website.

The antiquarian and topographical drawings from the 1779 tour of Connacht should be of interest to all those concerned with Irish art, architecture and history. For this reason, the National Library is pleased to support the present publication as part of a continuing programme designed to focus attention on the great storehouse of treasures which the Library contains.

Brendan O Donoghue
Director
National Library of Ireland

ACKNOWLEDGEMENTS

This book would never have come to fruition had it not been for the enthusiastic support of Brendan O Donoghue, Director of the National Library, and I would like to express my deepest thanks to him for having made it happen. Equally, my gratitude goes to his predecessor, Dr Pat Donlon, whose acquisition of the Cooper Collection for the National Library was the catalyst for the idea for this book, in which the Collection plays such a crucial role. Joanna Finegan, curator of the Prints and Drawings Section of the National Library, has gone far beyond the call of duty (as did her predecessor, Colette O'Daly) to facilitate my every wish in regard to all the drawings in their care, and Elizabeth Kirwan of the Manuscripts Department equally went out of her way to help me with the manuscripts and plans which she curates. My thanks are also gratefully extended to the former owner of the collection, Austin Cooper, who, with his wife Peg, allowed me to stay in their home long enough to be able to study the collection — and to realise the importance of its contents which his family had preserved so carefully for generations. Further pictorial material in this volume has been willingly supplied by the Royal Irish Academy, which I would like to thank here for its permission to reproduce it, given so graciously on the Academy's behalf by its Chief Librarian, Siobhán O'Rafferty. I am also much in the debt of her staff, Bernadette Cunningham, Deputy Librarian, Patrick Kelly, Karl Vogelsang, Petra Schnabel, Dympna Moore and Marcus Browne, for having been so helpful in providing me with information, books, and the photographs so obligingly taken and supplied by John Kennedy of the Green Studio. I would also like to express my grateful thanks to Andrew Bonar Law for his unfailing courtesy and help in supplying me with engravings, particularly of the hand-coloured variety, and whose Neptune Gallery is a treasure house of ancient prints. To Professor Pádraig Ó Macháin of the Institute for Advanced Studies my special thanks for having gone to the trouble of providing me with both a transcription and a translation of the Terrence McGuire text on Clonmacnois, which is an unexpected treasure of this work. Derek Cullen and Clive Brooks of Bord Fáilte have facilitated my use of photographs of paintings in Westport House, and I would equally like to express my gratitude to their owner, Lord Altamont, for acquiescing so readily in my reproducing them here. Among the many people who have been so forthcoming with assistance and information of one kind or another in the preparation of this volume, I would like to single out particularly Tim Boland, Gerry Bracken, Professor Anne Crookshank, Maurice Craig, Mairéad Dunlevy, Fr Vincent Kelly, Heather King, the Knight of Glin, Avice-Claire McGovern, Dr Edward McParland, Bernard Nurse, Michael O'Hara, Professor Nollaig Ó Muraíle, Noel O'Neill, Michael O'Sullivan, Moira and Christy Tighe of Cromleac Lodge, Martin Timoney, John Warren, David Willis and his wife Mary, and Professor Barbara Wright, as well as John Grimes, Rodney and Trudy Lomax, Ken Henry and Peter Walsh for facilitating the necessary trips to islands visited by Beranger and Bigari in 1779. A special word of thanks to Kathleen Roche, who, as if by magic, produced a clean text on disc from my over-corrected and many-times-changed typed versions.

The production and design of this book owe a great deal to the work of Nick Maxwell and his team at Wordwell, in particular Emer Condit, Maura Laverty, Niamh MacKenzie and Rachel Dunne. Also Xat and Stephen at Atomic Ltd for their work and advice on the duotone reproductions of Josephine Shields's photographs. Finally, I would like to express my gratitude to my wife Edelgard for her kind-hearted indulgence and goodwill during the long period of parturition of this book. To her, and all those mentioned above, my most heartfelt thanks.

Josephine Shields wishes to thank Dermot O'Hara and Rose and George Macnamara for their hospitality, her father, William F. Shields, for his support, and her daughter Isabel for her patience and understanding. But, most of all, she would like to express her indebtedness to Kathleen Rose for her unfailing technical assistance and constant encouragement, without which this photographic project would not have been possible.

PICTORIAL ACKNOWLEDGEMENTS

National Gallery of Ireland Frontispiece

Tim O'Neill Map pp ix–x

Kildare Street and University Club Fig. 1

Royal Irish Academy Figs 2, 3, 27, 52, 85, 86, 88, 90, 122, 141, 143, 144 and 149; Pls 3, 5, 7, 8, 10, 11, 12, 13, 14, 15, 16, 17, 19, 20, 21 and 23

After William Wilde, *Memoir of Gabriel Beranger* (1880) Fig. 4

National Library of Ireland Figs 5, 6, 9, 10, 11, 18, 21, 23, 29, 30, 32, 33, 35, 37, 38, 44, 46, 50, 53, 59, 61, 65, 67, 69, 71, 73, 74, 77, 80, 82, 83, 96, 100, 103, 106, 109, 111, 114, 119, 123, 126, 127, 130, 131, 134, 135, 140, 145, 150, 153, 154, 158, 160, 162, 165, 170, 171, 174, 177, 178, 180, 181, 182, 184, 185, 186, 189, 192, 195, 197, 200, 201, 203, 204, 205, 208, 210, 211 and 214; Pls 2, 4, 18 and 22

Josephine Shields Figs 7, 8, 12, 15, 17, 19, 20, 22, 24, 26, 28, 31, 39, 40, 43, 45, 47, 49, 51, 55, 57, 63, 66, 70, 75, 76, 79, 81, 87, 89, 91, 93, 95, 97 (both), 98, 101, 104, 105, 108, 110, 113, 115, 118, 124, 132, 137, 138, 139, 142, 152, 156 (all three), 157, 164, 167, 169, 172, 173, 175, 179, 183,188, 196, 198, 199, 202 and 213

After Grose's *Antiquities of Ireland* (1794–6) — engravings kindly supplied by Andrew Bonar Law of the Neptune Gallery, and the National Library of Ireland — Figs 13, 14, 16, 25, 36, 48, 54, 56, 60, 64, 68, 72, 78, 84, 92, 94, 99, 102, 107, 112, 116, 117, 125, 129, 133, 151, 155, 159, 161, 163, 166, 168, 176, 187, 191, 193, 206, 207 and 212

Peter Harbison Figs 34, 41, 42, 62, 128, 136, 146, 147, 148, 190, 194 and 209; Pls 9 and 24

Paul Caponigro Fig. 58

Bord Fáilte Éireann, by courtesy of Lord Altamont Figs 120 and 121

Mrs Pauline Mossop Pl. 1

Brian Lynch Pl. 6

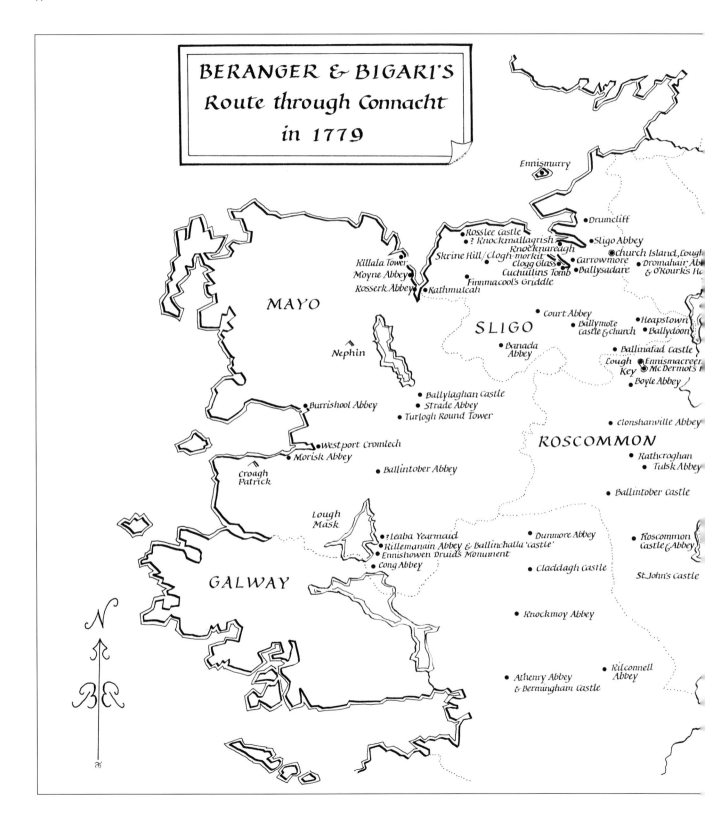

BERANGER & BIGARI'S Route through Connacht in 1779

Ennismurry

Drumcliff

Rosslee Castle
? Knockmallagrish
Knocknareagh
Sligo Abbey
Skrine Hill/Clogh-morkit
church Island, Lough
Killala Tower
clogg Glass
Carrowmore
Dromahair Ab
Moyne Abbey
Cuchullins Tomb
Ballysadare
& O'Rourk's Ha
Rosserk Abbey
Rathmulcah
Finnmacool's Griddle

MAYO

Court Abbey
SLIGO
Heapstown
Ballymote
Castle & church
Ballydoon

Banada
Abbey
Ballinafad Castle
Lough
Ennismacreen
Key
McDermots
Nephin

Boyle Abbey

Ballylaghan Castle
Burrishool Abbey
Strade Abbey
Clonshanville Abbey
Turlogh Round Tower

ROSCOMMON

Westport Cromlech
Rathcroghan
Morisk Abbey
Tulsk Abbey
Croagh
Patrick
Ballintober Abbey
Ballintober Castle

Lough
Mask
? Leaba Yearmaud
Dunmore Abbey
Roscommon
Rillemanain Abbey & Ballinchalla 'castle'
Castle & Abbey
Ennishowen Druids Monument
Cong Abbey
Claddagh Castle
St.John's Castle

GALWAY

Knockmoy Abbey

Kilconnell
Abbey
Athenry Abbey
& Bermingham Castle

N

Map by Tim O'Neill of the places visited on the tour of 1779.

1 . INTRODUCTION

'Our treasure of Antiquities', the title of this volume, was a phrase used in a letter from the artist Gabriel Beranger to Col. William Burton of Slane, dated 3 August 1779 (Nat. Lib. MS 1415, p. 100), to describe the collection of drawings which he and his friend Bigari had already produced in the course of an antiquarian sketching tour of Connacht — the most extensive archaeological survey undertaken in Ireland before the Ordnance Survey began its comprehensive fieldwork in the 1830s. Together with Vallancey's journal *Collectanea de rebus Hibernicis*, it was a core activity of the short-lived Hibernian Antiquarian Society, which focused amateur interest on extolling the physical remains of the country's past in the years leading up to the foundation of the Royal Irish Academy in 1785. This expedition, therefore, played a seminal role in the early development of archaeological endeavour in Ireland, and deserves a fresh and comprehensive study, particularly now that new pictorial material has come into the public domain which allows a much more vivid reconstruction to be made of the tour than that which Sir William Wilde so nobly attempted in the 1870s without any original illustrations at all.

The dynamo behind both the whole scheme and the Society was William Burton (*Fig. 1*) himself, privy councillor, teller of the Exchequer, antiquarian, entrepreneur and first treasurer of the Royal Irish Academy, whose career was fully examined in an article by C.E.F. Trench in the 1985 volume of the *Journal of the Royal Society of Antiquaries of Ireland.*

Born William Burton in Buncraggy, Co. Clare, in 1733, he dropped his family name in favour of Conyngham when he inherited Slane Castle — and a fortune — from his uncle in 1781, but the frequently used combined form, Burton Conyngham, is the name generally used here. He had seen Frederick Grose produce volumes of engravings illustrating British antiquities during the mid-1770s and, though we have no evidence, it is even possible that the two may have met when Grose paid a short visit to Ireland in 1770. But, more pertinently, the views of Ireland, almost all based on drawings by the Hon. John Dawson (later Lord Carlow), which were engraved for Paul Sandby's *Virtuosi's Museum*, dated 1778, may have put into his

Fig. 1
William Burton, later the Rt Hon. William Conyngham (1733–96) of Slane Castle, Co. Meath, from an eighteenth-century engraving.

head the 'intention of publishing a large work on ye Antiquities and Curiosities of Ireland' (Nat. Lib. MS 1415, p. 131) at a time when rediscovery of the past was burgeoning in Irish minds only a few short years before Grattan's Parliament began to make its own decisions independent of Westminster. A letter probably addressed to Burton Conyngham by Edward Ledwich, vicar of Aghaboe in County Laois, dated 6 April 1779 (MS 1415, p. 122), indicates that Burton was considering the possibility of publishing a specimen, just to test the waters of public interest, and a follow-up letter of 1 May (*ibid.*, p. 130) intimates that he may even have been harbouring the notion of having a separate volume of engravings for each county — an idea which Ledwich thought 'might be too voluminous'. But a much earlier letter from Ledwich, of 26 November of the previous year (*ibid.*, pp 120–1) — this time probably written to Col. Charles Vallancey, who had been a member of the Royal Dublin Society's antiquarian Select Committee of 1772–4 — makes it clear that, already in 1778, a collection of pictures was being assembled (presumably for potential engraving), some of which had been copied by Gabriel Beranger from the work of other artists. These copies Ledwich thought to be a disfigurement rather than an embellishment of the source material, 'a propision of daubing, which injured the truth and perspective of the original' that was 'more calculated for the ignorant and superficial than the intelligent and lovers of virtu'. He had a point when he said that he thought that, when engravings were to be made, they should be based on originals rather than on Beranger's copies, but the latter were probably executed so that at least some of the illustrations being gathered for a potential volume of engravings should be ensured of a fairly uniform style and format (though compare the Paul Sandby comment on p. 216). In this same letter, Ledwich stated that Beranger was not a genius, had but little taste, 'and besides he is poor'. 'Let Beranger be paid for his trouble', Ledwich continued, 'and let him be employed in what he can be usefull, but let not an hungry artist swallow up whatever profits may arise, when those profits, judiciously applied, will promote the work, by paying for new drawings, etc.' Presumably wanting to get into Burton Conyngham's good books so that he could be rescued from his rural vicarage and brought to Dublin, where his talents could be used to advantage in writing texts for an Irish version of Grose (as they were to be more than a decade later), Ledwich was obviously jealous of the head start that Beranger already had in helping Burton Conyngham to fulfil his dreams.

To further his 'very laudable plan in rescuing from oblivion the antiquities of this country' (MS 1415, pp 115–16), Burton Conyngham brought together a small group of serious-minded people over dinner at his townhouse in Harcourt Place in Dublin one evening in February 1779, and formed the Hibernian Antiquarian Society, with himself as president and Vallancey playing a valuable supporting role. Ledwich — who, some months previously, had suggested, apparently to Vallancey, the idea of appointing a committee (MS 1415, p. 121) — was also a founding member, and Walter D. Love, whose definitive history of the Society appeared in the Autumn 1962 edition of the Jesuit magazine *Studies*, pointed out that Ledwich's inclusion 'from the beginning was portentous; for it was he who was to provoke fatal discord' that was to lead to the virtual collapse of the Society after a life of only four years. No one was more surprised to be asked to join the Society than Charles O'Conor (*Fig. 2*) of Belanagare in County Roscommon, the famous Gaelic scholar and collector of manuscripts, who found himself to be the only Catholic member among Ascendancy Protestants at a

Fig. 2
Portrait of the well-known antiquarian and Gaelic scholar Charles O'Conor of Belanagare (1710–91) which hangs in the Royal Irish Academy. He guided Bigari and Beranger to the venerable site at Rathcroghan, near his County Roscommon home.

time when his brother was using 'anti-popery' laws to take his land and livelihood away from him, simply because he was a Catholic. In a letter preserved among the O'Conor manuscripts at Clonalis, quoted by Walter Love, Charles O'Conor — whose biography was written by Diarmaid O Catháin in the 1989 volume of the *Journal of the Royal Society of Antiquaries of Ireland* — said that, at the founding dinner in February, a plan had been laid for rescuing Irish antiquities from their obscurity, and that, if Col. Burton could infuse his own spirit into others, the plan would surely succeed.

Writing presumably to Burton Conyngham from his Dublin address at 58 Pill-lane on 10 April 1779 (MS 1415, pp 135–6), O'Conor expressed the honour of being

as assistant as I can, in your scheme of bringing to light, all that can be recovered of the Antiquities of this Country. To search into our Carns, Raths and other antient structures above ground, as well as into our artificial caves (structures under ground) is to begin well. Such a search would not, I conceive, end in the gratification of pure curiosity; it may lead us to useful knowledge also, by giving us as far as it will go, a true idea of the state of the Arts, and consequently of manners in the earlier ages of civil Government in Ireland.

His cooperation had doubtless been sought because of his expertise in Gaelic manuscripts — an interest which Burton Conyngham encouraged him to pursue — and, in the same letter, he wrote that

a critical review of our antient writings would come on of course, and enable us to discover the true era of Authentic History, by separating the fabulous from the historical.

A further letter of his on p. 139 of the same manuscript, written five weeks later, on 14 May, states that he was delighted at the prospect of spending a vacation attending to Burton Conyngham's commands 'relatively to the Antiquities of this Country, so long neglected, and so little patronized', and added that he was setting off in a day or two for the County of Roscommon, 'where I expect soon to meet with M. Berenger, and attend him in excursions which will be partly under as well as over ground'.

Even if it was to be some months before the two were to meet on Roscommon soil, it is obvious that plans were already being laid by March of 1779 at the latest to undertake a tour of Connacht. That Beranger himself was involved in the planning and preparations for the trip at this early stage is seen in a letter (p. 36 below) from Col. Lewis Irwin of Tanrego, about eight miles west of Sligo, dated 26 March 1779. In it he confirmed that he had received a letter from M. Berenger, written by the 'Directions' of Burton Conyngham, asking for his (Irwin's) assistance for the artists employed by the Antiquarian Society, and requesting details of anything that may be deemed worthy of notice. In a letter of 10 April of that year (same manuscript, p. 136), Charles O'Conor had recommended Irwin to Burton Conyngham as someone who could be 'very useful to your draughtsmen'. Whether they were called 'artists' or 'draughtsmen', it is clear that, from as early as March of 1779, Burton Conyngham had decided that there should be more than one of them undertaking the tour. Irwin, incidentally, already seems to have been acquainted with Beranger, for in a letter — presumably to Burton Conyngham — of 23 April 1779 (once again MS 1415, this time pp 155–6) he says that

> I hope my acquaintance Berenger may be employed on this circuit, as from my knowledge of him, he would make the party more agreable to me, as over and above his qualifications for such an undertaking, he has a general discernment and manners to recommend him.

As we shall see, Beranger's admiration for Irwin grew daily as the tour progressed. But it is perhaps appropriate to pause at this juncture to ask why there should have been a 'tour of Connaught' only and not of any other province, and who and why were the two artists selected to undertake it. The answer to the first question probably lies in the portfolio of drawings that Burton Conyngham had already amassed by the early months of 1779. Some day I hope to be able to reconstruct, as far as is possible, the contents of his collection — original drawings and plans, as well as other artists' work which, as copied by Beranger, came in for such criticism from Ledwich's somewhat poisoned pen. But the likelihood is that it contained little material from Connacht. I suspect that Ulster was not very well covered either, and so a tour of that northern province should also possibly have been considered — but the fact that there is no sign that any thought was given to the matter would suggest that there was more northern material in the collection than one might suspect.

It is apparent from a letter from Ralph Ousley, written at Dunmore, Co. Galway, on 16 April 1779 (MS 1415, p. 169), that Burton Conyngham had posted off to various members of the landed gentry multiple copies of a 'printed scheme', presumably looking for information about antiquities worthy of notice, accompanied by a request that the sheets should be 'dispersed' to 'the most likely people' in the neighbourhood. In addition, Burton Conyngham's 'printed scheme' must have asked that he be sent or lent any drawings of antiquities which may already have been in existence, of which Ousley (MS 1415, pp 169 and 179) — in answer to Burton Conyngham's request — sent four views, and subsequently a further three (subjects unspecified). But, other than these, I know of only three Connacht drawings which were probably in Burton Conyngham's collection before the start of the tour in June 1779. One was of a detail of Sligo Abbey, which we know about because of an entry on p. 4 of the National Library's manuscript 4162 to be quoted below (p. 39), telling us that Col. Burton had given the artists a drawing of the tombs of the O'Connors in Sligo Abbey (without, however, saying whose work it was). He had presumably given it to them so that they could check its accuracy

Fig. 3
Sir William Wilde
(1815–76), from a
photograph after a
drawing by B.
Mulrenin.

on the spot, as this was certainly the case with the second drawing, one of Boyle Abbey on p. 52 of the National Library's album 1958 TX, illustrated in my book *Beranger's Antique Buildings of Ireland* (1998). It is a watercolour by Beranger based on an original by Major John Corneille, on which the copying artist wrote 'I have compared this drawing on the spot with the original & found it Exact in 1779'. The map on p. 223 of *Antique Buildings* showing the geographical locations of the sites covered in this album only underlines what a glaring void Connacht was — except for Boyle, where the abbey may have offered an interesting subject to draw for soldiers stationed in the barracks there. The same abbey was also the subject of the third drawing, executed by J. Warren, sen., which Beranger copied into p. 42 of the companion album in the Royal Irish Academy (MS 3.C.30), where he likewise noted on it 'I compared this with the original on ye spot in 1779 & found it exact', suggesting that he also had this drawing with him on the tour. If, therefore, Burton Conyngham and the Hibernian Antiquarian Society wanted to give coverage to the whole of Ireland, and to cherish all the provinces of the island equally in the proposed volumes of engravings, it would have been absolutely necessary to mount an expedition to Connacht to remedy the lack of any considerable corpus of readily available material from the province. By the spring of 1779, Burton Conyngham had probably already selected the two artists he needed for the tour — Beranger and Bigari — and to these we must now turn.

Of the two, Beranger (*frontispiece*) is certainly the better known, thanks primarily to the efforts of Sir William Wilde (*Fig. 3*) who, in a series of articles in the *Journal of the Royal Historical and Archaeological Association of Ireland* in the early 1870s, dragged him out of the oblivion into which he had fallen after his death in 1817. These articles were subsequently collected by his widow 'Speranza' and published in book form in 1880 with the grandiose title *Memoir of Gabriel Beranger, and his labours in the cause of Irish art and antiquities, from 1760 to 1780*. It was this work of Wilde's which permitted the piecing together of the details of Beranger's fruitful and active life. He was born in Rotterdam of French Huguenot parents around 1729, and came to Dublin, according to Wilde (3), 'in order to unite by marriage the two branches of his family' — the Irish branch being perhaps the Berangers who are known to have lived near Carbury, Co. Kildare, in the eighteenth century. He kept a print shop and artist's warehouse at No. 5 South Great George's Street from 1766 until at least 1779, and was probably fully occupied in Burton Conyngham's employ during the active years of the Hibernian Antiquarian Society (1779–83). When, presumably, it could no longer put his talents to use, Beranger decided to set up shop again at another address in George's Street, where he placed on offer an unexpectedly wide range of goods, as we know from a fascinating advertisement in *The Volunteer Evening Post* of 25–27 November 1783, which I came across through the work of John Andrews and which runs as follows:

BEAVER NIGHT-CAPS, GLOVES and STOCKINGS, just imported
BY GABRIEL BERANGER, Painter, No. 67, Great George's-street, South, who acquaints the Nobility, Gentry and his Friends, that he has opened an Artist's shop, where the Lovers of the Fine Arts may be supplied with the under-named articles, the goodness of which, together with his constant endeavours to please, will, he flatters himself, insure him their countenance and favour.

Water colours in shells	Carmine
Do. in drops	Ultramarine
Do. in boxes	Drop lake
Do. liquids	Paintings in oil
Reeves's colours in cakes	Do. in watercolours
Italian and French chalks	Flowers painted from nature
Tools for painters	Tracing paper
Camel hair pencils	Elephant paper
Pallets for oil colours	Imperial do.
Ivory do. for watercolours	Super royal do.
Ivory do. for miniatures	Royal do.
Pallet knives	Medium do.
Pencil sticks	Ink stands
Indian rubber	Pocket ink-horns
Blacklead pencils	Ivory paper-cutters
Port crayons	Pounce boxes
Flags and mullers	Pen knives
Indian ink, and marble for do.	Sealing wax
Rules	Wafers

Maps of surveys copied and ornamented, —framing and glazing done in the neatest manner. Mr Beranger teaches Ladies and Gentlemen to paint and draw landscapes and flowers.

Seemingly everything there for the aspiring artist, you might think, but Beranger's new business may not have prospered, and he appears to have rounded off his career with a steady (if possibly slightly dull) position as assistant ledger keeper in the Government Exchequer Office, procured for him, no doubt, by Burton Conyngham.

His first wife was a cousin and, after her death, he married *en secondes noces* a French lady named Mestayer, who seems to have had enough private means to enable Beranger to live in comfortable retirement until his death at No. 12 St Stephen's Green on 18 February 1817. He was buried in the Huguenot cemetery in Peter Street, but, when it was needed for building purposes in 1967, Beranger's remains were transferred to Mount Jerome Cemetery, where they now lie.

To judge by Beranger's surviving watercolours, he began to visit and sketch antiquities in the Dublin area in the 1760s, and it was his penchant for making drawings of ancient buildings (only two or three of which were ever published in his lifetime) that probably brought him to the attention of Burton Conyngham, and led to his being chosen for the Connacht trip. We know that he exhibited seascapes with the Society of Artists in the 1760s and early 1770s (A.M. Stewart (ed.), *Irish art loan exhibitions, 1765–1927* (Dublin 1990), 49), though none of these can now be recognised, and Wilde (29–30) enthuses about his flower and bird drawings, which I have not been able to locate. He has left us hundreds of watercolours of antiquities in many parts of Ireland, some his own compositions (including a number of duplicates), others copied from original works by other artists. These were preserved in two companion albums, one in the National Library (1958 TX) and the other in the Royal Irish Academy (MS 3.C.30), which also houses two similar but smaller postcard-size albums of 'Rambles in County Dublin etc'. In addition, there are a great many of his drawings scattered in private collections, mainly in and around Dublin.

Beranger was a good-looking man, with an eye for the ladies. This we can infer from his appreciation of the embraces from the fair sex which he got at Inishmurray (p. 58) and Rathmulcah (p. 113), as well as wanting to leave the gentlemen at their bottle so that he could escape to the ladies at a family gathering in Castle Kelly, Co. Galway (p. 192). As made clear by the remarks quoted above in a letter from Lewis Irwin, he was obviously a genial companion who, as Wilde (28) noted, 'appeared to relish Irish fun'. Wilde gives an excellent thumbnail sketch of him, as if he had known him all his life (though the two never met):

> spare in person, of middle height, his natural hair powdered and gathered into a queue; he had a sharp, well-cut brow and good bushy eyebrows, divided by the special artistic indentation; a clear, observant, square-ended nose, that snuffed humbug and took in fun; clear, quick, brown eyes; a well-cut dramatic mouth, eloquent and witty [Wilde, 28]

— not all of which can be seen in the miniature self-portrait in the National Gallery of Ireland which acts as the frontispiece here.

Wilde suggests that he was self-taught as an artist, which, he says, may account for the sense of undoubted stiffness in his drawings, and his shortcomings as a painter of landscape and trees. But, for us, the great value of Beranger's drawings lies in their depiction of buildings as they were in the eighteenth century, and they are imbued with an even greater historical value when those buildings have either partially disintegrated or totally disappeared in the meantime. In addition, Beranger's watercolours give us a glimpse of the social elegance of the eighteenth century, and occasionally even provide vignettes of the more mundane side of rural life at the time. Beranger was obviously well-read on matters historical in Ireland, as can be seen from his remarks quoted below about Rathcroghan (pp 182–3) or the cromlech at Westport (p. 136), where he is not averse to criticising strongly the views of scholars where he thinks that there is justification for doing so. He also had an enquiring mind and, after a visit probably to Moyne in County Mayo where he was not able to find out what the surviving domestic rooms in the monastery were used for, he requested Burton Conyngham (MS 1415, p. 91) to procure 'a plan from France, of one of the old abbeys which are inhabited and intire' because, he thought, 'it would help greatly to determine by comparison what our remains were formerly'. Given that his parents were Huguenots, it is very probable that he spoke good French, coming out with the occasional French phrase in his correspondence with Burton Conyngham preserved in the National Library's manuscript 1415. In addition, this was probably his means of communication with his companion Bigari, who knew no English. Speaking French to one another led to some amusing incidents on the tour, when visiting places like Clones (p. 28) and Burrishoole (pp 132 and 137), where they were looked at askance and taken for French spies, because England was at war with France and Spain at the time over the American colonies. As Beranger put it in a letter to Burton Conyngham from Dunmore on 28 July 1779 (MS 1415, p. 97):

> We are known thro Connaught by the name of the french spies & fame spreads our renown in the towns longtime before we arrive in them. On all our expeditions we are surrounded by a hundred or two of spectators who sometimes obstruct our operations by the croud hindering us to act, as quick as we should do, if the place was empty. There is no driving them away, and as very few of them speak English we are, only sometimes troubled with their questions.

Beranger's travelling companion, Angelo Maria Bigari, came from Bologna and was described in Beranger's diary as a painter and architect (Wilde, 34). It may have been in his capacity as an architect that he apparently prepared a design for a grotto at Slane Castle in 1779, as we know from a letter in Italian (kindly translated for me by Professor Corinna Lonergan) sent by Bigari to Burton Conyngham and preserved as p. 111 of the manuscript 1415 in the National Library. According to Strickland's *Dictionary of Irish artists*, I (Dublin/London, 1913), pp 61–2, it was probably as a scene-painter that he came to work in Ireland, a career already followed successfully in London by his brother Francesco in the 1760s and early 1770s. Strickland says that he was employed by Thomas Ryder at Smock Alley Theatre shortly after it opened in 1772. According to pp 10–11 of an article by Sybil Rosenfeld and Edward Croft-Murray on eighteenth-century scene-painters working in Great Britain and Ireland published in *Theatre Notebook* vol. 19 for 1964 (for the reference to which I am grateful to Professor Anne Crookshank), Bigari was painting stage scenery in Dublin again in 1783–4, copying models sent from Covent Garden for *Castle of Andalusia* in 1783, painting scenery for *Harlequin Foundling* and making transparencies for *Medea and Jason* in the same year. Furthermore, according to the *Hibernian Journal* of 5 May 1784, he designed and executed a scene of Pluto's palace, as well as designing a Temple of Love and Hymen for Giordani's burlesque opera *Orpheus and Eurydice* in 1784. We last hear of him being complimented in the *Dublin Evening Post* of 22 January 1788 (for the reference to which I am grateful to Edward McParland). There it is stated that the ceiling of the New Theatre Royal 'on Crow Street, does honour to the masterly pencil of Bigari, as do two capital figures of Comedy and Tragedy which ornament the sides of the middle gallery'. What happens to him after that we know not, and no portrait of him is known to survive, but the tradition reported by Wilde (32) that Bigari painted the allegorical panels on the state coach of the lord mayor of Dublin (1790/91) has been scotched by Strickland and, more recently, by McEvansoneya.

His sense of theatre and drama was probably just what Burton Conyngham was looking for to create pictures of Irish antiquities that would be lively enough to appeal to lovers of engravings on both sides of the Irish Sea. Certainly one of the notable characteristics of his drawings is his sense of the dramatic, as in the group attending the funeral at Banada Abbey in County Sligo (*Fig. 71*), and, if the picture of 'Leabui Yearmaid' near Ballinchalla (*Fig. 140*) were copied after an original of his, which seems likely, it could almost be seen as a stage setting by itself. He also has the gift of imparting a sense of depth to buildings which — as shown by comparison with Josephine Shields's splendid on-the-same-spot black-and-white photographs reproduced here — are in reality not as extensive as he makes them out to be (e.g. Boyle and Ballintubber). The style of his pen and wash drawings is instantly recognisable because of his characteristic juxtaposition of horizontal and vertical blocks of masonry.

In a letter from Belanagare ('Balinagar'), dated 3 August 1779 (MS 1415, p. 101), Beranger praises his friend and fellow artist's abilities to Burton Conyngham when he writes:

> I am sure you will be pleased with Bigary's views, the excellent perspective deceives the eye, and one thinks to see the buildings themselves. Piranesy can not do better

— though it remains to be seen how pleased Piranesi would have been with the comparison. In talking of the frescos at Abbeyknockmoy (see p. 164), Beranger mentions that Bigari possessed 'the art of Fresco painter', and one intriguing reference in a letter which Beranger sent from Westport to Burton Conyngham on 19 July 1779 (MS 1415, p. 92) could suggest that he also did large landscape paintings in oils:

> There is a charming view from milord's house of an archipelago of islands called Achill 400 in number, some with immence hills, on the left is the main shore with the mountain of Croagh Patrick, rearing its lofty and picturesque head above all other hills. Milord has desired Mr. Bigary to draw this view, & when in Dublin, to paint it in oil as a large picture.

Around the late 1780s, Beranger added to the large Academy volume of watercolours (MS 3.C.30, p. 90) a copy of a Bigari picture illustrating what it calls Enniskillen Castle, but which is, in reality, Crom Castle on Lough Erne. It is shown from an angle similar to that seen on one of the four large unattributed landscape paintings created for and still preserved at Florence Court in County Fermanagh, where our two artists stayed during their tour. However, stylistic considerations pointed out to me by Professor Anne Crookshank and the Knight of Glin would make it difficult to ascribe any of these canvases to Bigari, and, in *The sublime and the beautiful, Irish art 1700–1830* (London, 2001), William Laffan has tentatively ascribed them to John Lewis.

In his letter of 3 August already quoted above, Beranger describes to Burton Conyngham how the two artists divided the workload between them, saying that Bigari

> has drawn most of the views, and my share has been the parts and doors, windows, monuments, circles of stone, cromliaghs and greatest part of the plans.

He continues by surmising that

> if the engraver does justice to the views, your work will have the advantage over most of those published. I am charmed with them every time I look them over.

However, a note of caution must be sounded at taking the views at face value as portraying what the artists actually saw. In a letter from Sligo, dated 2 July (MS 1415, p. 79) and thus early in the tour, Beranger admitted that

> we are become most terrible levellers. Since in our drawings we level without quarter, all those vile walls, with which ignorance had spoiled the elegance of Antiquity, we restore every thing on its ancient footing, opening arches, doors and windows

and they were still doing the same thing near the end of the tour at Tristernagh (see p. 207). Furthermore, close comparison of the views with the photographs taken by Josephine Shields from the artist's standpoint shows certain discrepancies, making us realise that a 'nice picture' was sometimes considered more desirable than absolute accuracy.

Being months away from home made Beranger a little uneasy about leaving his wife for so long, particularly as he thought that she would be a little shy about her want of money in his absence (MS 1415, p. 105). However, he would easily have been distracted from his domestic anxieties by the fact that the two artists were rarely without company on the tour, including that of their interpreter, Ter(r)ence McGuire, from near Swanlinbar, famous for its spa in the eighteenth century. He was 'a descendant of the princes of Fermanagh, and reduced to the station of schoolmaster of a little village' (Wilde, 38), who was obviously happy to earn a little extra money during his summer vacation. Four years earlier he had already shown an interest in history by writing a regnal list 'for the Revd. Father John Maguire, Parish Priest of Glinaly Anno 1775. August the 19th', as recorded in the supplementary sheets of the manuscript Advocates 72.3.1 in the National Library of Scotland (for the reference to which I am grateful to Pádraig Ó Macháin of the Dublin Institute for Advanced Studies). During the tour he continued to gather Irish traditions assiduously, as Beranger noted in a letter from Sligo of 25 June:

> we have also recovered the Irish poem of the Feast of O Roirk, which the priest of Drumahair has dictated to our Irish Literator. Said virtuoso is busy at present to write in Irish the traditions of Ennismurry or Island of Saints [Nat. Lib. MS 1415, 76]

and, in another letter of 12 July from Castle Gore, he speaks of the literator also having got some of the songs of the island, which contain the feats of Cuchullin (MS 1415, p. 86). Sadly, however, none of these has been preserved. Probably his only contribution from this tour to survive is a single sheet in Irish (*Fig. 204*) preserved in the Cooper Collection (shelf-mark Acc 4841, Folder 18 in the National Library), which contains information he recorded at Clonmacnois (see below, pp 201–2). He parted from the artists after having been exactly two months with them and, in appreciation, Beranger wrote to Burton Conyngham describing him as 'our honest interpretter who has attended us thro our tour, since the 17th of June, and which has behaved with all honesty and zeal, taking care of our horse and our self as much as in his power' (MS 1415, p. 108).

The other more sporadic company that the two artists had during their tour were the hosts with whom they stayed and who had apparently been asked to supervise them. Some of these actually accompanied them on their excursions. It seems likely that Burton Conyngham had not only planned the artists' tour carefully, giving instructions where to go, but had also given the travellers letters of introduction to their various hosts, many of whom would have been at least his acquaintances, and some even his friends who would have shared his antiquarian enthusiasms. The extracts from Beranger's Diary of the tour as published by Wilde show the pair of artists going from one large country house to another, and usually dining with the gentry who owned them.

Of the list of names thanked in a newspaper after the tour had concluded (pp 213–14), a number come in for special mention in the letters written by Beranger to Burton Conyngham in the course of the tour (collected together in the National Library's manuscript 1415). These include James Cuffe of Newtown Gore, who (according to MS 1415, p. 85) had some brass heads of ancient spears and battleaxes which he intended to present to Burton Conyngham; Lord Altamont of Westport, who opened a cromlech on his land to prove a theory of Beranger's; Ralph Ousley of Dunmore, who placed his horse at their disposal; and Sir John Browne of the Neale, who lent them money to keep their coffers filled and a coach for their excursions from his Mayo mansion. But none comes in for greater praise than Lewis Irwin of Tanrego House near Beltra, who, in his letter to Burton Conyngham of 23 April (MS 1415, pp 155–6), promised all in his power 'to promote the object of their Expedition', offering to meet the artists at Enniskillen and, should his affairs permit, 'accompany them so far, and to the extent of my acquaintance procure every assistance in their designs, and accomodations for themselves'. He did, in fact, accompany them enthusiastically in Fermanagh, Leitrim, Sligo, Roscommon and Mayo for over a month and, had not a letter from Sligo called him home on some important business, he would doubtless have stayed with them even longer. MS 1415, p. 80, would suggest that he had let his house for the summer, thus allowing him time to accompany the tourists while at the same time being able to make occasional use of the house — a handy arrangement.

Beranger and Bigari had such complete trust in Lewis Irwin's ability to guide that they knew they would miss nothing, and for them he was also 'a good ingenier, and helps us with indefatigable alacrity in taking up plans of the antiquities' — to the extent that his is the name printed on the plan of Rosserk (*Fig. 102*) in Grose's *Antiquities*. They were also grateful to him for helping them to distinguish between what is old masonry and what was added later (MS 1415, p. 79). He dined them 'like princes, so that, our table is rather too elegant, but such is the man, *un très galant homme*' (*ibid.*, p. 80). When the inhabitants of Inishmurray presented their landlord Irwin with a mether — one of those ancient Irish drinking-cups, square-topped so that four people could each have a corner for quaffing — he was generous enough to give it to the two artists to take back to the Antiquarian Society as a present (*ibid.*, pp 76–7). In Beranger's letters he is described as an 'indefatigable' man of 'iron' and 'steel', one who spared 'no pains, trouble or expense' in forwarding Burton Conyngham's undertaking and, on parting from him with the greatest of regret, Beranger said:

> we cannot enough express our sorrow in being deprived of him. he not only was an agreeable companion but an excellent guide and assistant in planning and measuring, in all our collateral excursions whether on sea loughs, or by land he provided saddle horses, or boats & provisions, and in all the inns where we were sometimes 4 days as headquarters, he treated us sumptuously and would never suffer us to pay a single farthing. his men had orders to mind our horses, he rubbed them with goulard & has cured them, in a word, never was greater attention [MS 1415, pp 87–8].

Certainly the help of a man like that was needed with coach and horses, because the coach kept breaking down: the axle-tree snapped at Strade (p. 128), and the mainspring, which they had had repaired at Clones, snapped again in County Galway, where they got it tied with iron at Athenry, and another clamp was put on it at Dunmore (MS 1415, p. 99). That notwithstanding, down it came again, and Mr Ousley got a 'fork made of iron at the Castle of Ballintober, in this county 15 miles from Dunmore, which held out until within 2 miles of this place [Belanagare] when it gave way again' (*ibid.*, pp 99–100).

The one thing our pair were determined to do was never to lose sight of

> our chaise which contain *our treasure of antiquities* [my italics], which in this rainy weather which we have got, must be kept dry [MS 1415, p. 100].

But it was not the rain threatening the proper storage of the drawings that troubled them most, it was the heat. What Beranger (MS 1415, p. 92) described as the 'broiling heat' affected the coach so much that it 'split our panels and shrivelled the apron in a lump'. It was not just the carriage which suffered, it was the humans too, who found the 'immence hot weather' so difficult to 'support' that 'in our chamber work we sit in our shirts only'. The heat, which Bigari thought was equal to that of Italy, has almost 'overpowerd us, and deprived us of part of our strength in preventing us from eating and sleeping. We live upon liquids only' (MS 1415, pp 87–8). Nevertheless, they were normally able to cover between sixteen and twenty (presumably Irish) miles in a day (*ibid.*, pp 80 and 85), usually in their chaise but sometimes on horseback. Bigari was obviously not much accustomed to riding, and occasionally lost his mount. Having 'undertaken to pilot us thro our tour' he had made wonderful progress in horsemanship by 25 June (*ibid.*, p. 75) but, having fallen off again on 1 July, Beranger reported on the following day that 'he blesses himself a thousand times' when he is to mount his horse, and preferred to 'drive in the chaise' (*ibid.*, p. 82). But, despite the occasional mishaps and misadventures, the travellers, in Beranger's own words written to Burton Conyngham, enjoyed their tour perfectly and

> find by experience that one must not believe the foolish tales with which ignorant people love to entertain one, the roads are excellent thro Connaught, & if sometimes mountainous, they repay the trouble of ascending by the most delightful prospects and enchanting scenes, which indeed caused a certain rapture in me when I beheld them, which I cannot express so well as I have felt them [MS 1415, pp 96–7].

The 'ignorant people' mentioned in that extract presumably included a side-swipe at one Dr Twiss, who, in a recent travel book (*A tour in Ireland in 1775*), had stung the people of Connacht by his unfair criticism without ever having set foot in the province (see also below, p. 126). In contrast to the detestable Dr Twiss, our travellers found that the inhabitants

> are the most hospitable people, even the poorest sort, when we beg a drink of water during the broiling heats, bring us milk, with the greatest pleasure [MS 1415, p. 93].

The gentry, too, were so pressing with their invitations that, had our pair accepted every one, they 'could not travel 2 miles a day without stopping' (MS 1415, p. 81) and 'would not be at home this year' (*ibid.*, p. 93). So impressed was Beranger that, having only got as far as Westport, he was already begging Burton Conyngham to do him a favour which was

> to compose a paragraph as part of a letter to you from Mr. Bigary and my self acknowledging the excellent roads & hospitallity of the inhabitants and get it inserted in ye Dublin Evening Post which is the favorite paper in Connaught. It will not only rejoice them, but procure us all the good will and assistance in the places where we are going. You might also mention that the

Romantick and Picturesque views would make a traveller regret not to have seen them, as it is a real fact [MS 1415, pp 93–4].

The outcome of that excellent bit of public relations for the province was apparently printed in a Galway newspaper, the final wording given below on p. 213.

2 . THE SOURCES

When Sir William Wilde first reconstructed the 1779 Antiquarian Tour in the 1870s, he had the inestimable advantage of having at his disposal Beranger's Diary of it, which cannot now be found, but we are fortunate that he published extensive extracts from it, which are a very important element of the chapters which follow here. For illustrations, all Wilde could do was refer to engravings in Grose's *Antiquities,* and bemoan the fact that he could not find any of the original drawings.

The situation has now changed dramatically with the emergence into the public domain of the Cooper Collection, which contains most of what is now known to survive in the way of original drawings, plans or later copies of these. Taken together, they now make it possible to recreate the tour not just with words, as Wilde did, but also with many of the pictures that it produced. However, before proceeding further, it is appropriate to look at the sources which enable us to do so, firstly those of a literary nature, followed by the pictorial material.

Literary sources

1. **MS 1415 in the National Library**, which contains valuable letters by Beranger (pp 75–110) written to Burton Conyngham from the field. They provide revealing and fascinating personal details which form the basis of much of the preceding chapter, and which augment to our great advantage the material in the lost Diary (No. 2 below), as quoted by Wilde. The letters are contained in a volume which may well have been bound by their recipient, Burton Conyngham, and later formed part of the Phillipps Collection (No. 6473) before coming to the National Library. The manuscript also contains other letters relevant to our present enquiry, including a long one which Beranger wrote to Colonel Charles Vallancey about Inishmurray (pp 61–74), a number from Ledwich to both Burton Conyngham and (presumably) Vallancey (pp 120–30), and two others from Lewis Irwin (pp 149–56), as well as one written in Italian at Slane by Bigari (p. 111). There are, furthermore, letters from Charles O'Conor to Burton Conyngham (pp 135–40), and one significant letter (pp 175–8) from Paul Sandby to Lord Carlow (the Hon. John Dawson before he ultimately became earl of Portarlington), which the latter must have passed on to Burton Conyngham because of its relevance to his project (see pp 215–16). Correspondence going from Burton Conyngham to the writers of these various letters does not seem to have survived.

2. **The lost Diary.** Beranger kept a detailed Diary of the whole tour, not just for himself but clearly for others as well, as can be seen when he says 'I can assure the reader that not even the least trace of such a building is to be seen' (Wilde, 75). Lady Wilde believed that it was written with the intention of publication (Wilde, 143). Wilde calls it a 'Note Book' or 'Journal' (terms also used for it here) and describes it as 'an impressive tome', saying of it:

> Among the materials that have come into my possession is a large quarto Ms. book of 118 pages, in double columns, on one side (and with 'Notes and Anecdotes' on some of the blank pages), of several tours made in Ireland from 1773 to 1781. It is most beautifully written in a clear, distinct hand, without a blot or erasure, and contains several small illustrative sketches. The work itself is a diary and itinerary, evidently written from day to day, but the 'Notes and Anecdotes' and historic extracts appear to have been added subsequently, when the author had access to libraries, &c. The book, which is bound and shuts with a clasp, is a foot long, and 9½ inches broad [Wilde, 5].

Here Wilde states that it was actually in his possession, but it does not appear to be mentioned in the catalogue of Wilde's library when it was sold after his death in 1876. Michael Ryan and I, and doubtless many others as well, have looked in vain for this important document — and I keep on hoping with every book I publish on Beranger that it will one day turn up, dusted down from where it has wasted its sweetness on some deserted shelf or attic air for more than a century. But it looks as if I will have to keep on waiting.

The Diary clearly was not the actual one written in the field, but a later, clean copy designed to include an account of all the tours that Beranger had made hitherto — Wicklow in 1773, Connacht and Glendalough in 1779, Wicklow and Wexford in 1780, and Dundalk in 1781, but how long after that the Diary was written remains an open question. It certainly does not include what may have been his final trip, undertaken to Moira, Co. Down, in 1799 to visit a Miss Sharman, who was probably his pupil. The disappearance of the Diary for well over a century now is a great loss to Beranger studies, but we can be fairly confident that Wilde's acumen and sense of the relevant would have ensured that the extracts he published from it (in duly edited form) left out little that would have been of any consequence. As a result, almost all of the extracts are quoted again here in the pages that follow, because they help to give us so much of the atmosphere of the tour, the social scene and the interaction between the two artists and others whom they encountered *en route*, be it their hosts, the common people or their interpreter. It is anything but a dry description of the monuments they visited and drew, which is what is contained in the next manuscript to be discussed; the latter was probably designed to be closely linked to the Diary in style and purpose.

3. **MS 4162 in the National Library.** Entitled 'Journal of a Tour thro' Connaught & Wicklow and Wexford' on the cover, this was written no earlier than October 1780 — the month of the last entry. The first page is headed

Tour Thro' Connaught in 1779
by order of the Society of Antiquarians under
the Direction of ye Rt Honble Wm Burton

though the words 'by order of the Society of Antiquarians' was crossed out by a later hand — perhaps because it should have read 'Hibernian Antiquarian Society'! Another copy of the same text was owned by the son of Roger C. Walker, Q.C., of Rathcarrick, Co. Sligo, which is almost certainly now MS 5628 in the National Library. Yet a third copy survives in the Royal Irish Academy's manuscript 12. I.19, which is no earlier than 1816 — the date of the watermark.

Rather than being 'a meagre paraphrased abridgement', as Wilde (33) thought, it is much more likely to be a copy of Beranger's original brief discussion and list of illustrations submitted along with the drawings to Burton Conyngham shortly after the end of the tour, presumably for passing on eventually to an engraver. Certainly, parts of the descriptions in this manuscript are sometimes found repeated, almost verbatim, in the letterpress accompanying the engravings of Bigari's original drawings from this tour in Grose's *Antiquities*, demonstrating that the latter's editor, Edward Ledwich, must have had access to its contents or another version of it, and found it suitable for use as text material to accompany engravings. At the end of most of its entries, the drawings for each site are given a consecutive number, and what Beranger calls the 'parts', that is, the details, are frequently allotted additional letters within that numbering system. These numbers and, on occasions, even the letters are found in the top right-hand corner or on the back of some of the original illustrations (from the Cooper Collection), showing that the contents of this manuscript are directly linked into the numbered drawings (of both Bigari and Beranger). This supports the notion that we should see the manuscript as a commentary accompanying the worked-up illustrations to be considered for engraving, and as part of the programme of the Hibernian Antiquarian Society. The phraseology of the text often corresponds with that of the Diary extracts as published by Wilde, whose comment that 'no mention is made of the name either of Beranger or Bigari' (Wilde, 33) is best explained by the virtual certainty that the text was written by Beranger himself. Because we know from a handwritten note by Austin Damer Cooper on p. 49 of the Cooper family's copy of Wilde's book on Beranger (now in the Prints and Drawings Department of the National Library) that Austin Cooper 'purchased all Colonel Conyngham's drawings, books and works of art' in 1810, we may presume that this manuscript — doubtless originally commissioned by Burton Conyngham — was part of that purchase, and was later item 35 on p. 55 of the catalogue of 'the Antiquary' Austin Cooper's library when it was put up for sale in 1831. It was bought by Sir Thomas Phillipps, in whose catalogue it bore the number 6476. After such an odyssey, we can be happy that it has come home again and landed in the safe hands of the National Library.

The punctuation and use of capital letters used in the manuscript does not always conform to modern usage, but Beranger's spelling has been retained in order to give a flavour of his style of writing — which, it may be said, is extremely fluent for someone who was born of Huguenot parents in Amsterdam, making one suspect that Beranger was in an English-speaking milieu or country long before 1750, the year when Wilde (3) says he came to Ireland. Comparison of the description of Clonmacnois given on pp 28–9 of this manuscript and the version printed by Wilde (84) in his book on Beranger — No. 4 immediately below — shows just how much Wilde 'tidied up' Beranger's text in order to make it more easily readable.

4. **Sir William Wilde's** *Memoir of Gabriel Beranger and his labours in the cause of Irish art and antiquities from 1760 to 1780*, published by M.H. Gill in Dublin in 1880. This is a reprint of a series of articles written by Wilde in volumes 11 and 12 of the *Journal of the Royal Historical and Archaeological Association of Ireland* in the years 1870–4, together with a concluding memoir commenced by Wilde and completed by his widow in vol. 14 for 1879, fortunately publishing the manuscript which Wilde had left incomplete at his death three years earlier. The word 'literature' in the heading of the Journal articles ('labours in the cause of Irish art, literature and antiquities') was — probably wisely — left out in the title of the book, but the omission was more than made up for by the insertion of new material at the end of the volume, including the following.

(i) List of watercolour sketches contained in three small postcard-sized albums entitled *Rambles through the County of Dublin and some others*, two of which are preserved in the library of the Royal Irish Academy (MSS 3.C.31–2). A third (Wilde's No. 2) has, like the Diary, sadly gone missing since Wilde's day, and there was also a fourth, which was owned — and lost — by a Mr Clarke, in whose father's house Beranger had died in 1817 (Wilde, vi and 31).

(ii) List of drawings by Gabriel Beranger included in the catalogue of Austin Cooper's collection. It is curious that no original drawings have survived in the Cooper Collection from the places on the list that were included in the 1779 tour (Inishmurray, Dunmore, Killala, Ennismacreery, Ballymote Church and Ballindoon), and that those places of which we do have original views by Beranger from the Cooper Collection (e.g. Ballinafad and Ballysadare) are not mentioned on Wilde's list at all.

(iii) Copies of drawings by Gabriel Beranger, from a book of Irish scenery and antiquities in the possession of Huband Smith, Esq., M.R.I.A. This list contains nothing of relevance to the 1779 tour, but the collection to which the monochrome Indian ink drawings belonged (Wilde, 34 and Appendix, p. 7) seems to be similar to, though not identical with, a collection of Beranger watercolours largely dispersed in 1965 and to which I hope, some day, to be able to devote another book.

We owe an immense debt of gratitude to Wilde for, without him, we would not have the extracts from Beranger's lost Diary which are such an important part of the reconstruction of the 1779 tour in the following pages. Where Wilde's extracts or his commentaries on them are cited here, the page references quoted are those in the *Memoir of Gabriel Beranger* book, and not those of the original Journal articles.

Illustrations

We now come to the illustrative material, of which Wilde only had the engravings from Grose's *Antiquities* at his disposal when trying for the first time to reconstruct Beranger and Bigari's tour and make the world aware of its importance for the early evolution of Irish archaeological studies.

5. **Grose's *Antiquities of Ireland*.** The two volumes of this work were edited by Edward Ledwich after Grose had died in 1791, when the project to provide Irish equivalents for the Grose volumes of England and Wales (1773–6) was only in its infancy. Engravings made for Grose's *Antiquities of Ireland* included 31 which are acknowledged to have been based on originals by Bigari in Burton Conyngham's collection, along with a number of plans for which no authorship was given. Many, though not all, of the plans are likely to have been by Beranger, whose drawing of McDermott's Castle (*Pl. 8*) was engraved without admission of authorship. The letterpress for the various illustrations frequently borrowed ideas from Beranger's descriptions as contained particularly in the National Library's manuscript 4162 (No. 3 above). It is worth noting that some Bigari drawings were obviously proposed, but finally rejected, for use in Grose's *Antiquities* and, instead, Ledwich chose to use alternative drawings of the same places made by T. Cocking and Grose's nephew Daniel, who must have been sent out around 1791 to draw the same monuments that Bigari and Beranger had already covered twelve years earlier, but from a different angle. It is clear, therefore, that Ledwich relied heavily on Bigari and Beranger material in the collection of Burton Conyngham, to whom *The antiquities of Ireland* is rightly dedicated.

Since Wilde's day, a considerable amount of original pictorial material has emerged that emanated primarily or secondarily from that tour, and it is this that has provided the impetus to prepare the present volume, encouraged specifically by the National Library's acquisition of the Cooper Collection, to which we must now turn.

The National Library

6. **The Cooper Collection** drawings were given the general number 2122 in the Prints and Drawings Department of the National Library after they had been acquired in 1994. The collection gets its name from Austin Cooper (1759–1830), known in his family as 'the Antiquary' because he had been elected a Fellow of the Society of Antiquaries of London shortly before his death in 1830. He was a gentleman civil servant born in the family home at Killenure, Co. Tipperary, and his job brought him around many parts of the country, where he made sketches of antiquities, which I have recently published in *Cooper's Ireland* (2000). These, and other (usually slightly inferior) drawings by members of his family, form one particular part of the Cooper Collection; a second is material from the 1779 tour to be discussed immediately below, and the third is a miscellaneous collection of engravings and watercolours (for some of which see *The Irish Arts Review* for the year 2001).

Cooper bought the original material of the 1779 tour from Burton Conyngham's heirs in 1810, according to notes which the antiquary's grandson, Austin Damer Cooper, added to pp viii and 49 of the Cooper family copy of Wilde's *Memoir of Beranger*, now kept in the Prints and Drawings Department of the National Library. It comprises by far the greatest number of the original drawings by Bigari and Beranger surviving from the 1779 tour, with the division of labour between the two artists quoted above (p. 10) being very much in evidence. There are 31 pen and wash views by Bigari, together with half of another showing part of the tomb at Strade (*Fig. 111*). Because Bigari spoke — and presumably, therefore, wrote — no English, he put the Italian words *'scala di piedi'* to his scales of length, whereas the captions to these would have been provided in Beranger's hand. No more than five views can be ascribed to Beranger, who concentrated more on the details of buildings spread over ten separate sheets, but he was also the one who specialised in the prehistoric tombs and their plans, of which only three originals survive intact. Most of the plans of medieval castles and abbeys were done by Beranger (see above, p. 10), and, of these, eight survive in the form of drawings, original or copied.

Many of the original drawings have disappeared, probably during the course of the nineteenth century, but those which have survived did so thanks to several generations of the Cooper family, who kept them together for 184 years. What has disappeared can be judged, at least to some extent, by copies made of the original material by members of the Cooper family (see below), but also by eight engravings in Grose's *Antiquities* showing images that are not present among the original drawings. In fact, a total of 32 engravings spread over the two volumes of Grose's *Antiquities* illustrate views (almost all Bigari's) from the 1779 tour, in addition to which there are also other plans (including one of Rosserk Abbey prepared by Lewis Irwin) which emanated from the tour.

Fortunately for us, a considerable number of lost original drawings were copied by various members of the Cooper family, thus giving us a more extensive insight into material gathered by our two artists, whose authorship is acknowledged by the presence of their name or initials, placed usually in the bottom left-hand corner of the copy. On the whole, the copyists concentrated on reproducing Beranger's material more than Bigari's, thus redressing the balance created by the survival from the tour of more original drawings by Bigari. Austin Cooper himself was one of the more prominent and diligent of the copyists, usually signing himself A.C. at the bottom right. Another is J.T., who, I believe, was Cooper's brother-in-law Joseph Turner, a clergyman. A third is someone with the initials S.C., probably the same hand that signs itself what looks like J.S.C.; this is likely to have been Austin Cooper's cousin Samuel, with whom he is known to have gone on sketching expeditions. The copying of original material from the tour otherwise largely lost was concentrated, for some unexplained reason, in the month of October in the two years 1794 and 1799, though April 1794 also produced a few copies. Cooper was a man who kept diaries over decades, but sadly those two years are not among the annual diaries that have survived. Why the family seems to have foregathered at these times five years apart for what looks like a feast of copying we do not know. It should be noted, however, that 1794 was only two years before the death of Burton Conyngham, who was obviously happy to allow members of the Cooper family to copy drawings in his collection, in the same way that he had facilitated Ledwich in making engravings from them in the early 1790s for use in Grose's *Antiquities*.

Perhaps Cooper may have been afraid that he might not have access to the drawings after Conyngham's demise, and got his family to copy at least some of them in 1794. The fact that 1799 was one year before the passing of the Act of Union is probably unconnected with the concentration of Cooper family copies in the dying months of the year. Perhaps a better explanation is that Joseph Turner is likely to have been active as a clergyman in Slane at that time, and the obvious availability of Conyngham's material at Slane Castle nearby, three years after his demise, may have been a magnet for artistic activity when Cooper would have come to visit his sister, who was married to Turner. Incidentally, what I take to be Cooper's wife, Sarah, put her signature to a not-very-good copy of a Bigari drawing of Inishmurray; this and other poor copies of Bigari's views made by both Turner and Samuel Cooper, which are preserved in the National Library's album 2122 TX(2), are neither illustrated nor mentioned further here, though they are listed on p. 281 of *Cooper's Ireland*. That Cooper was obviously very attached to the antiquarian drawings in Burton Conyngham's collection, and presumably had a very high respect for their historical value, is shown by the fact that he not only wanted to copy them lest they be lost or perish, but was also prepared to purchase them, which he did in 1810.

His grandson, Austin Damer Cooper (1831–1900), pasted a number of original Bigari views into an album (now 2122 TX(3) in the National Library) in 1875, shortly after Wilde had published his series of articles on Beranger and the 1779 tour (No. 4 above), yet there is no indication in Wilde's posthumous reprint volume of 1880 that Cooper ever appraised Wilde or his widow of the existence of these drawings.

7. **MS 671 in the National Library**, which describes itself as '28 Views and Plans from Col. Conyngham's collection' — a title probably written when it formed part of the Phillipps Collection, where it bore the number 20865. Sadly, all the views are missing, but, of the sixteen plans that survive, seven can be associated with the 1779 tour (compare *Figs 109, 134, 154, 192* and *210*). An entry in the catalogue of *The Phillipps Manuscripts* (2001), with an introduction by A.N.L. Munby, states that the plans were 'supposed to be made for Capt. Grose's Antiquities, as they were found in a Collection of Grose drawings', and references to 'reduced drawings' — and a date of 'May 1791' on one of them — supports the suggestion that they were intended for Grose's *Antiquities*, but presumably rejected in the final selection of engravings. We will probably never know whether material emanating from the 1779 tour was included among the missing views, which can have numbered no more than twelve, though it is possible that they included the view of Enniskillen Castle and the three watercolours mentioned immediately below under No. 8.

8. **Miscellaneous items** in the Prints and Drawings Department of the National Library which are of relevance here include one drawing (by Bigari?) of Enniskillen Castle (*Fig. 9*) and a Cooper copy of a Beranger drawing of 'Ballinchalla Castle' (*Fig. 145*). But more attractive are the watercolours (*Pls 4* and *22* and *Fig. 178*) which have a note added at the top to say that the building 'was engraved from another view'. These were presumably prepared for the engravers of Grose's *Antiquities* but rejected in favour of other material. The artist did not sign his name.

Royal Irish Academy

9. **MS 3.C.29**. In this manuscript there are watercolours depicting buildings encountered on the tour, copied by an as yet unidentified artist and obviously prepared for engraving in Grose's *Antiquities*. The three watercolours just alluded to as being in the National Library presumably belonged to the same series. Some of the subjects, e.g. Claddagh (*Figs 158* and *159; Pl. 19*), Murrisk (*Figs 123* and *125; Pl. 17*) and Turlough (*Figs 114* and *116; Pl.14*), have the advantage that they are also present in the form of original drawings and engravings, so that we are in the enviable position of being able to follow an illustration from original pen and wash drawing to the stage of being made into a watercolour preparatory to being sent for engraving, together with the final engraving itself.

10. **MS 3.C.30**. This, the larger album of Beranger watercolours in the Academy's library, contains a single illustration relevant to the 1779 tour — that of Rathcroghan on p. 79 (*Pl. 21*).

11. **MS 3.C.31**. One of the two smaller albums of watercolours housed in the Academy, this preserves two views of the Westport area (*Pls 15–16*) and one of Nephin (*Pl. 12*).

12. **MS 3.C.33**. This album of drawings by the Revd Joseph Turner contains two copies (not illustrated here) of drawings of Killemanain (alias Inishmaine), the Bigari and Beranger originals of which are contained in the Academy's manuscripts 3.D.4 and 12.T.16 respectively (Nos 14–15 below).

13. **MS 3.C.42**. This comprises a variety of loose or mounted drawings, illustrating, among other things, some of the prehistoric monuments of Sligo and Mayo encountered by the two artists. One is an original Beranger, the others are Cooper family copies of original material of his that does not otherwise survive. These drawings lay for years in a drawer in the Department of Archaeology in University College Dublin, where they had been deposited probably by Dr Françoise Henry, who had possibly acquired them on the art market or was presented with them by someone who shared her interest in archaeology. Some of the sheets bore old stamps of the Royal Irish Academy, from whence they had, at some stage, been taken. One of the miscellaneous drawings in the Academy (see below, *Fig. 197*) had marked on the back of it that it was returned by Miss Stokes's brother in December 1901 — the year of her death. It is quite possible, therefore, that it was she who borrowed this collection of drawings, perhaps in connection with her study of Petrie (who also possessed Beranger material, according to Wilde), and was never able to return it. Now it has been returned to the Academy, thanks to Professor Barry Raftery and his colleagues in the Department of Archaeology in University College Dublin, who agreed in the year 2000 to restore the drawings to where they had come from. One of the items was a plan and cross-section of a monument called 'The Druids Temple on the Island of Ennishowen', which will be mentioned below (No. 16).

14. **MS 3.D.4.** Among the miscellaneous drawings in this portfolio are two Beranger originals showing details of Killemanain (*Fig. 144*) and Clonmacnois *(Fig. 197)* respectively.

15. **MS 12.T.16.** Bigari's original plan and view of Killemanain (*Figs 141* and *143*) are preserved here among a collection of drawings otherwise largely concerned with the work of the Ordnance Survey in counties Galway and Mayo.

Author's collection

16. **Drawing of 'Druid's' Temple on the Island of Ennishowen**. During the summer of the year 2000 I was approached by a German art historian, Dr U. Middendorf, who asked whether I knew of the existence of a Druid's Temple on the Island of Ennishowen because she had not been able to find it mentioned in my *National Monuments Guidebook*. The reason behind her enquiry was that she had an original drawing of the subject, signed by GB and dated 1784 (*Fig. 148*). When she sent me a copy of it, I realised that this was the only drawing of its size by Beranger, larger than all the others illustrating monuments visited on the 1779 tour, and the only one to bear the year 1784. On my inquiring how she had come to be in possession of it, she told me that she and an art dealer had bought it from a dentist in northern Germany who had inherited it, and that it had been part of a large collection of drawings (devoid of any other Irish material) which had been looted from a Belgian castle at the end of the First World War. How it got there we do not know, but the hope may be expressed that it could well be a stray sheet from some larger collection of drawings of 1784 which may some day turn up in Belgium or elsewhere, and provide us with more copies of material from the 1779 tour which has since got lost. Having been able to assure Frau Dr Middendorf that the monument did indeed exist, I decided to acquire the drawing myself and repatriate it, lest it be lost again to Ireland.

3. FROM DUBLIN TO INISHMURRAY

'We set out from Dublin, June the 9th.'

With these words, written in the large, lost manuscript Diary (p. 16), Beranger announced his and Bigari's departure for their tour of Connacht in what, for them, was to be the hot and productive summer of 1779. Their mode of conveyance was an open chaise, which Beranger sometimes called a chair, that was to give the pair considerable trouble in the months ahead, as the springs and harness frequently malfunctioned, causing inconvenience and annoying delays. The state of the roads did not help. Their first day's journey brought them along the Slane road, which had to be subsequently smoothed and straightened. The reason for that, according to legend, was to allow King George IV, on his brief visit to Ireland in the summer of 1821, to be transported all the more hastily to Slane Castle to visit the chatelaine there, who was his lady-love. However, in a letter to *The Irish Times* of 4 September 2000, Chalmers Trench claimed that it is John Foster, the Speaker of the Irish House of Commons, that we have to thank for the improvements — probably because the road needed them. At the end of their 30-mile journey, the two artists finally arrived at Slane Castle, where they had 'orders to halt and study the route given to us' (Wilde, 34).

The castle looked different in those days, before Wyatt began to make considerable changes to it in 1785. This can be seen in an attractive oval watercolour of the castle (*Pl. 1*) by Beranger — not done on the tour but based on an original by Thomas Roberts (1748–78) that was perhaps a preliminary sketch for his painting of the castle recently published by Anne Crookshank and the Knight of Glin in *Masterpieces by Irish artists 1660–1860*, the fine catalogue of an exhibition in the Pyms Gallery in London, where the Roberts oil was exhibited in 1999. The castle still had the square corner-towers at the time, but these had conical caps rather than the crenellations we see today, and both the roof and the chimney-stacks were taller than they are now.

Burton Conyngham was probably a genial host to many an artist in his day, as contemporaries such as Jonathan Fisher are known to have painted subjects of historical interest in the vicinity of Slane, probably while they were enjoying his hospitality there. A happy omen of the success of things to come occurred on our pair's first morning at the castle. In his Note Book, Beranger illustrated one of those curious bronze objects which we call latchets (*Fig. 4*) — something of a euphemism for admitting that we do not know what they were used for — and, in an accompanying report beneath it, wrote:

> An unknown instrument found at Slane, Co. of Meath in the year 1779; this copy same size of the original, and same colour, the whole machine being made of brass. As I was sitting at

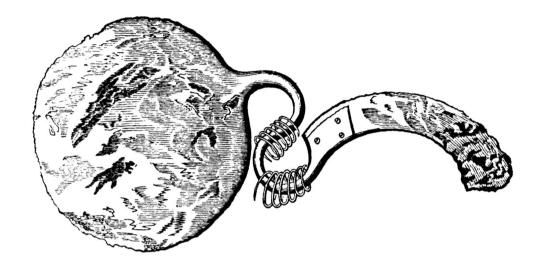

Fig. 4
A bronze latchet of the kind found in the grounds of Slane Castle on the day that Beranger and Bigari were receiving their instructions from William Burton before setting out on their tour of Connacht. From Wilde's *Memoir of Gabriel Beranger*.

breakfast with the Right Hon. William Burton, at the Castle of Slane, the stuart came in, and brought an antiquity like the above, but much damaged and broke, which was found in digging a trench in the park. He had ordered the men to stop the work until further orders. After breakfast we went to the spot, and ordered the diggings to go on carefully. After a few minutes the above was found, very little damaged, and just as I have represented it. It is of brass, and as thin as a card [Wilde, 35].

Kells

Having presumably been briefed *in extenso* by Burton Conyngham, the two set out the following day, 11 June, and

> arrived at Kells, a borough of the County of Meath; here we designed the square and round towers, cross, and St. Kevan's Cell [Wilde, 36].

The second-last word should have read 'Columb's' or 'Columba's', a mistake rectified in the text of the very first page of the *Tour Thro' Connacht*, manuscript 4162 in the National Library, which is as follows:

> The Antiquities of Kells consist
> 1st   in a square tower pretty wel built, which has four kind of buttrasses at the angles, there is a kind of offsett about ye middle of the hight
> 2nd   A round tower of 90 feet high and 16 feet Diamr the walls of which are 3 feet So that

the inside is 10 feet in ye clear. The tower is of good workmanship

3rdly   A small Round Tower at the back of the Town which might have been a Turret of a Wall of the Town. 16 feet diamr & 30 high

4ly   A cross Loaded with carvings 9 feet high base 2 ft in all 11 feet, on which a mutilated inscription tells it was re-errected by the Sovereign and the Corporation of Kells in 1688

5ly   a small stone building arched and covered with Flaggs instead of slates, called Columb Kill's cell where we were told the archdeacon is obliged to take possession before he goes to the church, it is at present used as a Stable is enclosed in a garden & the proprietor not being at home, we could get no access and drew it from a wall of the garden. See Drawings plan etc. No. 1.

These five antiquities are still preserved, though the 'cross loaded with carvings' — now known as the Market Cross — was removed from its position in Cross Street after a bus had struck the modern base in 1997, and is now displayed near the entrance of the new Heritage Centre. It is curious, however, that Beranger did not list the tower-house castle close to it which was demolished early in the nineteenth century, or mention any of the other crosses or cross fragments in the Church of Ireland churchyard, of which that near the round tower is likely to have been standing when Beranger and Bigari visited Kells in 1779.

Clones

It is much to be regretted that none of the drawings executed at Kells can be traced, a fate which also applies to those that illustrated the antiquities at the next stop on the journey, Clones in the County of Monaghan, which Beranger listed as follows on p. 2 of MS 4162:

The Antiquities of Clones consist

1.   of a rath at some small distance from ye town composed of earth and covered with grass, it has 3 fosses and parapets, the lower one much worn by time. [This is, in fact, a Norman motte.]

2.   A round tower of good masonry 60 feet high, & 15 diamr. The door, 5 feet high by 2 wide, and at present but 4 feet from ye ground, which is much raised by burrials.

3.   A small church called of the Angels 20 feet broad in front, 42 in lenght & 19 high to the top of the gabel end. the walls 2 feet 8 thick, it is all of hewn (mountain) stone and the foundation for 3 or 4 feet from the ground has its stones curiously cut and let into one another. [A later hand adds that this is the burying-place of the McMahons of Dartrey.]

4.   A cross in the market loaded with carving much defaced. See dimentions on the drawings, we could not mesure the top for want of a ladder and as we were cursed and insulted here (being taken for French spies) they would not grant us the least assistance for love or money. Mr. Cross to whom we had letters being out of town, & the priest with whom Mr.

Bigary scraped an acquaintance, & who was of some use to us being that day gone out of town.

That Beranger and Bigari, being of French/Dutch origin and Italian nationality respectively, should be suspected of being spies comes as no surprise because England at the time was at war with France, Spain and Holland, who had allied themselves with the rebelling American colonies, and it was the fear of a French or Spanish invasion which gripped Ireland in 1779 that led to the Irish nobility organising themselves into volunteer groups to defend the country in the absence of any government inclination to do so. A further insight into the artists' plight can be found in Beranger's lost Note Book, as quoted by Wilde (37):

> Sunday 13th June, went out early to reconnoitre the antiquities about the town; drew the Rath at some distance from it, and measured it, also the Round Tower in the churchyard. Mr. Bigari went to mass, after which the priest came to visit us, and offered his service to conduct us to the antiquities, which we accepted. I went with him, and measured with Jacob's staff the height of the Tower. Great commotions in the town; the Protestants gathered, and, taking us for spies, were very clamourous; on the other hand, the Romans, seeing us with their priest, assembled about us, so that the churchyard was full of people. Great debates among the two parties — one was for sending us to jail, the other to prevent us. Returned to our inn, followed by the crowd, and stayed at home for the rest of the day.

Wilde tells us further in his own words that the priest went to visit them again in the evening, giving rise to a pleasant party with the landlady, which Beranger apparently described in graphic terms — making us all the more aware of how much we are missing through the loss of Beranger's Note Book! He obviously explained that one of the company present informed them that there was an opinion prevalent in the town that they had come to remove the round tower, and fix it on top of the rath with a machine of a hundred horsepower. The rumour machine would appear to have been even stronger! With no hint of a hangover, Beranger recorded for the following day:

> June 14th, went out at 6; drew an old church and the market cross; followed by a crowd, some abused us by words, and called us spies … As we could not go abroad even to walk without being followed by a crowd, we amused ourselves within, and dined with our landlady and her daughters [Wilde, 37].

Rescue, however, came at last in the shape of Mr Cross, who by now had returned to town, and, as soon as he

> heard the emotions of the people at our sight, he desired us to take a walk with him through the town; and as soon as it was known we were under his protection and recommended to him (he being a Protestant), every one dispersed, and followed us no more [Wilde, 37].

Fig. 5
Florence Court, Co.
Fermanagh, by J. J.
Barralet, as engraved for
Milton's *Seats* in 1786.

FLORENCE COURT.
Most Humbly Inscribed to Lord Visct. Enniskillen, by Thos. Milton
Published as the Act directs. March 1st. 1786, by Thos. Milton, London.

After this ordeal, we can sympathise with an artistic soul like Beranger describing Clones 'or Clownish as the inhabitants pronounce it' as a place which he found to be 'indifferent enough', remarkable only for its round tower and rath. To him, the counties of Cavan and Monaghan looked poor, the land coarse, the cabins as if going to ruin, half-thatched, several bogs close to the road, and digging turf going on almost everywhere (Wilde, 36).

An additional reason why the artists had a protracted stay in Clones — from 12 to 15 June — was that it took a long time to repair the chaise, which had broken down a few miles short of the town, forcing them to go the remainder of the way on foot. Little better luck awaited them on the road to Enniskillen, where another spring broke. As if to make up for their misfortune, they were cordially received by Lord Enniskillen at his home in Florence Court (*Fig. 5*).

Devenish

It was from Florence Court that they set out on 16 June for a boat trip on Lower Lough Erne where,

Fig. 6
'Abbey & round Tower on Devenish Island in Lough Erne' — a pen and wash drawing signed by A. M. Bigari, No. 2122 TX(8) in the National Library.

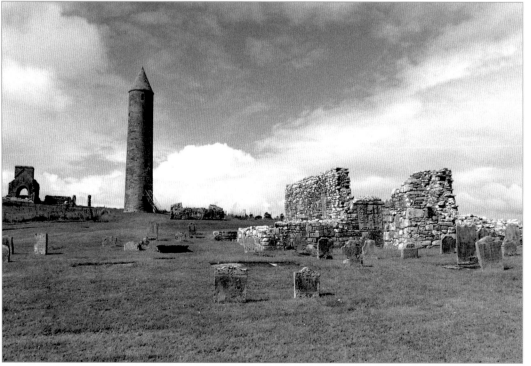

Fig. 7
The round tower dominates the old monastic site on Devenish Island in Lower Lough Erne, Co. Fermanagh, where so much less survives of St Molaise's House and Teampall Mór than in Bigari's day (*Fig. 6*).

as Beranger recorded in the lost Note Book, they landed on Devenish Island and

> Drew the Abbey and Round Tower. Prodigious warm day, almost broiled by the heat of the
> sun. Coming back visited Portsorey Castle, and drew en passant the Castle of Enniskillen. No
> expenses here, my Lord having ordered the boat, &c. Returned to Florence-Court where we
> arrived past 6; found a dinner ready for us; dined by ourselves, after which joined the family
> at tea; supped with them and retired at 12 [Wilde, 37].

Devenish, one of ancient Ireland's most important and picturesque monasteries, was founded by St
Lasrén or Molaise in the sixth century and, partially with the aid of Augustinian Canons, it continued
in existence for a thousand years. In Beranger's own words on p. 3 of MS 4162:

> Devenish Island Lyes in that part of Lough Earne which is N.W. of Enniskillen and about 1½
> miles from the town. Its antiquities are
> 1st   a large building which might have been the monastery of good masonry [St Mary's
> Priory]
> 2.   A Round Tower [blank] feet high 15 feet Diamr & the walls 3 feet thick, of pretty good
> masonry,
> 3.   A Cell [St Molaise's House] with a piramidal roof of flags instead of slates, the inside of
> this cell has in the roof the mark of the whattles which served for center when it was building
> [an interesting comment, suggesting a late medieval repair].
> 4.   A lesser building [called now, in contrast, *Teampull Mór*, or large church] which might
> have been the church of the monastery, the window of this church was fine but is broke at
> present. Next of this window to the right about 10 feet from the ground is a stone in the wall
> with an inscription of raised letters round which is a frame somewhat raised, which had also
> an inscription of which only the lower line is legible. See Drawg.
> For the severall parts as Doors, windows etc.
> See Drawings No. 3.

According to a letter from Beranger to Burton Conyngham written from Sligo on 25 June (Nat. Lib.
MS 1415, p. 76), Mr Irwin 'decyphered' the inscription mentioned under No. 4 above, but was not
able to make it out, so Beranger enclosed it and left 'Coll Vallancey to accomplish' it.

Even though the sketches of the architectural details are not preserved, it is from this section of
the journey that we begin to encounter surviving drawings. The first of these to be mentioned is one
signed by Bigari, and preserved as 2122 TX(8) in the National Library (*Fig. 6*). Captioned 'Abbey &
round Tower on Devenish Island in Lough Erne', this pen and wash drawing shows the large church
on the right and, behind it, St Molaise's House with a window high up in the east gable and its stone
roof heavily covered in ivy while, receding on the hill slope in the left background, we can see the
round tower and St Mary's Priory. As if on an island in the foreground is a tall and dominating tree,

beneath which is a figure with a stick or staff (probably Beranger), but the most remarkable feature of this drawing is the way in which the figures at a lower level in the middle ground are represented at a Lilliputian scale in comparison to the buildings — presumably to give the latter a greater sense of size. The large tree in Bigari's drawing is doubled in W. Beauford's engraving of the same scene published as plate XIII in Edward Ledwich's *Antiquities of Ireland* of 1790, though there the two trees are close to the wall of the large church, and the individual monuments are clustered more closely together than they are in reality (*Fig. 7*). Viewing them from a different angle, as Beauford does, has the advantage that we see more of the sides of the structures, but his placing of a doorway in the east gable of St Molaise's House is unlikely, and the tall and thin nature of the priory tower on top of the hill makes us query the accuracy of some of his details in comparison to Bigari's. The engraving of Devenish seen from the mainland, reproduced as plate 16 in vol. 2 of Grose's *Antiquities of Ireland* and based on 'an original drawing in the collection of the right honourable William Conyngham', could well have been a product of the 1779 tour, but as it is not ascribed to anyone in the accompanying letterpress, it is omitted here. Beranger's note quoted above mentions that he visited Portsorey Castle on the way back from Devenish. This is now normally spelled Portora, and is a Plantation fortress standing high up on the eastern bank of the Erne just below Enniskillen, before the river opens out into Lower Lough Erne. The National Library MS 4162 does not list Portora/Portsorey as one of the castles drawn on the tour but, having visited it, Beranger must have been happy to make a watercolour copy of a drawing of it by his employer William Burton Conyngham that is now preserved in the Ulster Museum in Belfast.

Enniskillen Castle

Only a short distance upstream is the Castle of Enniskillen (*Fig. 8*). Its Watergate, the town's most famous landmark, overlooking the River Erne, was built shortly before 1620 and consisted of a rectangular tower bearing high corner-bartizans that are corbelled below and have a conical roof above, the whole standing on a batter sloping outwards to the water flowing around its base. The drawing of the Watergate which Bigari or Beranger executed *en passant* (*Fig. 9*) is preserved as No. 991 TB in the National Library, which acquired it from the Phillipps Collection, where it bore the manuscript number 24466. It shows the Watergate derelict within, and with the outer walls in a perilous state, but the drawing is of great value in showing what the fortification looked like before the castle was refurbished as a barracks in 1796. The boat shown being apparently rowed upstream may be carrying turf as its cargo. On the top right of the sheet is written 'No 3' and this, together with an inscription on the left of the drawing, ties in neatly with Beranger's entry in MS 4162 describing the monument he had visited:

> Castle of Enniskillen. Consist of a square Castle with two turrets on consoles at the angles the whole is in ruins. Took the view from ye Lough, it was ruined by the owner Philip Maguire in

Fig. 8
Enniskillen Castle stands
picturesquely on the banks
of Lough Erne, Co.
Fermanagh.

Fig. 9
The Castle of Enniskillen, a
pen and wash drawing by
or after Beranger or Bigari,
now 991 TB in the Prints
and Drawings Department
of the National Library.

1508 to prevent O Donnel chieftain of Tirconnel his Ennemy to take possession of it.
Annals of Connaught Ms in possession of Chs O'Connor, Esqr.

The presence of the number 3 corresponds well to its placing between numbers 3 (Devenish) and 4 (Sligo) in the catalogue MS 4162, and would suggest that it may well have been the actual original that Beranger would have presented to Burton Conyngham when the two artists returned home at the end of their tour in August 1779.

According to Wilde (38), the lost Note Book/Diary contained Beranger's description of Florence Court, Enniskillen and Lough Erne, as well as of his hospitable host, Lord Enniskillen. In his demesne lay the Marble Arch, one of Ireland's finest caves, which the two artists visited but found dangerous because of the water within. Having scrambled out of them and back up to the open air, Beranger describes how he and Bigari

> were met by two men at variance, who came to have their case decided by his lordship; halted; a servant was detached on horseback in quest of a prayer book, which being procured, and the plaintiff sworn, the case was heard, and tried, and decided. This was the first time I assisted at a court of justice on a mountain [Wilde, 38].

On 17 June Beranger and Bigari left for Manorhamilton, where they apparently spent the night and set out early next morning for Sligo. Beranger was surprised to find that each hill he climbed brought another equally high one into view, but felt that his effort had been amply rewarded by the beauty of the scenery that he encountered:

> All the mountains of Cavan, Monaghan, and Fermanagh, which we thought once high, are nothing in comparison to those we passed this day. We looked forwards from the top of the first we ascended, and were astonished to see others as high before us succeeding one another in chains, piled up so that no horizon could be seen. Thinking it impossible to pass over them, we fancied that we had strayed from the right road, and sent our Irish interpreter to inquire, who soon confirmed that we were to pass them. Went on; but if we had the trouble to walk over them, we were amply repaid by the variety of charming prospects every hill afforded, particularly one where we had a distant view of Lough Gill, with its hills around it, and some of its wooded islands. I could not withstand the temptation to take a sketch of it, which see, Plate [Wilde, 39].

This piece of landscape drawing is not known to survive, but the Cooper Collection does contain one sheet of a manuscript (*Fig. 204*) written by the interpreter whom Beranger mentioned, and who had been provided for them by Lord Enniskillen before they left Florence Court. Beranger described him thus:

Fig. 10
Tanrego House, near Beltra in County Sligo, where Col. Lewis Irwin hosted Beranger and Bigari on their tour of Connacht in 1779. This view was prepared for a brochure when the house was offered for sale through the Incumbered Estates Court in 1855.

Mr. Terence M'Guire well versed in the Irish language, which he writes and reads, whom his lordship had engaged at the desire of the Antiquarian Society to accompany us as an interpreter, and to copy the Irish inscriptions we should chance to meet. This person is a descendant of the princes of Fermanagh, and reduced to the station of schoolmaster of a little village; he was to receive 2s. 2d. per day for him and his horse, half of which was to go to the owner of the beast, as it was a hired one [Wilde, 38].

Wilde (39) notes that Beranger's description of the scenery and manners of the area is interesting, graphic and well worthy of general perusal, but space sadly prevented him from preserving it for posterity. He does, however, record that during the period 19–28 June which the two artists spent in Sligo they were hospitably received by William Ormsby of Willowbrook, the collector of Sligo, and Lewis Irwin of Tonrego or Tanrego House near Beltra (*Fig. 10*). Of the two, Irwin was much the more attentive, probably because he himself had a particular interest in the antiquities of Sligo and its adjacent counties. Probably a grandson of the Colonel John Irwin (1680–1752) for whom Carolan had composed a planxty, he was a genial companion who was to accompany the two artists for more than three weeks, sparing no time, trouble or expense to ensure a fruitful outcome of the tour in his home county. Beranger had already been in correspondence with him during the previous March to acquaint him of the artists' impending visit and asking for suggestions about monuments that would be worth sketching (see above, p. 4). Because his reply in the form of a letter (presumably written to

Burton Conyngham) dated 26 March 1779 (Nat. Lib. MS 1415, pp 149–54) contains what is perhaps the earliest surviving description of County Sligo's antiquities, and can act also as a suitable introductory preamble to the next ten days of the tour, it is worth quoting here in its entirety:

Tanrego, March 26th 1779

Sir,

I this day received a Letter from Mr. Berenger, as he informs me by your Directions, to acquaint me that the Antiquarian Society had wished my assistance for the Artists to be employed by them, as also a communication of such particulars as in my mean Capacity may be deemed worthy of notice.

In this County, the Barony of Tireragh seems most replete with objects worthy the attention of an Antiquarian, not that the rest are destitute of Vestiges not to be overlooked, but that being maritime retains the traces of the earliest Inhabitants. Should the artists begin their Progress from the northward by Ballyshannon, thro Carbury Barony, which also lies on the sea, the first and greatest Object is the Island now called Innismurray, and perhaps always as dedicated to the Virgin, although Usher or rather Author of the Addenda spells it Inis Comera (see the Dublin Edition de primordiis Ecclesiarum AD 1639, page 1066) this lies about three leagues in the Sea between that coast and Killibegs and as the first asylum of Columbkille after the Battle of Clunderub [? Culdreimne] is really the Mother Church of the famous Island Hy or Iona in Scotland, so celebrated by Johnson and other Travellers. It is full strange rude antiquities and superstitious Legends, to long here to enumerate, next in that barony on the Shore is Drumclief said once to have contained fifty religious Houses, many traces of edifices are visible, but nothing to throw any distinct Light; it was formerly a distinct bishoprick, but now incorporated with Elphin. The Abbey of Sligo is next in Place, and near the town up the river two large cairns, or cromleach, and westward a Number of small circles of large stones surrounding three others supporting a still larger, just beyond those on the top of a great Hill, the immense cromleach, by much the largest I ever saw. About five or six miles up the river is the old castle of Drumahaire, where the famous Hall wherein O Rorks noble Feast was celebrated, is to be seen, and the ruins of an old abbey beautifully situated over a fine water fall. Higher up the country in that direction nothing interesting is to be seen. Pursuing the sea coast westward the five Waterfalls at Ballisadare present themselves and some Ruins of an old Augustine Abby. Two miles farther is a large strand, to this day called Cuchullen Strand, and a Burial place shewn for his on a Rock, and all the Denominations environing it correspond with the names recorded in [Macpherson's] Fingal. crossing that Tireragh is enterd, I think more fertile in old remains than any country I ever saw; It is a narrow stripe four and twenty miles long, and not three broad between the ridge of mountains and the Sea, at each miles end runs a River and stands a Castle, and the Vestiges of old circular Forts called Danish, with subterraneous caves, stand as thick and close almost as the Foundations of Houses in many cities; some considerably large, some of those circular arrangements of stones already mentioned like Stonehenge, but much smaller, here and there some structures which appear to me like some Druidical alter or place of Worship, they general Consist of six large stones, sometimes four, of a vast size near six feet above ground, placed three on aside enclosing an area of perhaps ten feet by six, open at one end, on the other nearly closed by an odd stone of the same size, sufficient however to afford Entrance for a man, just before this stone placed another with a flatt face uppermost above the heighth of the Knee; this I supposed was the altar and the apperture an entrance for the priest, whilst the other extreme was open to the assisting Congregation. In one place, on a high Hill is a large rock, which I cannot avoid conjecturing to be a Rocking stone, it is as I recollect about six feet Diameter, irregularly roundish, and supported on the Point of a Rock, on one side elevated above two feet from the surface, and the other gradually declining a little, without any such near it; nature could not form it there, chance could not stop, nor Art without violent Efforts, stop any Efforts in a progressive Motion there, and for what other Purposes Men could erect it there, I am not sufficiently informed to decide. In this Barony and apart almost inaccessible for Bogs and Morasses, stands Fin Mac Coils Gridle as called by the common people, eight long narrow flag shaped stones, thin but sufficient to support the incumbent Weight, and fixed on the End in the ground, on the outside where the soil has grown up they are visible for about four feet, within where sheep have worn away the soil for shelter, above five; on these is placed on the convex side a larger, about nine feet in length, and six feet in breadth, having the appearance of a perpendicular and lesser segment of a cylinder, not through the axis but the third of the Base, with the plane Surface layed uppwards and horizontally, on these four stones, having in fact the Appearance of a Gridle, it can scarcely be doubted to be an altar, and probably for some druidical Holocaust. This process through this Barony terminates the County at the influx of the river Moy, which separates it from the County of Mayo, on the opposite Banks of which are the ruins of the fine Abbeys of Moyne and Rosserk, with the old tower of Killalla, with these limits my Information Ends. Farther than that the inland Baronies of the County of Sligo offered little that I have perceived for the Antiquarian Enquirer, some Danish Forts excepted, a Crumleach at Heapstown, the Castles of Ballymote and Moigara, and Abbeys of Court and Banada; Boyle Abbey tho in another county is so near, it is worthy inspection; I have seen two views of the latter but none interesting farther than an Antient Ruin; whereas the Style of Gothick architecture is peculiar and the most airy and elegant, with more real Strength than I ever saw: from the high surrounding Walls this is only discernable at the Inside, and to be communicated by an internal perspective of the Edifice; I have twice lately when there unfortunately interrupted by heavy Rains, but shall repeat my Attempts till I succeed, should not the artists employed by the Society anticipate me. This is said by Cambden to be built in 1152.

As I wished to communicate the earliest Information of the particulars that the Society did me the honour to demand I have as briefly as the Space for and Compass of a Letter permits acquainted them with such particulars as in the short Period occurred to my Recollection, many I know I have omitted, and many not sufficiently dwelt upon, but which will all occur in the trail I have prescribed, which I think had best commence either from the Westward by Ballina in the Barony of Tyrawley in the County of Mayo, Northwest by Ballishannon; as the County of Roscommon is sterile in Matter, the Castles of Roscommon, & Ballintober, the Residence of our last Monarch of Ireland & a very few others excepted. For many obvious reasons maritime Counties or Districts were most thickly inhabited, and most subject to Invasion, consequently most fitted with indigenal, as well as foreign antiquities. Indeed from Circumstances and Geographical Probabilities, as well as such Vestiges, I cannot avoid conjecturing that this county if not the first, at least the most frequented Avenue of Danish incursions. Of the proper Rout however the Society will be best Judges from their Informations and objects, I must however beg that you may assure them, that on proper Notice some days previous to the Artists entering the County, and at what approach, I shall meet them and afford every assistance and protection in my power. One thing I must beg leave to promise, that a clerk conversant in the Irish language will throughout be a very necessary attendant on the party, and such Books as can aid them or the Gentlemen of the County through which they pass, from the matters therein suggested, to make further Enquiries from those Inhabitants where such Places have stood, of the particulars worthy remarking.

Mr. Berenger in his Letter seems to imply that you yourself propose makeing a tour of this Country, when you are determined on the time it shall take Place, I must entreat that you will honour me with the earliest notice of the time and from what quarter, as I shall do myself the Pleasure to wait on you before you enter it, to offer my Services as a Guide, on which Occasion I shall only premise that altho you may find more qualified and respectable, you will not find a more assiduous or attentive Conductor. From a person totally unknown, this Profession may seem extravagant and outrée, but the Gentleman who has avowed not only the Patron, but acts as the first Spring in so laudable Enterprize, which had I powers or Abilities, it would be my Pride to emulate, must receive my Applause and esteem, with high Sentiments of both I therefore subscribe myself
Sir
Your most obedient
and most humble servant
Lewis Irwin

Time would scarce permit me to
Write, & cannot read over this.
Your own good Understanding must
supply Defects, it will of course excuse

Sligo Abbey

The first Sligo antiquity in Irwin's compilation to which the two artists turned their attention was the abbey in Sligo town, which had been founded for the Dominicans by Maurice FitzGerald, second baron of Offaly, in 1252–3. It survived local political upheavals of the thirteenth and fourteenth centuries before it was accidentally burned in 1414, but rebuilt two years later. The Sligo branch of the O'Connors used it as a burial place for their dead, and succeeded in preventing the friary from being dissolved under King Henry VIII, on condition that the friars became secular priests. During the Elizabethan wars the woodwork was removed, but worse was to happen in 1641 when the friary was sacked and all the friars killed. Members of the order returned later in the century and remained at least in partial occupation until 1760, when they were removed elsewhere — less than two decades before Beranger and Bigari arrived there.

On p. 4 of MS 4162, Beranger gives quite a long description of the 'Abbey':

> The Abbey at Sligo is most pleasantly situatd on the banks of the river Garrowoge, which originates in Lough Gill, it was a spacious and magnificent building as much as we could judge by its remains, of very good workmanship, the east window is beautifull. See drawing, the altar under it, was covered with bones & skulls in such quantity that it would serve for load of a small vessel, the cloysters of which three sides are extant, were magnificent, the arches & pillars being of exellent workmanship, and a few of these pillars adorned as is seen in the drawing. The cloysters are still covered by an arched roof, in the corner to the right as one looks to the Altar and marked A in the Plan. Up severall feet from the ground, is the Tombs of the O Connors, which was very exact, in the drawing (which Coll. Burton give us). The tower in the center of the building is pretty Entire except the Battlements at the Top, we could not discover any stairs to get up, which must have been stoped up or destroyed by time. we were told that the building extended to the river side but could not trace it.
> The monument of which see Drawing is situated at B in the plan
> See Plan Drawings &c No 4

The only original drawing to survive from the day's sketching activity in Sligo Abbey is Bigari's view taken from near the south-western corner of the church, and preserved as 2122 TX(7) in the National Library (*Fig. 11*). It shows the cloister to the left and provides a long view through the church, under the tower arch to the half-blocked traceried east window in the background. Interesting is his representation of the fragments of the rood-screen just short of the tower on the right-hand side, which has since been largely restored (*Fig. 12*). The drawing was engraved as plate 107 in the first volume of Grose's *Antiquities* (*Fig. 13*), which omits a figure standing near the south wall but otherwise remains faithful to the original that Ledwich, the book's editor, stated was 'in the collection of the Right Honourable William Conyngham'. Plate 108 presents a plan of the 'Abbey' which is remarkably accurate, though curiously careless in allowing too few windows in the south wall of the

Fig. 11
'The Abbey at Sligo', signed A.M. Bigari and now 2122 TX(7) in the National Library.

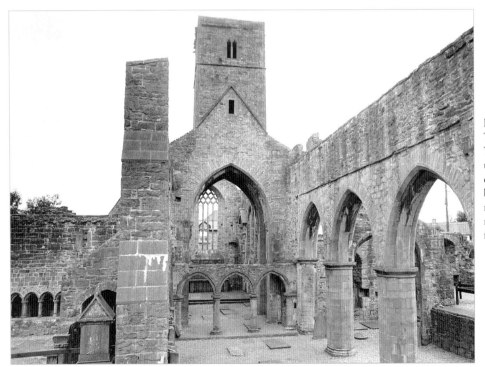

Fig. 12
The interior of Sligo Abbey. The O'Connor tomb is on the right-hand wall of the choir, and the cloister can be seen on the left. The rood-screen has now been reconstructed in the centre foreground.

Fig. 13
'Sligo Abbey, Co. Sligo',
engraved in 1793 after a
Bigari original for plate 107
of vol. 1 of Grose's
Antiquities of Ireland.

choir. Among the architectural details illustrating the introduction to the second volume of Grose's *Antiquities of Ireland*, no. 21 on plate 26 gives details (*Fig. 14*) of three different styles of pillar forming part of the cloister which, though unascribed, provides a good rendering — probably by Beranger — of what still survives today (*Fig. 15*).

On the following day, 20 June, it was not to antiquities that Lewis Irwin brought them, but to one of Leitrim's most celebrated beauty spots. This was what Wilde (40) described as 'a famous cataract at Glan' (almost certainly Glencar), where the intention presumably was to view the waterfall now known as Sruth-i-nagaidh-an-áird. They 'arrived after much fatigue, and Mr. Bigari (a bad horseman) after some falls, at the place, when behold there was no water, occasioned by the excessive heats and droughts'. But, in recompense, the artists experienced what Wilde described with wistful nostalgia as a 'good old Irish rustic festivity' near the bank of a pleasant lake (presumably Glencar Lough) and which Beranger portrayed as follows:

> A great crowd, and went up to see the occasion of it; found it to be a dance for a Cake — stopped some time to see the diversion. The scene was pleasing — gentlemen and ladies, on horseback and on foot, being mixed with the country people, and forming a triple ring round the dancers, whilst a fellow standing on some bench or barrel held up a pole, at the end of which the cake was hung in a clean napkin, adorned with ribbands, to be given as a prize to the best performers [Wilde, 40].

Fig. 14
Architectural details
engraved after Beranger and
Bigari drawings on plate
126 of the second volume
of Grose's *Antiquities of
Ireland* include Cong (2–7),
Ballintubber Abbey (8–11),
Boyle (20), Sligo (21),
Rosserk (22 and 24) and
Dromahaire (26–7) — the
latter two places confused
in the original caption.

Fig. 15
Detail of the most
ornamental part of the
cloister of Sligo Abbey.

Dromahaire (Creevelea) Abbey and O'Rourke's Hall

June 21st, though not a Sunday, gave the artists a respite from their work, but on the following day Irwin must have kept them busy, bringing them over his county border into Leitrim again, where the artists

Entered a river, which had a hedge of trees and underwood on each side which seemed to grow out of the water. Had a cold dinner, and drank the health of the Miss Ormsbys under the name of the Three Graces, which was one of our standing toasts. Walked to Drumahaire, drew and took the plan of the famous O'Rourke's Hall, where he gave the great feast, which the Irish poets have celebrated in a song, of which Dean Swift has given a fine translation. Baited at a gentleman's house; and on hearing that the priest had the original Irish song, sent our interpreter to transcribe it. Went to the Abbey, drew it, and plan, &c.&c. [Wilde, 41].

The letterpress accompanying the engraving of O'Rork's (or O'Rourke's) Hall, plate 35 in the second volume of Grose's *Antiquities* (*Fig. 16*), runs as follows:

Fig. 16
'ORourks Hall, Co. Leitrim', engraved in 1793 after a Bigari original for plate 35 of vol. 2 of Grose's *Antiquities of Ireland*.

Dromahaire castle has before been mentioned; it was on a hill close to the village. Somewhat lower down the hill was O'Rork's hall, or castle, with the stones of part of which the new castle of Dromahaire was constructed, by Sir William Villiers, about 1630.

O'Rork's hall was a much older building; for, in 1588, the Earl of Clanricard, and Sir Richard Bingham, surprised the Irish at Dromahaire, that is, at O'Rork's castle, and slew many of them.

From the circumstance above related, much of the original fortress was carried away; but from what remains, it appears to have originally been an oblong building. There is a room, at the upper end of which are loopholes for the windows; this rendered it very dark. This has been called the cellar. The whole is at present in such a state of ruin, that nothing but conjectures can be formed respecting the different parts of the edifice.

This view was taken from an original drawing by Begari, in the collection of the Rt. Hon. William Conyngham.

Fig. 17
The ivied, ruined window of O'Rourke's Hall at Dromahair contrasts with the splendour it must have seen at the great feast held there by Brian O'Rourke over 400 years ago.

The comments about the structure itself must have been culled from an account by Beranger, who, on p. 5 of MS 4162, wrote:

> O'Rourke's hall Drumahare an oblong square building, very much ruined, seems at present, of middling workmanship as the morter is fallen from between the stones. There is a closet at the upper end with small loop holes for windows, which made that place very dark when covered & from thence got the appellation of the cellar. See plan No. 5

Bigari's hand-coloured original drawing (*Pl. 2*) survives as 2122 TX(66) in the National Library, and differs little from the engraving in Grose except for the door at the end of the right-hand wall, which is round in Bigari's drawing and pointed in the engraving; the latter also adds a man and a woman in the foreground who are far too small in scale. The long, rectangular building, with its unusually tall

Fig. 18
'Plan of O Roirke's Hall at Drumahaire' and 'Windows of the Abbey of Drumahaire', signed by G. B(eranger) and now 2122 TX(89) in the National Library.

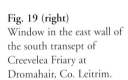

Fig. 19 (right)
Window in the east wall of the south transept of Creevelea Friary at Dromahair, Co. Leitrim.

Fig. 20 (far right)
The east window of the friary at Dromahair, Co. Leitrim — little changed since Beranger drew it in 1779.

window embrasures in both side walls, does not look as if it formed part of a castle originally, and was almost certainly built specifically as a hall. Though close to the seventeenth-century Plantation castle, the building (private property) is now, unfortunately, so overgrown and full of brambles that it is impossible to make out architectural details (*Fig. 17*) — a great pity, considering that it is the only surviving medieval building of its kind in Connacht and, indeed, one of little more than half a dozen in the whole country. It would be wonderful to see it restored to its original function as a banqueting hall, particularly as it is so closely related to the tradition of hospitality in the province. This comes about because of a great feast already mentioned by Beranger, which was given to poets (and presumably others) by Brian na Murtha O'Rourke, chieftain of Breffny, who had given succour to at least one survivor of the Spanish Armada in the form of Captain Francisco de Cuellar and who, after much resistance to the English, was finally brought to London, where he was hanged and quartered in 1591. Pages 24–5 of the first volume of Grose's *Antiquities* say that

> on his submission, he went to England and was introduced to Queen Elizabeth, but refused to bend his knee. Being asked why he did not, he answered that he was not accustomed to it. How, says a smart English Lord, not to images? Aye, replied O'Rourk, but there is a great deal of difference between your Queen and the images of Saints. He gravely petitioned the Queen, not for life or pardon, but that he be hanged with a gad or withe, after his country fashion, a request, which no doubt, was readily granted to him.

The story about bending the knee comes from Philip O'Sullivan Beare's *Historiae Catholicae Iberniae compendium* (Lisbon, 1621) and the account of the interview with Queen Elizabeth stems from one of Bacon's Essays. This information we glean from a John O'Donovan footnote in his edition of *The Annals of the Four Masters,* which, under the year 1591, state that

> The death of this Brian was one of the mournful stories of the Irish, for there had not been for a long time any one of his tribe who excelled him in bounty, in hospitality, in giving rewards for panegyrical poems, in sumptuousness, in troops, in comeliness, in firmness, in maintaining the field of battle to defend his patrimony against foreign adventurers, until his death on this occasion.

O'Rourke's reputation for hospitality praised by the Four Masters remained legendary, and a Christmas feast he is said to have given was the subject of *Plearaca na Ruarcach*, a laudatory poem written in Irish by Hugh MacGauran around 1700, later put to music by his friend Carolan, and further immortalised by Swift, who translated it into English around 1720. Beranger may have heard of it from Col. Charles Vallancey, one of the members of the Antiquarian Society, who, on pp 128–31 of the second edition of his *A grammar of the Iberno-Celtic, or Irish language* published in Dublin in 1781 (only two years after the Tour of Connacht), gave the poem as one of his linguistic examples, and provided alongside it Swift's translation, a part of which runs as follows:

O'Rourke's noble fare
Will ne'er be forgot,
By those who were there
Or those who were not.

His revels to keep
We sup, and we dine,
On seven score sheep,
Fat bullocks, and swine.

Usquebaugh to our feast
In pails was brought up,
An hundred at least,
And a madder our cup....

Come, harper, strike up;
But first by your favour,
Boy, give us a cup:
Ay! This has some savour.

O'Rourke's jolly boys
Ne'er dreamt of the matter,
Till rouz'd by the noise,
And musical clatter.

An unattributed plan of the hall from the Burton Conyngham Collection is preserved in MS 671 in the National Library, but an original (*Fig. 18*), signed by Beranger and bearing the number 5D on the back, is also housed there as 2122 TX(89), and a faithful copy by Austin Cooper of April 1800 can be found on p. 20 of 2122 TX(4).

In both of the latter instances, it shares the sheet with details of the windows of what Beranger calls the Abbey of Drumahaire, but which is more correctly described as a friary, now generally known as Creevelea, founded by Margaret O'Brien for the Franciscans in 1508 — one of the last religious houses opened in Ireland before the Reformation. Beautifully sited overlooking the River Bonet, it has the typical Franciscan layout of a long, hall-type church with tall, off-centre tower and adjoining cloister, but having details that Killanin and Duignan described in *The Shell Guide to Ireland* as being 'curious and degenerate rather than beautiful'. The mild asymmetry in the north range of the cloister buildings is not apparent in the unsigned copy plan of the friary preserved as 1976 TX(26) in the National Library (*Fig. 21*), and subsequently engraved as plate 56 in the first volume of Grose's

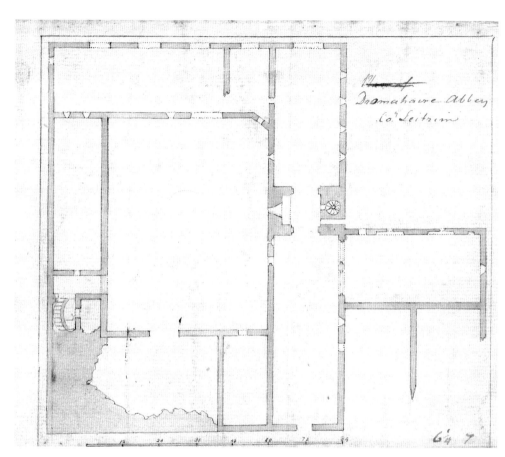

Fig. 21
'Plan of Dromahaire Abbey, Co. Leitrim', prepared for engraving in Grose's *Antiquities of Ireland* and now preserved as 1976 TX (26) in the Prints and Drawings Department of the National Library.

Antiquities, which — though unattributed, like most of the plans in the book — is likely to have been based on an original by Beranger. The lack of any remnants of a cloister arcade on the plan is explained by Beranger's account of the buildings preserved on p. 5 of MS 4162 in the National Library:

> This abbey is pretty extensive well built of a blackish stone. The arches round, part of the tower is broke down and the whole abbey much in ruin, nothing remains of the cloysters, not even the foundation can be traced, the aria which we suposed to contain them being covered with grass. There were some good stone windows. See Plan, view and parts No. 5.

The details of those 'good stone windows' are preserved in the Beranger 2122 TX(89) drawing (*Fig. 18*) mentioned above as bearing the number 5D, and represent — going from left to right — probably one of the windows in the east wall of the south transept (*Fig. 19*), the west window and the east window (*Fig. 20*) respectively. The latter two are reproduced as nos 26 and 27 of plate 126 of the second volume of Grose's *Antiquities* (*Fig. 14*).

The plate preceding the friary plan in the first volume of Grose illustrates an exterior view of the

Fig. 22
The Abbey of Dromahair as seen from the south-east.

friary seen from the south-east and 'taken from an original drawing by Bigari, in the collection of the right Honourable William Conyngham' — the whole little changed today (*Fig. 22*). It shows us the fine traceried east window in the centre, the south transept on the left, and the outside wall of the cloister and its corner building towards the right. The original drawing on which the engraving was based cannot now be found, but p. 14 of the Royal Irish Academy's manuscript 3.C.29 preserves a charming watercolour that was doubtless a copy (*Pl. 3*). It was prepared for the engraver, as was also another watercolour of the interior of the 'Abbey' — 1976 TX(61) in the National Library (*Pl. 4*) — that is ascribed to Bigari by an unidentified later hand, but which was rejected for Grose's *Antiquities* because the engraving chosen was 'from another view'. His original, though unsigned and probably captioned by Beranger, is also preserved in the National Library as 2122 TX(3), p. 6 (*Fig. 23*), and bears the original Beranger No. 5 on the top right. This view is taken from the western end of the church in what is a slightly twisted perspective, and provides a look into the south transept and — through the tower arch — to the east window, shown here without the tracery visible in the watercolour of the exterior (*Pl. 3*). Unusually for Bigari, the central tower is made broader than it actually is (*Fig. 24*), thereby reducing the effect of its height. Two tall and elegant male figures — could they be Irwin on the left, and Beranger with his Jacob's staff or measuring stick on the right? — form the focus of the centre foreground.

The Abbey of Dromahair Co. of Leitrim 7 miles from Sligo

Fig. 23
Unsigned Bigari view of the
interior of 'The Abbey of
Dromahair, Co. of Leitrim',
now 2122 TX(3), p. 6, in the
National Library.

Fig. 24
Interior view of Dromahair
Abbey, Co. Leitrim, looking
eastwards towards the tower
and chancel.

Church Island on Lough Gill

Having finished their drawings of the friary, the two artists went to sit down on 'O'Rourke's chair of marble, against a pillar where he used to judge causes', and then proceeded to Church Island on Lough Gill, 'where we landed and drew an ancient church' (Wilde, 41). This Beranger described on p. 5 of Nat. Lib. MS 4162 as

> A small oblong church, seemingly ill built with loophole windows very few in number and when roofed must have been a dark place. There is a recess at one end with only a loophole which when covered admitted hardly light enough to see the place, the door has some rude carving like dentiles on the arched part. See Plan & Drawg No. 6.

Echoes of Beranger's wording can clearly be seen in the letterpress accompanying the engraving of a lost Bigari drawing reproduced as plate 98 in the first volume of Grose's *Antiquities* and which runs as follows (pp 58–9):

> This island is usually called Innismore, and is situated in Lough Gill and barony of Carbury. Colgan says, St. Loman founded a church here in the time of Columba. Whatever the tradition may be it was certainly one of the old establishments of the Culdees, whose hostility to Romish tenets and innovations made the writers devoted to them deprive them of the honour to which their learning, sanctity, and zeal had just claim. In the year 1416 the abbey was destroyed by an accidental fire, in which the annals of the four masters mention some valuable MSS. of O'Curnin were destroyed. He was a religious of that church. The isle is about two miles long, and in some places half a mile broad; the abbey is at the east end of it, and in former ages was the burial-place of the parish of Calry. In a rock near the door of the church is a cavity, called Our Lady's bed, into which pregnant women go, and turn thrice round, which they believe prevents their dying in labour; at the same time they repeat certain prayers. Both rock and church are now covered with ivy.
> The church is an oblong, with a few loophole windows, which most of the very old Culdean edifices have. There is a recess at one end, lighted by a similar window. The door has some rude carving like dentils.

This view was taken from an original drawing by Bigari, then in the collection of the Right Honourable William Conyngham. Bigari's drawing, preserved only in the engraving reproduced as plate 98 in vol. 1 of Grose's *Antiquities* (*Fig. 25*), shows the interior of the church looking westwards, with a large tree growing inside, and gives a hint of the 'dentils' in the doorway (*Fig. 26*).

Fig. 25
The interior of the church on Church Island, Lough Gill, Co. Sligo, as engraved in 1793 after a Bigari original for plate 98 of vol. 1 of Grose's *Antiquities of Ireland.*

Fig. 26
Comparatively undisturbed, the church on Church Island in Lough Gill has changed little in the centuries since Bigari sketched it.

Carrowmore

On the following day, 23 June, attention was turned to monuments of a much remoter past, for which Sligo is famous, namely megalithic tombs at Carrowmore and on the summit of Knocknarea. To quote Beranger's own words:

> Mr. Bigary not wishing to ride, I went with Mr. Irwin and his son on horseback to Knocknareagh mountain, — seen on the lands of Carrowmore, in the space of a quarter of a mile, eighteen circles of huge stones, some with their Cromleghs in the centre standing, some down, but stones lying on the spot; designed and planned the largest one. Sure it is, that they are not Temples, nor the Cromleghs altars, as the antiquarians pretend, but burial places of chieftains. These eighteen together (I think) settles the matter, and prove this place to have been either a cemetery, or the spot where some famous battle was fought, and the heroes which fell to have been interred on the field where they were slain; but I believe, if some of the antiquarians had heard of eighteen being together in one spot, they would not have called them Temples [Wilde, 41–2].

Good reasoning on Beranger's part! Wilde (42) says that, under the heading Cromleagh, Beranger made a note in the Diary of the discovery of these Carrowmore monuments, and quoted a passage from Vallancey's *Collectanea* of 1791 — presumably, therefore, added later to the manuscript — to the effect that they 'pass with some for Druidical altars' before adding the following comments himself:

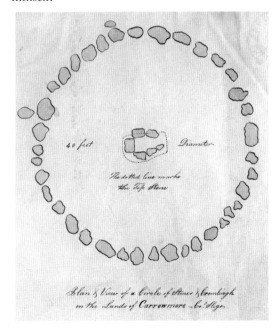

Fig. 27
A 1790s plan of Tomb 7 at Carrowmore, Co. Sligo, probably by Austin Cooper after a Beranger original, is now part of sheet 12 of the Royal Irish Academy's manuscript 3.C.42.

If the Cromleaghs and circles of stones were altars and temples, they would surely have been destroyed by the Christians, as they demolished all the religious monuments of the Pagans; but being known by them to be but burial places, or Mausoleums of the dead, they respected them, and left them untouched [Wilde, 42].

George Petrie, usually hailed as the founder of Irish archaeology, knew of Beranger's Sligo commentary (probably through the manuscript referred to above on p. 17, which was at that time probably in the possession of Roger C. Walker of Rathcarrick), and realised that there were many more tombs at Carrowmore than the eighteen (or fifteen — see below) mentioned by Beranger. He gave them a numbering system which is still in general use today, and it is almost certainly his No. 7 which was the subject of Beranger's catalogue entry on p. 6 of MS 4162, as follows:

> This circle of stones with a Cromliagh in the center is the most remarkable and most entire of 15 which are situated in the space of a square ¼ mile. It is 40 feet in diameter within the clear, and the circle is composed of 40 rough stones from 2 to 5 feet high & from 2 to 5 & 8 feet Diamr. The Top stone of the Cromliagh is 9 feet by 5 feet 8 inches and stands on 6 suporters 4 feet 4 high. The remaining circles are not so compleat and most of them have their Cromliagh demolished. See Plan and View No. 7.

A watercolour view of the tomb by J. T(urner), 1799 (*Pl. 5*), but based presumably on a lost Beranger original, is now on sheet 12 of MS 3.C.42 in the Royal Irish Academy (formerly in University College Dublin). It is pasted down on a sheet which also bears an unsigned and undated plan of the tomb (*Fig. 27*) and an early Academy stamp. The accompanying caption is almost certainly in the hand of Austin Cooper, who probably copied a Beranger original some time in the 1790s. The monument has not changed much in the meantime, but was carefully excavated by an interdisciplinary Swedish team in 1977–8 (*Pl. 6*).

Misgaun Mewe

The second major tomb which Beranger was to sketch on 23 June was Misgaun Mewe as he calls it, the great mound of stones on top of Knocknarea which so dominates the north Sligo landscape (*Fig. 28*). In the lost Note Book, Beranger described what he experienced, saw and did:

> Went on, ascended with much fatigue some part on horseback, and part on foot, that high mountain; arrived on the summit, on which is the tomb of Queen Maud, wife of Olioll, King of Connaught in the fourth century. This monument is a huge cairn of small stones, sixty feet high; drew and plan, and measured. On the top we had a fine view of the Atlantic Ocean, and all the neighbouring country [Wilde, 43].

In a note on Knocknarea carne, he relates further:

> On the top full of little houses like the children make of slates. Mr. Irwin told me that every one that came there erects such a one, and according to custom we took stones like slates, of which the hill is composed, and made one apiece [Wilde, 43].

In his description of 'Misgan Mewe', Beranger says on p. 6 of MS 4162:

Fig. 28
The dramatic mound of
Misgaun Mewe on the
summit of Knocknarea, Co.
Sligo, where 'the wind
bundles up the clouds', in
Yeats's phrase.

Fig. 29
View, plan and section of
Misgaun Mewe on
Knocknarea, Co. Sligo,
signed by G. B(eranger),
and now 2122 TX(4), p.
34, in the National Library.
The changes and additions
were probably made by
Charles O'Conor.

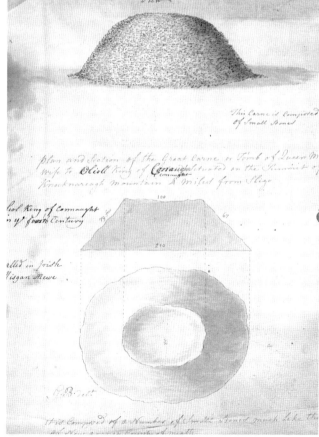

This carne said to be the Tomb of Queen Maud wife to Olioll King of Connaught in the fourth century, is situated on the top of Knock-na-reagh mountain, which is a headland on the south side of Sligo Bay, it is called in Irish Misgan Mewe and is composed of an enormous heap of small stones, & is of an oval figure of 630 feet circumference at the base; 79 feet slope on one side, 67 at the other and the area at the top 100 feet in its longest diamr & 85 in its shortest, it is seen at a great distance. See Plan and section No. 8.

Though not actually bearing the number 8, there is an original Beranger view, plan and section of Queen Maeve's Grave preserved as 2122 TX(4), p. 34, in the National Library (*Fig. 29*). The main caption states 'Plan and Section of the Great carne or Tomb of Queen Maud Wife to Olioll King of Conaught. Situated on the Summit of Knocknareagh mountain 4 miles from Sligo'. Underneath the word 'Conaught' the spelling has been corrected to 'Connaught' by a different hand — likely to be that of Charles O'Conor (compare below, p. 181) — which also wrote 'Oliol King of Connaught in ye fourth century'. At the bottom of the sheet, Beranger wrote 'It is composed of a number of small stones much like that of Newgrange County of Meath' — surely one of the earliest observations to connect the two monuments, both of which almost certainly belong to the same class of megalithic tombs known as passage graves. A good copy prepared by J.T. (presumably Joseph Turner) in 1799 is among the material recently returned by the Department of Archaeology in University College Dublin to the Royal Irish Academy, where it now bears the accession number of 3.C.42, sheet 9.

Drumcliff

The island of Inishmurray was the objective of the journey on 24 June, but before reaching it the artists stopped *en route* at Drumcliff, a site associated with St Columba. On p. 6 of the catalogue, MS 4162 in the National Library, Beranger says

> The Antiquities at Drumcliffe are a stump of a round tower dimentions on ye plan No. 9, and two crosses, the one plain, and the other with basreliefs, not very decent. What is remarkable in this cross is a frogg in relief on the side. See Drawing No. 9.

He need not have worried about the indecent carvings, as they represent Adam and Eve! An unsigned drawing (*Fig. 30*) of the two crosses and the round tower — almost certainly by Bigari, to judge by the tower's masonry – is preserved in the National Library as 2122 TX(79). Its main antiquarian interest lies in the head of the small cross in the background which has disappeared (compare *Fig. 31*), and this may be the only recorded drawing of it. The 'dimentions' mentioned by Beranger presumably refer to the caption on the back of TX(79), which reads:

> Crosses and broken round tower at Drumcliffe, 3½ miles from Sligo. Tower 27½ feet high.

Fig. 30
Unsigned pen and wash drawing, probably by Bigari, of the round tower and high crosses at Drumcliff, Co. Sligo, preserved as 2122 TX(79) in the National Library of Ireland.

Fig. 31
The head of one of the Drumcliff high crosses drawn on the 1779 tour (*Fig. 30*) no longer survives.

Inishmurray

Wilde (44–8) gives a number of valuable extracts about the Inishmurray visit taken from Beranger's lost Diary/Note Book, but Beranger's best overall description is found in a letter written from Dublin — to Col. Charles Vallancey — on 26 May 1785, and now preserved as pp 61–74 of MS 1415 in the National Library. As such, it is worthwhile quoting in its entirety:

> Sir,
>
> According to your desire, here follows the history of my trip to Ennismurry with the description of that Island, its inhabitants and its Antiquities. On the 24 of June 1779 we embarked in the Bay of Sligo about 3 o'clock, with Lewis Irwin of Tonregoe Esq., and as the wind was contrary we were obliged to make several tacks, so that we did not reach the Island until nine in the evening. We landed in a small and narrow harbour, the only one in the place where a vessel of the size of ours could ride in safety, having on each side rocks jetting out into the sea, which at first sight I took for the work of men, and tho' I was assured of the contrary, I cannot but think, considering its regularity, that it is nature improved. The inhabitands seeing us make towards them were collected on the shore and received us with open arms, and being warned by Mr Irwin to imitate him, we followed his example and embraced the females, who returnd the civility with as much cordiality as if we had been their nearest relations. We were immediately conducted to one of their houses where we staid until a large barn was prepared and some deal tables fixed together on which the cloth was laid and there we went to eat our supper which consisted in various sorts of fresh fish broiled and plenty of lobsters for desert. We did not want [for] liquor, Mr Irwin having provided wine, spirrits and porter. Our illumination consisted in four rushes dipt in grease put in as many old Irish wooden candle sticks of above two feet high, intended to serve only on the ground, which not showing light enough when standing on the table, we contrived to fix on stools between us, which with the oddity of our situation, the remarks and the gaity of the company, made us spend the evening in merryment and satisfaction; after supper we were conducted to another barn where we found clean straw spread on the ground over which four chaff beds were laid, with clean coarse sheets, on which Mr. Irwin, his son, Mr. Bigary and I, laid ourselves down, after which the door was shut and every crevisse or opening stopped with straw on the outside by the islanders, to keep out the air. They then returnd to the eating barn to finish the remains of our supper with our interpreter, Mr. Irwin's servant and the crew of our barge.
>
> We got up at five next morning and walked round the island examining the shore which we performed easily in ½ of an hour; we then began our operations by taking the plans of its antiquities. went to breakfast and returned to make drawings untill 3 o'clock.
>
> Ennismurry is an island of the Athlantick Ocean situated about 9 miles distance west of the shore of the County of Sligo. The western side is bold and rocky and appeared to me on looking down more than a hundred feet above the level of the sea. Some of the rocks projecting

like capes are perforated in the form of huge arches through which the sea foams continually, even in the calmest days, and must appear if it could be beheld from below in tempestuous weather most romantic and picturesque; the eastern side has not the grand apearance, as the rock of which the Island is composed goes shelving down on that side in almost regular steps to the edge of the water where the little children walk down with ease to wash themselves or to swim. About 130 acres of the surface is covered with a thin soil 5 or 6 inches deep, and produces grass enough to feed 5 cows, as many horses and 30 sheep, all the arrable produce about twenty barrels of corn, besides potatoes and garden stuff.

The collony at that time consisted of forty-five inhabitants children included, which compose five famillies inhabiting as many houses. They have besides five large buildings, who serve as barns, stables and stores. The males are all fishermen and they sell their cargoes on the main. They intermarry among themselves and have inhabited the Island in succession these 5 or 6 hundred years (as they told us); when they find themselves overstocked, they send their children, when able, to ye main to provide for themselves, who do not return but on visits to their parents, or to take possession of an inheritance.

All the inhabitants look neat and decent, the men having good coats or jackets, and most of the women wearing cotton or linnen gowns, their houses within are clean, and tho' not overstocked with furniture, the tables, benches and stools are whole and entire, and it seemed to me that this people are blessed with all the necessarys of life and that their wishes do not extent to the superfluities of it.

Comfortably situated during the summer, their situation in winter is most desolate, being secluded from all intercourse with the main, their small boats not being able to live in that most boysterous occean, the fury of which is such, that we were shown on the high western shore a stone four feet long and 3 thick every way, which the force of the billows had rised from below (two years ago) and carried to the top of the Island a hight of at least 100 feet. During this season they live upon dry or salted fish, potatoes, milk and now and then upon a sheep which is killed and devided among them. They are all of the Roman Catholick Religion. They appear devout, kneeling or bowing to all places which they hold as sanctified, but superstitious and credulous to the highest degree. On my enquiring how they would do, if a priest was wanting during the winter season for some ceremony, which absolutely required one, our conductor answered me gravely, that in that case any one of them went to the seaside and launched his boat, which as soon as she had touched the water, the sea would become calm, and the wind cease, untill the boat had brought the priest to Island, back to the main and was returnd and hauled on shore, that then the tempest would rage again and continue as violent as before. I was tempted to ask him if this miracle had been done in his time, but reflecting on the mortification my question might occasion him, I thought it would be ill repaying his trouble and hospitality towards us, so that I did not put my query to him. He observed also to us, that tho' they had neither priest, lawyer nor phisician, they were devout, just and healthy, of which we were in no doubt; to conclude the caracters of the inhabitands, they refuse all payments from their visitors for whatever treatment they have given them and, on our landing, they were going to kill a sheep to entertain us, our servants and crew, if Mr. Irwin had not prevented them by showing our provisions, which were in plenty more than we could consume.

The antiquities of the Island are called Stations by the inhabitants. They are visited by the roman Catholicks on certain occasion who recite some prayers at every Station. They rank them in the following order

1. monument of the Trinity, built by St. Molash
2. monument of St. Columb Kill
3. monument of St. Patrick
4. Loughtyroory
5. Tubberbrick
6. Tranew
7. Clushmore
8. Altbuy
9. Classahmore
10. Small loughties or circles of stones
11. Temple murry
12. The Abbey

for all of these see the Explanations in Irish by our Interpreter Terrence Maguire, the manuscript being in the hands of the Rt. Hon.ble Wm. Conyngham, president of the Society to whom I delivered them.

The first elleven Stations consist in pieces of ground enclosed by a wall of dry stones breast high, containing a kind of stone altar, a cross, or a well. The principal and largest one is that of the trinity, which I designed (see plan and view). Temple Murry is a small oblong church or chappel, the walls of which are standing, but the roof is gone. It is built with mortar, but of rude workmanship and very plain. Its situation is at some distance from the abbey (vide plan).

The abbey, as it is called, is the most rude and irregular of all the structures, being no more than a wall enclosing a pretty large piece of ground which contains 2 chappels and four cells. This wall is from 8 to 10 feet in hight, composed of large long stones piled upon one another without mortar; the thickness is unequal being in some places 5 in others 6.7.8 and 10 feet. The entrance is by 2 doors so narrow that a corpulent man could not enter it even side ways, which mode we used not to dirty our clothes. We were a longtime consulting to determine its figure to make the plan, having no other instruments than a 60 feet tape and a two foot rule, at length we determined it by angles as marked on the plan (which see), and performed our task as accurately as our poor tools would permit. Col. Irwin being a good Ingeneer was of great help to us. The chappel A stands by itself on a level ground which takes up 3 fourths of the enclosure, the other fourth is raised 4 and 5 feet above the level, and the earth is kept up by an iregular dry wall which part is shaded on the plan and contains the chappel B and the cells D D.E which, of course, are semysubteraneous; a passage like a trench is cut thro', lined with a drystone wall and gives access to them. Near the wall of this elevated ground in a corner but on the level stands the cell of St. Molash, which is entire, marked C, and near one of the doors is the cell F which, with the cursing altar, is what the enclosure contains.

The chappels A and B are built of stone and mortar, but of rude workmanship. The four walls only remains, the roofs being gone, but perhaps were arched like the cell of St. Molash C which remains entire, covered with its stone roof (See the drawing and plan). The cells D D and F are build without mortar in a rude manner, being arched, and have a hole at the top and a spike hole on one side. They contain nothing, only one has a stone bench or couch; they look horrid and gloomy. The cell E is fallen in or stopped. We could find no entrance. The inside of St Molash's cell contains a stone elevation about 4 feet high, which reigns along with two of its sides, not unlike a Taylors bench. What its use was I cannot conjecture. On this is placed a wooden figure of the Saint, about 5 feet high, of which Mr Bigary desiring to draw the portrait, we got him carried in open air. On sight of his Holiness, who was all over painted with vermillion, we could not abstain from laughing, to the great mortification of those who upheld them kneeling. But I hope they did forgive us, on telling them that it was for the honnour of the Saint that this portrait was to be made known to the world (See ye portrait). On considering the various buildings, mortar being employed in some, and none in the others, I am apt to think those last ones more ancient, but I leave to your great knowledge in antiquities to decide it. On the left hand, on entering the trench which leads to the semysubteraneous cells, stands the cursing altar about 4 feet square by 3 hight of stone and mortar. On it are placed several stones of various sizes of a circular form somewhat flatten'd. Our conductor told us that the miraculous propriety of those stones were such, that any person grievously injured by another, on coming devoutly to this altar and cursing his antagonist, specifying the evil he wishes to fall on him, and turning at the same time one of the stones, the said curse had its effect, and the wished evil fell on him who had injured the wisher, providing he had done it out of an evil design. But if the antagonist had not done it with a design to hurt or that he was not guilty, then the evil and curse fell upon the wisher himself, who was obliged to bear it without hope of relief, which added he keept everyone in such awe that seldom or ever a stone was turned. Thus, the altar is become useless.

To give you a compleat idea of the goodness of heart of those Islanders, I shall mention the manner of our departure, which I think is but doing justice to their hospitality and benevolence.

Having finished our drawings and observations we adjourned to our eating barn where, amongst the plenty of provisions Coll. Irwin had brought, the good people had added quantity of fresh fish, particularly exellent lobsters; notice was given to them that after diner, we should depart, and after our repast, on quitting the barn, we found all the inhabitants children included standing at the door with grief painted in their countenances, we walked slowly to the harbour followed by all; where being arrived Mr. Irwin made them sit on the grass in semy circular form, and opening a portmanteau distributed presents consisting in ribbonds, roll tabacco, and beads; after which his servant broched a small cask of whiskey, which was served round to the company, who drank to our healths wishing us a thousand blesses. The ceremony of embracing the females was renewd who returned the compliment with tears in their eyes, and with so much affection, that it seemed as if we were their nearest relations who parted never to return. We shook hands with the men who seemed not less concerned and we walked to the harbour and embarqued, whilst the people spred themselves on the piers, utering blesses, as soon as we unmoored, we saluted them with cheers which were answered from the shore, and both sides continued waving hands untill out of sight. There was something so affecting in all this, that for a long time we continued in a thoughtfull silence, out of which we were roused on entering Sligo bay, by our vessel striking on a bank, our crew consisting in five men, the Captain included, having found means to broach the whiskey cask unknown to us, the liquor of which operating on their brains, rendered them unable to do their business. We got of(f), however, by the help of poles, but running aground afterwards almost every five minutes Coll. Irwin was obliged, as it was already dark and for fear of accidents, to take the helm and steer us for Sligo; which he happily effected, and we arrived there at midnight. We observed during our navigation in the dark that phenomenon often mentioned in descriptions of voyages, namely the luminous wake of our vessel, and the fiery flashes occasioned by every stroke of our oars, which are thought to be occasioned by quantities of luminous sea insects. If it is so, Sligo bay abounds with them.

I have the honour to be, Sir,

Your Most obedient and most obliged Servt.

Gabriel Beranger.

Though these reminiscences were written almost six years after the visit to Inishmurray — probably to provide Vallancey with some material for his *Vindication of the ancient history of Ireland* of 1786 — Beranger must have been relying heavily for them on the notes he made at the time and which tally in certain instances almost word for word with the text of the letter quoted above. Yet Wilde (44–8) was able to reproduce extracts from the lost Note Book which are not repeated in the 1785 letter and which add some interesting domestic detail, such as travelling by currach, the nature of the candlesticks and quaffing from madders (methers), together with what amounts to a recipe for preparing a stew called 'olio':

> Mr. Irwin ordered our rabbits, a turkey, some fowl, and ducks, to be cut up with a leg of mutton, to which he added some greens, turnips and carrots, and a piece of hare, which being put in a large tosspan he had also brought with him, and having seasoned it properly, put it down on a slow fire, promising us the best olio we ever tasted [Wilde, 45].

Additional local colour was provided by a passing 'whale swimming in the ocean, spouting up water to a great height'. Irwin was presumably the island's landlord, and the islanders therefore his tenants,

Fig. 32
'St. Mary's church Ennismurry built of stone & mortar' — an original unsigned drawing by Bigari, now 2122 TX(77) in the National Library.

Fig. 33
'Ennismurry', Co. Sligo, an unsigned panoramic drawing of buildings in the enclosure, probably by Bigari and now p. 9 of 2122 TX(3) in the National Library.

and Beranger said that they loved 'Col. Irwin (by whose means they have been excepted from some county charges), and who every year pays them a visit by which they never lose' (Wilde, 46). One final small sample extract from the lost Note Book should, however, not be entirely omitted here:

> Saw distinctly the mountain of Croagh Patrick, in the County of Mayo, distance sixty miles. Went in every house, but could not converse with the females, as they only speak Irish; remembered the Irish phrase I formerly learned of '*Torum pogue Calinoge*' which I repeated to every girl, who immediately came to kiss me; how unfortunate it was I could ask no more! Finished our drawings; came home; adjourned all to the barn, where the olio was served up in the tosspan to have it hot; never did I taste of a better dish, nor ever did I eat so much; notwithstanding, when our dessert of fine lobsters appeared, we fell to again, so that we were obliged to drink a glass extra to wash it down [Wilde, 45].

We have two original drawings surviving from this island trip. One of these (*Fig. 32*) is of St Mary's Church and bears the number 2122 TX(77) in the National Library; inscribed 'No 10 E' on the back, it has masonry in the style of Bigari but the caption is in Beranger's hand. A hastily sketched copy by Joseph Turner, dated April 1794, is preserved on p. 32 of the second volume of Austin Cooper's drawings — 2122 TX(2). The church stands not at a great distance from the landing-place, but as its door is now permanently barred it is difficult to gain entrance. However, a glance over the western gable wall (*Pl. 24*) shows that, with the exception of the altar foundations and the flag that was flying

Fig. 34
View of part of the enclosure at Inishmurray, Co. Sligo, with Teach Molaisse in the left foreground and Teampull na bhFear in the background.

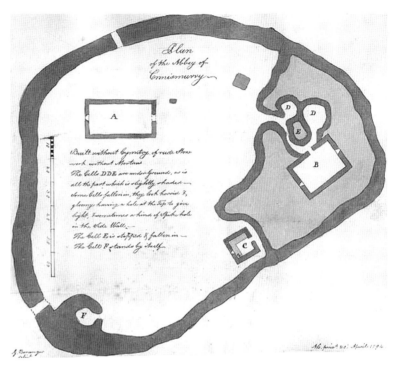

Fig. 35
'Plan of the Abbey of Ennismurry', signed A. C(ooper) in April 1794, copying an original by Beranger and now p. 35 of the Cooper album 2122 TX(2) in the National Library.

(perhaps to indicate the presence of the landlord on the island), things have not changed greatly in over two centuries.

The second drawing (*Fig. 33*), a dark pen and wash, is preserved as p. 9 of 2122 TX(3) in the National Library, and bears the original Beranger number 10 on the top right. It is almost certainly by Bigari, though again the caption seems to be in Beranger's hand, showing that the caption-writer is not necessarily always the draughtsman, as Bigari apparently knew no English. Taken from the top of the enclosure wall (compare *Fig. 34*), the drawing tries to give a panorama — and is almost certainly too ambitious in doing so — showing a beehive hut on the extreme left, St Molaise's House (too tall and thin) in the left foreground, the Men's Church and the doorway of the cashel to the right of centre, and the church known as Teampull na Teinidh on the extreme right. This drawing was copied —not very well — by Sarah Cooper, the wife of Austin Cooper, in the National Library's album 2122 TX(2), p. 31.

It is also thanks to the pen of Austin Cooper himself that we have at least copies of some of the Beranger drawings from the island expedition, referred to in Beranger's long letter to Vallancey quoted above. One of these is the 'plan of the Abbey of Ennismurry', preserved as p. 35 of Cooper's album 2122 TX(2) in the National Library (*Fig. 35*). Various letters designate the different buildings within the cashel (*caisil*) or oval enclosure which forms the kernel of the old monastery said to have been founded by St Molaise around the sixth century. The lost original of this plan was obviously the basis for the engraving forming part of plate 122 illustrating the 'Introduction to ancient Irish architecture' at the start of the second volume of Grose's *Antiquities* (*Fig. 36*). The engraving, however, alters the

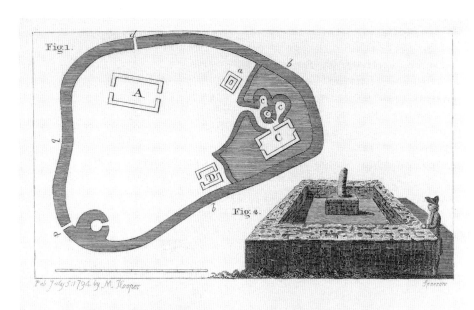

Fig. 36
'Innismurry Antiquities' — plan of the abbey and 'monument of the Trinity' forming plate 122 of vol. 2 of Grose's *Antiquities of Ireland* — both after originals by Beranger.

lettering and becomes confused in aligning it with the accompanying letterpress, which occasionally resorts to a wording which must have been borrowed from Beranger's original (e.g. the cells 'look horrid and gloomy, having a small hole at the top'). In MS 4162, p. 8, Beranger tells us of the tradition that the abbey was 'built by St. Molasse and Columb Kill' ('great saints' but 'horible architects,' he notes in MS 1415, p. 84!), 'but the latter being of a hot fiery temper could not agree with the former & left him and went to the mainland, leaving St Molasse in possession of ye island'. On the preceding page of the same catalogue (MS 4162), Beranger tells us that the abbey is an

> enclosure of dry stones from 5 to 7 & 8 feet thick. It is impossible to determine whether it is round or oval & never have I seen more rude workmanship. there are a few cells under ground which are lighted some at the top thro a hole & some thro a loophole in the side. they are so dark that they appear like horible dungeons.

He then goes on to describe some of the buildings, using the same letters for them as on the plan copied by Cooper:

> Chappels A–B on the Plan No 10 are built with mortar tho rude as is St. Molasse's cell C. The chappel B [now known as Teampull na Teinidh, the 'church of the fire'] is half underground and has a kind of trench to go to it. The chappel A [the Men's Church or Teampull Molaise] stands by itself, it has a window the arch of which is a rough natural crooked stone. See Drawg F No. 10, Letter A, and Plan of one of the cells [Nat. Lib. MS 4162, pp 7–8].

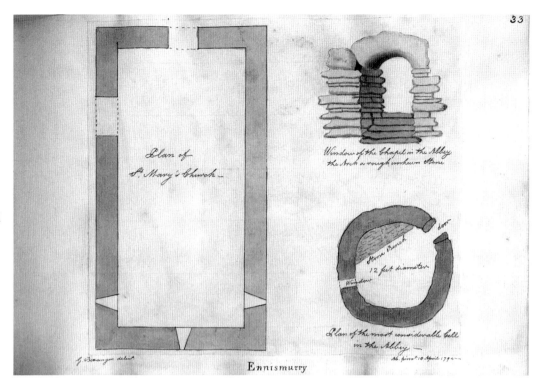

Fig. 37
'Plan of St. Mary's church', 'window of the chapel' and 'plan of the most considerable cell' on 'Ennismurry' in a 1794 drawing by Austin Cooper after Beranger originals and now preserved as p. 33 in the National Library's Cooper Album TX(2).

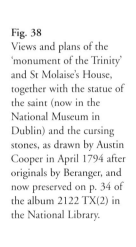

Fig. 38
Views and plans of the 'monument of the Trinity' and St Molaise's House, together with the statue of the saint (now in the National Museum in Dublin) and the cursing stones, as drawn by Austin Cooper in April 1794 after originals by Beranger, and now preserved on p. 34 of the album 2122 TX(2) in the National Library.

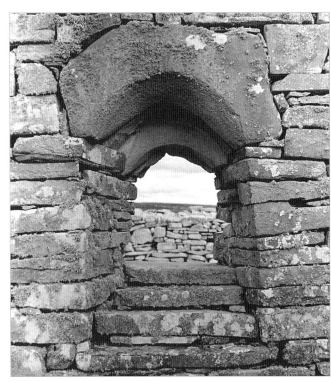

Fig. 39
Interior of the east window
of the Men's Church
(Teampull na bhFear) on
Inishmurray.

Fig. 40
'The monument of the
Trinity' on Inishmurray,
Co. Sligo.

Fig. 41
St Molaise's House (Teach Molaise) on Inishmurray, Co. Sligo. Comparison with Beranger's drawing (*Fig. 38*) suggests that the Office of Public Works may have lowered the roof angle in the nineteenth century.

Fig. 42
The cursing stones in the enclosure at Inishmurray, Co. Sligo.

This last-named drawing and plan refers to the second of Beranger's drawings copied by Cooper (*Fig. 37*), which is p. 33 in the National Library's Cooper Album 2122 TX(2). This shows the window of 'Chappel A', which is bridged by a single stone, and a plan of one of the cells which we would now call a beehive hut. On the same sheet is Beranger's plan of St Mary's Church.

The third Cooper copy of a Beranger drawing — p. 34 of MS 2122 TX(2) — packs in a lot of small detail (*Fig. 38*). On the right is a vertical drawing of the cursing stones, already described above and which, on p. 8 of the National Library's MS 4162, are compared by Beranger to Dutch cheeses. To their left is the statue of the saint which, as we know from the long letter reproduced above, was painted by Bigari — or, as the Diary put it, 'Mr. Bigarry described his holiness upon the spot' (Wilde, 46). Now in the National Museum in Dublin, this important medieval wooden figure was formerly kept in Teach Molaise or St Molaise's House, which is seen at the top centre of the drawing with, beneath it, a plan of the edifice, where the position of the saint's feet are marked on a ledge within. Finally, on the left, is Beranger's drawing and plan of 'the monument of the Trinity built of stone without mortar' as the caption says. The drawing, without the plan, was reproduced as fig. 2 on plate 122 of vol. 2 of Grose's *Antiquities* (*Fig. 36*). This is the only illustrated example of the first eleven stations listed in Beranger's letter and which, as he commented in his Diary,

> might have been made by any one as well as the saints they are said to be made by [Wilde, 47].

The cross-slabs on these stations are no longer in their original positions, having been taken in for safety, but otherwise things have changed comparatively little on Inishmurray (e.g. *Figs 39–42*). Finally, on the same p. 8 of the National Library's MS 4162 where Beranger wrote briefly of holy wells and 'some springs of water all consecrated to some saints', he reported that

> In the time we were drawing and planning, our interpreter gathered the traditions of each consecrated place and wrote them down in Irish as dictated to him. See his Ms.

Terrence McGuire's account of this island folklore is not known to survive, a loss which is all the greater because Beranger, in a letter to Burton Conyngham from Sligo, dated 25 June 1779 (Nat. Lib. MS 1415, p. 76), mentioned that Mr Irwin had told him that 'several poems exist here by tradition which almost prove the truth of those of Mc Pherson in spite of Johnson'.

Thus ends our account of Inishmurray, which, to judge by Beranger's long letter of 1785 quoted above, left a lasting impression, and where — as he described in his letter from Sligo to Burton Conyngham, dated 25 June 1779 (MS 1415, pp 75–6) — he had seen

> Irishmen in the true state of nature, hospitable, inocent and merry. I fancied to be at Ottaheite [Tahiti] since we found here the same good nature, but accompanied by modesty in the sex, who grants plenty of innocent embraces, since they could not enjoy our conversation.

4. MORE OF SLIGO AND SOME OF ROSCOMMON

As if to recover from their nocturnal adventures on the return voyage from Inishmurray, the pair stayed all day at an inn (probably in Sligo) on 26 June, and set out the following morning for Boyle.

Ballisodare Abbey and Church

En route, they stopped first at Ballysodare (as Beranger spells it), where they

> Viewed the cascade occasioned by several falls over rocks of the river Owenbeg: the principal one is about fourteen or fifteen feet high, very perpendicular, and with the rocks about it affords a most romantic sight. We sat down almost fronting it, and enjoyed for some time this charming scene. On the bridge we were shown a stone on which a beggar used to sit constantly, who, on receiving alms, used to bestow on the giver a blessing, which is become a famous toast, under the name of the *Beggar's benison* [Wilde, 48].

They also visited two separate monuments at Ballisodare which Beranger, in MS 4162, p. 9, calls the Abbey and Church respectively. Of the former — an Augustinian foundation dating from the fifteenth century in its present form — Beranger has this to say:

> The remains of the Abbey of Balisadare consist of the arch on which the tower was built & a very small remnant of the tower by the arch, and groining it seems to have been of good masonry of a blackish stone, it was once extensive, as we were told, but is now reduced to very little. See plan and drawing No 11 [Nat. Lib. MS 4162, p. 9].

Beranger's plan (*Fig. 46*) is preserved in an April 1794 copy by J.S. Cooper on the left of p. 47 of the National Library's album 2122 TX(2). Sadly, however, no original view is known to survive, and the engraving of the abbey in Grose's *Antiquities* was done twelve years later by T. Cocking, who shows the arch long before it became engulfed in waste material from the adjoining cement works that makes it look like Ireland's only subterranean abbey today (*Fig. 43*).

The other monument visited in Ballisodare stands on the site of a monastery founded by St Fechin

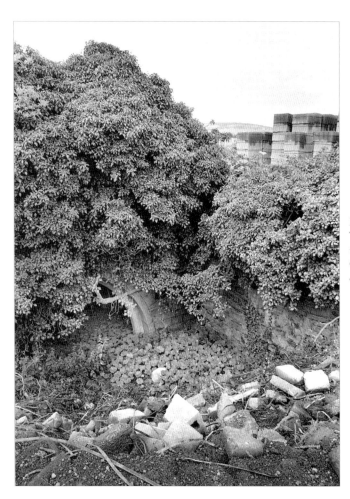

Fig. 43
The disastrous condition of
the 'Abbey' at Ballisodare,
Co. Sligo, which was visited
on the 1779 tour.

in the seventh century. It is a church with a Romanesque doorway of which we are fortunate to have
an original drawing by Beranger, catalogued as 2122 TX(62) in the National Library (*Fig. 44*), with
Beranger's original number 11D on the back. With a goat standing in the left foreground — unlike
the Cocking drawing engraved in vol. 1 of Grose's *Antiquities*, which shows a shooting party without
a bird in sight — the church is seen with the Romanesque doorway (*Fig. 47*) near the western end of
the south wall, which, like most of the rest of the exterior, is now covered with a heavy coating of ivy
(*Fig. 45*). In MS 4162, p. 9, Beranger describes the building briefly as follows:

> At some distance from ye abbey is a church or chappel, which has nothing extraordinary except
> the door, the arched part of which is adorned with heads, much worn, the arch part is stopped
> up with masonry so that it is impossible to see what sort of moulding is under the heads. The
> windows are of cut or hewn stone. Drawings etc. No. 11.

Fig. 44
'The church of Ballysadare, Co. of Sligo,' signed by Beranger and now 2122 TX(62) in the National Library.

The Church of Ballysadare Co. of Sligo.

Fig. 45
The old church with Romanesque doorway at Ballisodare, Co. Sligo, is now engulfed by ivy.

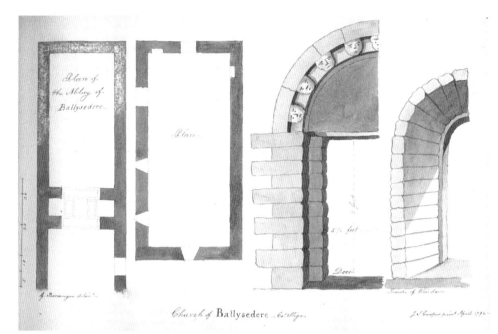

Fig. 46
Page 47 of 2122 TX(2) in the National Library shows plans of Ballisodare Abbey, Co. Sligo, and of the nearby church, together with details of the latter's Romanesque doorway with exterior heads and tympanum, and the inside of a window. All were drawn by J.S. Cooper in April 1794 after lost Beranger originals.

Fig. 47
The worn heads on the south doorway of the church at Ballisodare, Co. Sligo, probably date from the late twelfth century.

The buttress shown in the drawing was later used as one end of a tomb erected by his parishioners to the memory of the Rev. Walter Henery, but the ivy is now so thick that it obscures the nature of the windows so clearly delineated by Beranger. An interior view of one of these is preserved on the extreme right of p. 47 (*Fig. 46*) of the National Library's album 2122 TX(2), a 1794 J.S. Cooper copy of a lost Beranger drawing which also includes the plan of the church and half of the Romanesque doorway.

Ballindoon Abbey

Having passed through 'Coloony an indifferent-looking town' (Wilde, 48), their next stop was over twelve miles distant at what Beranger calls Ballydoon, but which is normally spelled Ballindoon, a Dominican priory built in the early sixteenth century on an entrancing site overlooking the northern end of Lough Arrow. Beranger's description of it is preserved in MS 4162, p. 9:

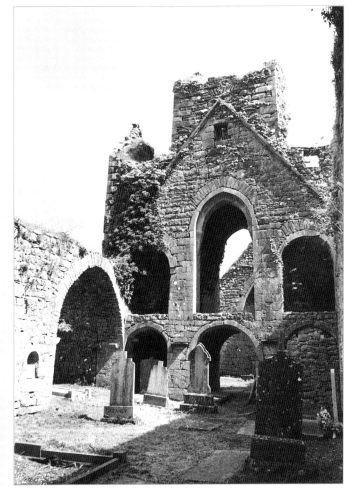

Fig. 48 (below left)
'Ballindown Abbey, Co. Sligo', an engraving of 1794 after a Bigari original, published as plate 86 in vol. 1 of Grose's *Antiquities of Ireland.*

Fig. 49 (below right)
Ballindoon Abbey on the shore of Lough Arrow, with its unique rood-screen little altered since Bigari sketched it in 1779.

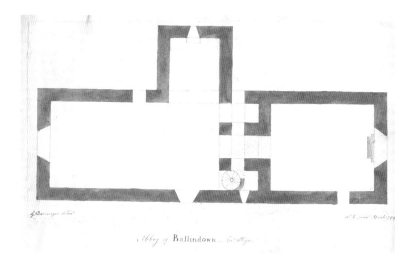

Fig. 50
The plan of the abbey of
Ballindoon, Co. Sligo,
drawn by J.S.C(ooper) in
April 1794 after a lost
Beranger original, is now
preserved on p. 45 of
2122 TX(2) in the
National Library.

This abbey is pleasantly situated near Lough Arrow, a pleasing sheet of water covered with well wooded islands, it seems well built of a blackish stone, the tower is not like the rest supported by one arch but has three to support it which once went through but one at present stopped up except the center one. Only a stump of the tower remains, the stairs seemed to us as if added in the spot they are, as the front of one of the arches has been stopped up for the purpose, two large kind of consoles stick out over the piers of the arches. What they supported we could not guess except it were statues of saints. See plan and drawing No. 12.

The building's most unusual characteristic is the two-storey triple-arched rood-screen supporting a tower, and it is, not surprisingly, this feature that was chosen by Bigari for his drawing, which survives in the form of the engraving reproduced as plate 86 in vol. 1 of Grose's *Antiquities* (*Fig. 48*). Little has changed today (*Fig. 49*), except that the left-hand arch in the first floor has now been unblocked (unlike its counterpart on the bottom right), the skulls have been removed from their niches, and the two unusually hatted gentlemen leaning on a headstone have moved on to their eternal reward. It must remain an open question as to whether it was Bigari or the unnamed engraver who inserted tall lancets in the east window seen through the central arches, instead of the switch-line tracery correctly shown in Cocking's engraving of the exterior of the church in Grose's *Antiquities*. Page 45 of the National Library's album 2122 TX(2) preserves a plan of the abbey drawn by J.S. C(ooper) after a lost Beranger original (*Fig. 50*).

Heapstown Cairn

Not far away, and less than a mile from the northern end of Lough Arrow, lies another great mound of stones (*Fig. 51*), a smaller version of Queen Maeve's Grave on top of Knocknarea, which is visible

Fig. 51
The mighty mound at
Heapstown, Co. Sligo,
probably hides a passage
grave within.

from it and, like it, almost certainly a Stone Age passage grave. It is called Carn Oliolla or Heapstown by Beranger, who noted in MS 4162, p. 10, that

> This carne said to be the burial place of Olioll King of Connaught in ye 4th century is situate in a plain near a village, which got from it the name of Heapstown. It is composed of stones somewhat larger than Misgan Mewe, to which it is inferior in circumference, but superior in height. it is of a circular figure. See plan, Sectn & View with Dimensions No 13.

The measurements are given in feet on the cross-section provided on a drawing by J. T. (presumably Joseph Turner) in 1799, which combines it with the plan and view referred to at the end of the text quoted above from Beranger, whose initials are given on the bottom left of this copy (*Fig. 52*). The drawing can be seen to have an old stamp of the Royal Irish Academy on the top, on the basis of which the drawing was recently returned to the Academy by the Department of Archaeology in University College Dublin, where it had lain for many years. Its accession number in the Academy is now 3.C.42, sheet 5, left.

In his diary, Beranger said that he 'baited or dined' in Heapstown 'at Mr. John M'Donnough's, farmer, and descendant of the princes of the country' (Wilde, 48), and

> went on, and passed the Curlieus mountains, which I do not think as high as they are represented. Stopped facing Kishcorren mountain; left our chaise and horses with the servants, and walked through some fields halfway up the hill, to examine the natural cave, the entrance

of which is by two openings, which appeared like two huge gothick arches. Got in as far as the light would permit us; but the slippery ground, and strong smell like that of cats, and the darkness, soon brought us to the mouth again. This cavern is said to communicate with that in the county of Roscommon, twenty four miles in distance, called the Hellmouth door of Ireland [at Rathcroghan], of which is told (and believed in both counties) that a woman in the county of Roscommon having an unruly calf could never get him home unless driving him by holding him by the tail; that one day he tried to escape and dragged the woman, against her will, into the Hellmouth door; that, unable to stop him, she ran after him without quitting her hold, and continued running until next morning. She came out at Kishcorren, to her own amazement and that of the neighbouring people. We believed it rather than try it [Wilde, 48].

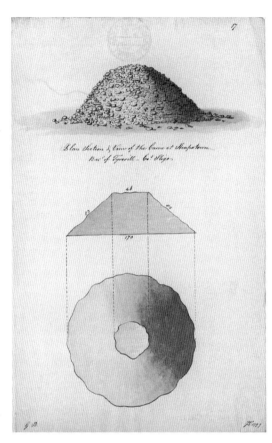

Fig. 52
'Plan, section and view of the Carne at Heapstown' in a 1799 drawing by J.T. (probably Joseph Turner), copying an original by Beranger and preserved in the Royal Irish Academy (MS 3.C.42, sheet 5, left).

Boyle Abbey

By 28 June the centre of operations had moved to Boyle, where the two artists first entered County Roscommon. Their focus of attention was, of course, the great abbey on the outskirts of the town, settled by the Cistercians in 1161. But, as Roger Stalley has made clear in his great book *The Cistercian monasteries of Ireland* (1987), it was not completed until around 1220, the progress of building from chancel in the east to the doorway in the west being reflected in the gradual change from Romanesque to Transitional style. This can also be followed in the pillars and arcade arches as drawn by Bigari in 2122 TX(64) in the National Library (*Fig. 53*), still bearing Beranger's original number 14 on the top right and followed closely in the engraved version on plate 75 of the first volume of Grose's *Antiquities* (*Fig. 54*), reproduced here from a contemporary hand-coloured version kindly placed at my disposal by Andrew Bonar Law of the Neptune Gallery in Dublin. Both present a splendid example of Bigari the stage-painter creating a much more dramatic sense of depth than the building itself provides, the east window seeming to be much farther away than it is (*Fig. 55*) from

Fig. 53 (above left)
'Abbey Boyle, Co. of Roscommon', an unsigned original Bigari drawing preserved as 2122 TX(64) in the National Library.

Fig. 54 (above right)
Boyle Abbey, Co. Roscommon, a 1792 engraving based on a Bigari original and published as plate 75 of the first volume of Grose's *Antiquities of Ireland*.

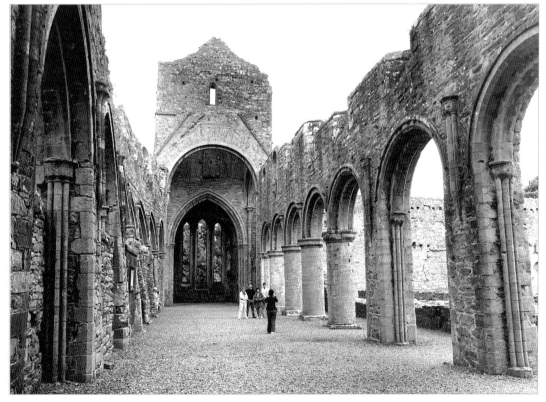

Fig. 55
Boyle Abbey, Co. Roscommon, is not as elongated as Bigari's drawing (*Fig. 53*) would suggest.

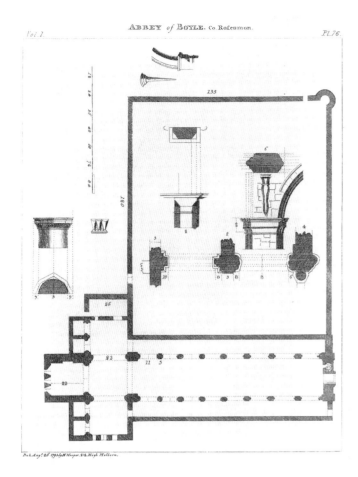

Fig. 56
Plan and (Bigari's?)
architectural details of
Boyle Abbey engraved in
1793 for plate 76 of the
first volume of Grose's
Antiquities of Ireland.

the artist's stance. That Beranger was obviously impressed by this great church is made clear by his calling it 'the phoenix of them all' (Nat. Lib. MS 1415, p. 98) and devoting to it an extensive commentary in MS 4162 (pp. 10–11):

> Abbey Boyle is the finest building we have seen as yet it is situated at the back of the town of Boyle, in Lord Kingston's concerns, who keeps it locked up, the whole structure, which is uncovered (except the chancel part & two small chaples on each side) is a complete forrest, covered with large trees, underwood and thorns, beside weeds, so that it was with infinite trouble and labour we could penetrate those obstacles to make the plan & measurements. The building is of exellent workmanship, the great arches which suported the tower were 45 or forty six feet high, the ground being raised so as to cover all the bases of the columns half of the arches are suported by round pillars of cut stones of various sizes masoned together, the rest are a group of small colums or mouldings and all those arches are joined by masonry to make a solid wall & we could just distinguish their moulding thro' a fracture, some of the capitals are

plain, some with carvings. The east window was grand and lofty, but is all stopped with masonry so that the mouldings cannot be assertained; over the pillars between the arches are ornaments, for which I do not know a name. See perspective view No 14, letter D. the chancel is yet roofed as are the small chappels on the sides, in which latter the groinings yet remain. The place only of the cloysters remain, that part having been a horsebarrack yard with stables about it and is among the cest? barracks at present. A stump only remains of the tower. See plan & drawings No. 14.

The substance of a lost drawing of the 'grand and lofty' east window was reproduced as no. 20 on plate 126 of the second volume of Grose's *Antiquities* (*Fig. 14*), and plate 76 of the first volume (*Fig. 56*) provides a plan of the abbey (unattributed) which, most unusually, is accompanied by architectural details — pillar cross-sections, springing of arches, consoles and capitals, many still surviving today (*Fig. 57*). They show how much Bigari in particular must have appreciated the carving which decorated the abbey, despite the physical inconvenience they encountered in carrying out their work. As Beranger put it in his letter to Burton Conyngham written from Castle Gore on 12 July 1779:

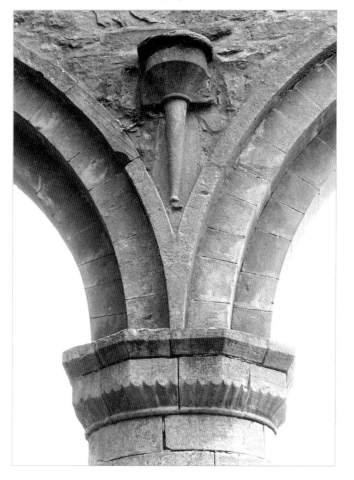

Fig. 57
Details of a capital and console on the south wall of the nave arcade of Boyle Abbey, Co. Roscommon.

As for the Ellegant and beautiful, the Abby of Boyle has the preference as yet. Mr Bigary was so delighted with it that, besides the plans and view, he will give you sections, etc. of it, as certainly it deserves it, the Ellegant Arches which suported the Steeple Being 44 feet high. it was impossible to find out all its beauties, being within a forrest, with large timber, underwood and weeds, and the walls so covered with ivy and of such a thickness that our 4 feet staff could hardly reach it, but notwithstanding, I flatter myself that never were more exact plans and views taken of it. Mr. Irwin was a great help to us, he is undefatigable [Nat. Lib. MS 1415, pp 84–5].

But even more remarkable is the prodigious amount of drawing and measuring they were able to do before finishing in mid-afternoon, as is clear from the brief extract Wilde gives from the Diary:

> Found the inside to be almost a forest, being overgrown with large trees, underwood, and weeds, and could not stir before we made our way through them. Drew and planned with difficulty, and it occupied us until 3 o'clock [Wilde, 49].

As the same Diary relates:

> Set out from thence for Kingston [site of the present Lough Key Forest Park], two miles distant, on foot, passing through a delightful forest. Arrived, and were by Colonel Irwin presented to the Earl of Kingston, and his brother, the Right. Hon. Henry King; dined, and were told by his Lordship that he had ordered his boat to be ready at our orders for the next day. Set out past nine, crossed by moonlight the same forest, and arrived at Boyle at 10 [Wilde, 49–50].

Ennismacreedy or Church Island, Lough Key

For the following day, 29 June, the Diary continues:

> Set out early; went to Lough Key; found his Lordship's boat ready, with four oars, and his sportsman acting as captain, who showed us some guns and fishing tackle which he had provided by his Lordship's order, without which nobody could sport on the lake. We embarked on this delightful sheet of water, which presents to view such a beautiful scene, that I confess to be unable to give a description of it, but only a faint sketch. The lake is about five miles across, being nearly of a circular form, surrounded by mountains covered with woods — some sloping to the water, others advancing a little like a promontory in the lake. Six islands, nobly wooded, are dispersed in it, which, by the brightness of the sun, and the clearness of the sky, struck our eyes with the lively variety of their greens, and represented to us an idea of the Elizian fields of the poets. We made for Ennis M'Creedy island, where, being arrived, we found it impossible to land — the weeds, particularly the hemlock, being two feet higher than ourselves, and so thick grown, that even the sight could not penetrate them. Kept a council of war, and resolved to make our way by knocking them down with clubs, in which operation the crew was a great help. Arrived at the church; drew and plan; also the little chappel, both overgrown with weeds [Wilde, 50].

The name of the island is given variously as Ennis Macreeny or MacCreedy, the Irish word for island (Inish) followed presumably by the name of a previous owner, long forgotten because it is now marked on the map as Church Island. The church itself had what was one of the last west gables of an Early

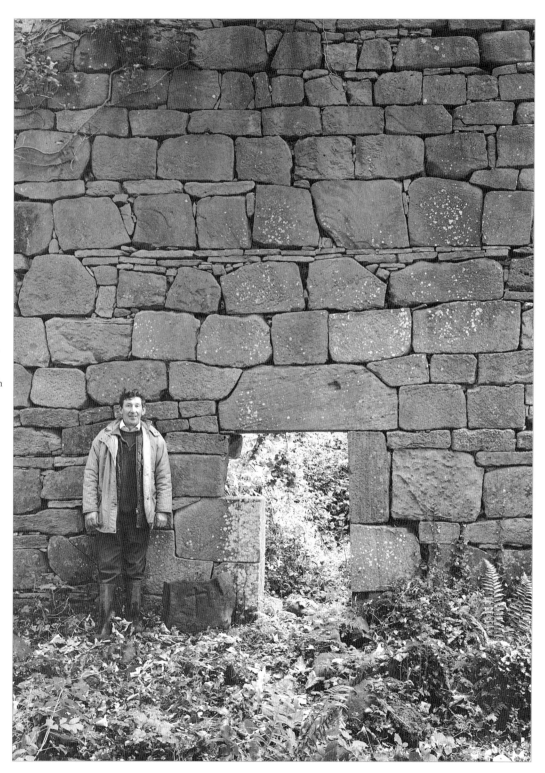

Fig. 58
The boatman Peter Walsh
in front of the west wall of
the church of
'Ennismacreeny' on Church
Island in Lough Key, Co.
Roscommon, as
photographed by the great
Paul Caponigro some 30
years ago.

Fig. 59
Bigari's unsigned drawing
of the church and shrine of
'Ennismacreeny on Lough
Key, Co. Roscommon', now
p. 12 of 2122 TX(3) in the
National Library.

Fig. 60
Interior view of the church
on Church Island, Lough
Key, with the tomb-shrine
on the right, as engraved in
1792 after a Bigari original
for plate 78 of vol. 1 of
Grose's *Antiquities of
Ireland*.

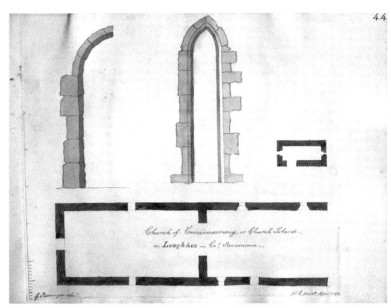

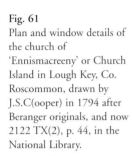

Fig. 61
Plan and window details of the church of 'Ennismacreeny' or Church Island in Lough Key, Co. Roscommon, drawn by J.S.C(ooper) in 1794 after Beranger originals, and now 2122 TX(2), p. 44, in the National Library.

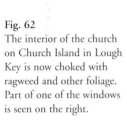

Fig. 62
The interior of the church on Church Island in Lough Key is now choked with ragweed and other foliage. Part of one of the windows is seen on the right.

Christian Irish church to have remained unchanged for centuries until it was recently repointed and its door partially restored by Dúchas. A photograph (*Fig. 58*) by the great American photographer Paul Caponigro shows the west gable as it was some 30 years ago, with Peter Walsh, the same boatman who will bring you out to the island today, standing beside the door. But Bigari's drawing (*Fig. 59*) shows us the interior of the gable because his view was taken from the eastern end of the church. It is No. 2122 TX(3), p. 12, in the National Library, bearing the inscription '*C No. 15 Bigary*' on the back. It served as the basis for the charming watercolour in the Royal Irish Academy's MS 3.C.29, p. 48

(*Pl. 7*), on which, in turn, was based the engraving plate 78 in vol. 1 of Grose's *Antiquities* (*Fig. 60*), where a third spelling — Ennismacreey — is used for the caption. At least the main features, including the west doorway and the windows of *c.* 1200 (compare *Fig. 61* — Nat. Lib. 2122 TX(2), p. 44) in the north wall on the right, can still be made out, even if less of the masonry now survives (*Fig. 62*). The curious structure on the extreme right, exaggerated in size and standing much higher in comparison to the church than in reality, is a small and unusual tomb-shrine of whichever saint was the original founder of the church or the hermit who lived on the island. The building as it exists today has no obvious entrance, but on the plan drawn by J. S. Cooper in April 1794 and preserved on p. 44 of the National Library's 2122 TX(2) the doorway can be seen near the western

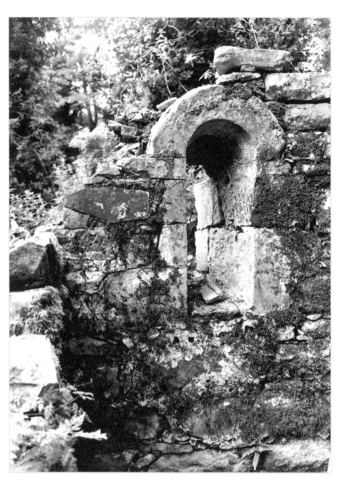

Fig. 63
The west window of the small shrine beside the church on Church Island, Lough Key, Co. Roscommon.

end of the south wall, as in its counterpart known as 'the Priest's House' in Glendalough, Co. Wicklow. Built sometime around 1200 to judge by the surviving west window (*Fig. 63*), it would have served as a focal point for visiting pilgrims, in much the same way that St Molaise's House did at Devenish, or Teach Molaise on Inishmurray. An excavation carried out by Heather King for Dúchas in 2000 revealed the remains of two human bodies inside, one of which, at least, we may take as that of an unrecognised and uncanonised Irish saint!

MS 4162, p. 11, provides us with Beranger's comments on the island and its buildings as follows:

> This abbey as they term it is an oblong building very much ruined and seemingly of ordinary workmanship. The building was devided in two parts its windows are of the loophole kind. At some distance is a little chappel with two small loopholes to give light which must have been admitted very sparingly and made the place dungeon-like when it was roofed. No traces of any tower could be found. The island is covered with wood, and the whole surface of the ground with weeds and hemlock seven feet high, without road or path, we were obliged to beat them

down at every step for ¼ mile, the inside of the church was the same so that the operation was laborious to plan and measure. We were sick with the odious effluvia of the hemlock which was knoked down. See Drawings etc. No 15.

Bigari must have had much of the hemlock beaten down inside the church before he put pen to paper, but things have changed little over the last two centuries because much of the island, including the church interior, is still covered with what would now be called ragweed, together with nettles and a variety of small trees.

Beranger's Diary, as quoted by Wilde (50–1), continues:

> Returned to our boat; went to another island, where we landed easily, as it was a fine continued lawn shaded nobly by a grove with some underwood, on which a temple was built, which has a large room to dine in, and a smaller to retire to to take a nap, with a kitchen separate from the building. From this summer house one has a charming view of the lake and its islands; re-embarked; went to another, also wood and lawn, where his Lordship keeps bullocks fattening, which were the largest I ever had seen. They put me in mind of elephants; they were very shy, and fled on our appearance to very thick thickets, where they hid themselves.

McDermott's Island

Then the party continued on to a fourth island,

> in which are the walls of a very large building, with various rooms erected in the last century by some of his Lordship's ancestors, intended to retire to with the whole family if the plague, which raged on some part of Ireland made its progress to this country. This island is well wooded, part lawn and part underwood. Refreshed ourselves here, and set out for M'Dermott's Island, the smallest of them all, of a circular form, and surrounded by a strong high wall, rising from the water edge, where it would be impossible to land, was it not for a breach on one side. In this island, thickly covered with trees and underwood, is a castle so covered with ivy that no stone can be seen on the outside. There is an eagle's or osprey's nest on the top, and we could hear distinctly the cry of the young ones from the top of some broken stairs which went formerly to the roof, but found no means of access to them [Wilde, 51].

In MS 4162, p. 12, Beranger gives further details:

> McDermots Island, is circular & fortified with a wall 14 or 15 feet high all round, so that there is no landing but at a breach. It is wooded and it contains a square castle so covered with ivy that absolutely no stone of it is to be seen on the outside, the inside is so ruined that no idea

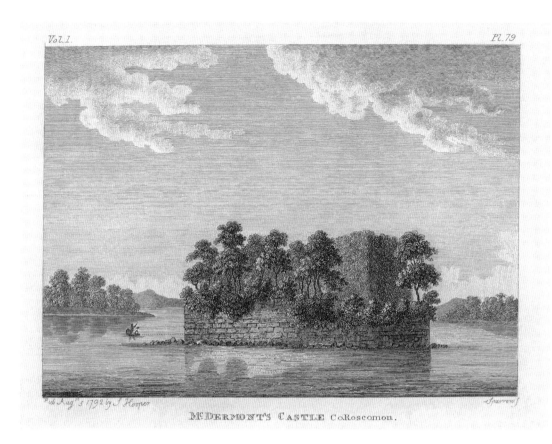

Vol. 1.   *Pl. 79*

Pub Aug.ᵗ 5 1792 by S Hooper   Sparrow f

M^cDERMONT'S CASTLE Co.Roscomon.

Fig. 64
'McDermont's Castle, Co. Roscommon', engraved in 1792 — probably after a Beranger original — for plate 79 of the first volume of Grose's *Antiquities of Ireland*.

can well be formed of the workmanship, it got the name of its founder, one of the Princes of the Country who tradition says was jealous of his wife which he used to keep here during his warlike operations. It is added that her lover like an other Leander found means to visit her by swimming over. See drawing No 16.

The illustration of this description is well known from plate 79 of the first volume of Grose's *Antiquities* (*Fig. 64*), where much of the accompanying letterpress is a repetition of Beranger's text quoted immediately above, with the additional comment that 'this view was taken from an original drawing in the collection of the Right Honourable William Conyngham'. Furthermore, the watercolour on p. 47 of MS 3.C.29 in the Royal Irish Academy (*Pl. 8*), which was presumably prepared for Grose's London engraver, says on the back that the drawing was by Beranger, who noted that they 're-embarked, lay on our oars at some distance, and drew a general view of the island and castle' (Wilde, 51). This gives us the probable authorship of the drawing which the Grose letterpress would not disclose. The castle to which Beranger referred was replaced early in the nineteenth century by a folly (*Pl. 9*) which was apparently used for dances and parties, but which also seems to have had living quarters for staff — if not for some of the guests themselves.

Ballymote Castle and Church

On 30 June our two artists left County Roscommon, whither they were to return at the beginning of August. Their next immediate goal was Ballymote in County Sligo, 'a small village inhabited mostly by weavers', where the two artists 'drew the castle and abbey' (Wilde, 52). It was here, as the well-informed Beranger duly noted, that the Book of Ballymote was written, a manuscript now in the Royal Irish Academy but at the time in the possession of the Chevalier O'Gorman in Auxerre, long after it had been owned by the Mac Donoghes who had paid 140 milch cows for it (see Wilde, 52).

Beranger describes Ballymote Castle as follows in MS 4162, p. 12:

> This was an extensive and strong castle of very good workmanship, flanked by six round towers, deprived at present of their battlements, and yet the highest is 55 feet from the top to the ground, the walls are 9 feet thick and I believe had a gallery or covered way in their thickness all round, at least it is so for some few paces on each side of the towers, we could not follow it, as part of the arch of this covered way is fallen in & stopp's up the passages on the top of the wall. all round is a way with a parapet of about 2 feet thick, the entrance was defended by some works, of which only 2 bits of walls remain, the inside is only a large aria, or Bawn, so that the dwellings must have been in the towers, one of which is half broke down. See plan and Drawing No 17 Letters C and D.

That plan is presumably the one reproduced as plate 91 of Grose's *Antiquities*, vol. 1 (*Fig. 84*), where the two engravings of the castle were based not on drawings from the 1779 expedition but on others by Daniel Grose and T. Cocking respectively. It is all the more to be welcomed, therefore, that we still have what we may take to be the original Bigari drawing in 2122 TX(15) in the National Library. The strongest castle in Connacht, it changed hands — Irish and Norman/English — many times over almost four centuries after it had been built around 1300 by Richard de Burgo. It is square in shape, with large drum towers at the corner and D-shaped towers in the middle of two of the sides (*Fig. 66*), as seen on the plan on plate 91 of vol. 1 of Grose's *Antiquities*. Bigari's view of the castle (*Fig. 65*) looks into the south-east corner-tower, where a figure (Irwin?) stands on the rubble, which has been removed and the tower repaired after David Sweetman excavated the castle in the early 1980s.

The other building in Ballymote which Beranger mentioned in his Diary is described as follows in MS 4162, p. 13, under the heading 'Ballymote Church':

> This building also named Abbey tho it does not appear to have been of larger extend then it is at present, is situated at the end of the town at a musket shot from the castle, is of good workmanship tho' much ruined, the east window was curious workmanship may be seen by the fragment remaining in the arch part; the lower part of the window is stopped up with masonry even with the wall, so that it is impossible to know if there are pillars or pillasters to suport it. See drawing No 17 Letters A and B.

Fig. 65
Pen and wash drawing of
Ballymote Castle, Co. Sligo
— unsigned but by Bigari
— preserved as 2122
TX(15) in the National
Library of Ireland.

Fig. 66
The massive bulk of
Connacht's strongest castle
at Ballymote, Co. Sligo.

BALLYMOTE CHURCH, Co. Sligo.

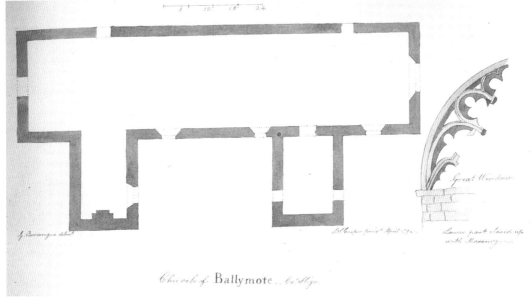

Church of Ballymote, Co. Sligo.

Fig. 67 (above left)
The church at Ballymote, Co. Sligo, in an unsigned pen and wash drawing by Bigari, now 2122 TX(73) in the National Library.

Fig. 68 (above right)
'Ballymote Church, Co. Sligo', in a 1794 engraving after a Bigari original and published as plate 99 in the second volume of Grose's *Antiquities of Ireland*.

Fig. 69 (right)
The plan of the church at Ballymote, Co. Sligo, and a detail of the 'great window' in the east wall were drawn by J.S. C(ooper) in 1794 after a lost Beranger original and now form p. 50 of 2122 TX(2) in the National Library.

The drawing referred to is preserved as 2122 TX(73) in the National Library (*Fig. 67*), where, on the back, the artist is erroneously named as Barralet, who was not on this tour, whereas the mix of upright and horizontal masonry clearly shows the drawing to be by Bigari — a fact confirmed by the letterpress accompanying the engraved version that is plate 99 of Grose's *Antiquities*, vol. 2 (*Fig. 68*). The old church as it stands today (*Fig. 70*) does not easily match that in the drawing, as the gabled south side-chapels are no longer visible and the western porch has been replaced by an arch. This suggests that a certain amount of reconstruction has taken place in the meantime, including the insertion over the west door of a curious head with three-tiered tiara, not noticed by Bigari or

Fig. 70
The ivied overcoat of the ruined church in Ballymote, Co. Sligo, has doubtless already caused part of the fabric to collapse — and will continue to do so if not checked.

Beranger but published in *The Irish Penny Magazine* of 5 February 1842 after an original drawing by Grose's nephew Daniel. J.S. Cooper's April 1794 plan after a lost Beranger original, as copied on p. 50 of the National Library's album 2122 TX(2), also illustrates vanished parts of the 'great' east window (*Fig. 69*) which Beranger referred to in his description above.

Having finished their field drawings, the two artists dined there and

> went to lodge for the night at the village of Tubbercorry, in which poor place Mr. Bigary and I were surprised to find an elegant supper served up, by the care of Colonel Irwin [Wilde, 52].

Banada Abbey

On the first day of July they proceeded to two abbeys — or, more correctly, friaries — which, because they are off the beaten track, are even today still comparatively little known. The first of these is Banada, some five miles west of Tubbercurry. Dating from 1423, it was founded for a community of Augustinian friars (rather than the more usual canons) and was the first Irish house of the order to promote the Observantine movement. In MS 4162, p. 13, Beranger describes it as

Fig. 71
The unsigned Bigari drawing showing a lively funeral scene in 'The Abbey of Banada, Co. of Sligo' is now 2122 TX(3), p. 13, in the National Library.

Fig. 72
The 1792 engraving of 'Benneda Abbey, Co. Sligo' that forms plate 95 of the first volume of Grose's *Antiquities of Ireland* states that Bigari drew the original.

Fig. 73
J.S. C(ooper)'s drawing of a doorway at Banada, Co. Sligo, after an original by Bigari, can be found on the right-hand half of p. 41 of the Cooper Album 2122 TX(2) in the National Library.

The only one as yet which we have seen of regular square hewn stone. The tower 70 feet high, tho mutilated at top is of the same materials and has an offsett at every story which are 3 above the ground floor. It is suported (like the other abbeys) on one arch, the east window is neat and not crouded with work. At the left side of the entrance at the door in the thickness of the wall is menaged a place for holy water with holes to put the hand in. no sign of cloysters but the aria where they formerly stood, there are two pretty ancient tombs in the church. See plan drawings etc. No 18.

Bigari, too, must have been impressed by the regular ashlar masonry of the tower because he prefers to show it as such in his drawing — 2122 TX(3), p. 13, in the National Library (*Fig. 71*), and bearing the original Beranger number 18 on the top right — rather than presenting us with his usual stylised combination of vertical and horizontal. But the appearance of well-built stability did not prevent the tower from crashing down in November 1897, weakened, it was said, because some of the lower blocks had been taken away for use as tombstones. A headstone is shown being carried on the back of a man in what is obviously a very lively, theatrical scene worthy of Hamlet, shown in the foreground in Bigari's version — and, for that reason, the one example of the artist's work chosen for illustration in Anne Crookshank and the Knight of Glin's splendid volume *The watercolours of Ireland* (1994). This burial drama was, sadly, not repeated in the engraved version reproduced as plate 95 of the first volume of Grose's *Antiquities,* where a man stands and looks motionless at a family group beyond the arch (*Fig. 72*). Yet another poorer version of the drawing survives in a copy hastily sketched by Austin Cooper on 18 April 1794 (Nat. Lib. MS 2122 TX(2), p. 39), and reproduced as illustration 117 of my *Cooper's Ireland* book. This, however, has the advantage of showing on the top right a detail of the two-tiered window in the uppermost storey of the tower, which was probably based on a lost sketch by Beranger. A more valuable drawing is that occupying half of p. 41 of the same Cooper album

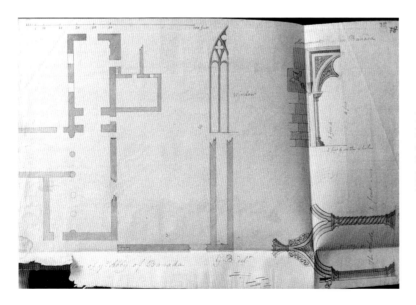

Fig. 74
Beranger's signed plan and details of Banada Abbey, Co. Sligo, are preserved on p. 35 of 2122 TX(4) in the National Library.

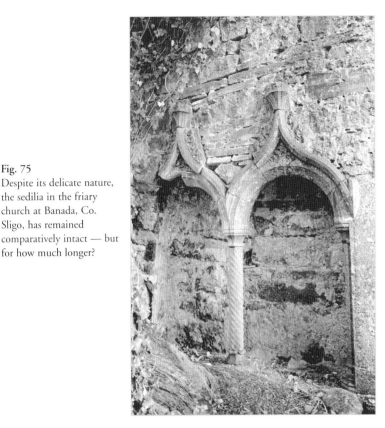

Fig. 75
Despite its delicate nature, the sedilia in the friary church at Banada, Co. Sligo, has remained comparatively intact — but for how much longer?

(illustration 119 in the book). It is signed J. S.C(ooper), acknowledging its indebtedness to a Bigari original (now lost), and showing a door (*Fig. 73*). The other half of the page is taken up with details of arches and a window copied from the Beranger original which, in this instance, fortunately survives as 2122 TX(4), p. 35, in the National Library (*Fig. 74*). This also preserves an original plan of the abbey, later copied by Austin Cooper on 18 April 1794 into Nat. Lib. 2122 TX(2), p. 40. Beranger's original number 18 (corresponding to that referred to in MS 4162) has been crossed out on the upper right-hand corner of p. 35, and, beneath it, is an arch belonging to a triple sedilia that survives in part (*Fig. 75*). But the cusped arch and traceried window which Beranger drew on the same sheet have disappeared — as has virtually all the masonry at the western end of the church, leaving behind it a sad and sorry sight in the present churchyard (*Fig. 76*). The east wall and the gabled extension to the south, seen in Bigari's original view, have also vanished.

Fig. 76
Where once the friary tower dominated the well-kept ruin at Banada, Co. Sligo, a scene of desolation now awaits the visitor.

Court Abbey

The second 'abbey' visited on 1 July was Court, about five miles north-west of Tubbercurry, founded for the Third Order of Franciscans around the middle of the fifteenth century. The tower shown in Bigari's original drawing, p. 3 of the National Library's album 2122 TX(3) (*Fig. 77*), bears the original Beranger number 19 and was faithfully engraved as plate 97 of the first volume of Grose's *Antiquities* (*Fig. 78*) after a watercolour on p. 28 of the Royal Irish Academy's MS 3.C.29 (*Pl. 10*). It still stands to a considerable height above the well-kept churchyard, while the arch leading to the north side-chapel and the east wall shown beyond it are also well preserved (*Fig. 79*). The choir, visible through the tower arch, has suffered more heavily in the meantime, and ivy has taken over so much of the building that the State should consider taking it into its care. Beranger describes it in MS 4162, pp 13–14:

> This Abbey is of good workmanship of a blackish stone. It seems not to have been larger than the plan represents it, it is in a field, the acces of it thro boggs, the tower on an arch is 58 feet

Fig. 77 (below left) Bigari's signed view of 'The Abbey of Court, Co. of Sligo' is now on p. 3 of 2122 TX(3) in the National Library.

Fig. 78 (below right) Court Abbey, Co. Sligo, in a 1792 engraving after a Bigari original that was published as plate 97 of the first volume of Grose's *Antiquities of Ireland.*

Fig. 79
Court Abbey, Co. Sligo, now sports more foliage than it did 223 years ago, and deserves to be taken into State care.

high, has two ofsetts and on the sides of the tower large stones are sticking out, but for what use we could not guess. On the sides of ye chancel northwards is an Isle which contains recesses, and kind of closets in the thickness of the walls, at present filled with skulls. the east window is entire and plain. See drawings etc. No 19.

The plan which Beranger refers to is preserved as 2122 TX(88) in the National Library (*Fig. 80*), and indicates a circular staircase within the tower wall (now blocked up) and the unusual arrangement of openings in the east wall of the north chapel. The west doorway, which the plan shows as open, is now largely walled up. Also on the same sheet — without the detailed measurements in 2122 TX(2), p. 43 — are the 'Great window' (now gone) and a second, smaller, two-light window now barely surviving in the exterior east wall of the north side-chapel.

Fig. 80
Beranger's signed plan and window details of Court Abbey, Co. Sligo, are now 2122 TX(88) in the National Library.

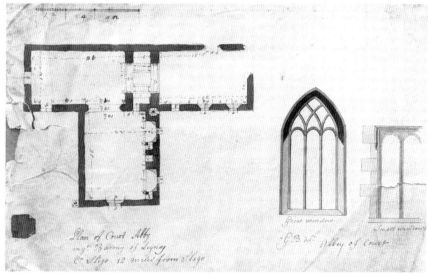

Fig. 81
The ruins of Ballinafad
Castle, Co. Sligo, are now
splendidly visible on the
new road from Collooney
to Boyle — complete with
rooks.

Ballinafad Castle

Our artists then returned to Collooney, where they worked at their drawings and sketches. Wilde (54), who had access to Beranger's Diary, said that they spent two days doing so before going to Mercrea (Markree) on the evening of 3 July. But this does not allow the pair to have visited Ballinafad Castle, which Wilde does not refer to but which Beranger includes after Court on p. 14 of MS 4162 without giving a date. He only gives a very brief description of it:

> This castle stands on the road to Boyle Co Sligo [*recte* Roscommon], is flanked by four towers, and was formerly all covered, the walls are 4½ feet thick, all of a reddish kind of stone. See plan etc. No 20.

The castle, now beautifully exposed to view on the new road going from Collooney to Boyle (*Fig. 81*), is a Plantation structure of *c.* 1590 where the rectangular core is visually engulfed by the large towers at each corner, of which one is round within and the others angular. This detail is well brought out by Beranger's original plan (*Fig. 82*) preserved as 2122 TX(13) in the National Library, which was engraved as plate 89 of the first volume of Grose's *Antiquities* (*Fig. 84*). It was also Beranger who

Fig. 82
Beranger put his initials to this plan of Ballinafad Castle, Co. Sligo, now 2122 TX(13) in the National Library.

Fig. 83
The signed view of Ballinafad Castle, Co. Sligo, now 2122 TX(105) in the National Library, is perhaps Beranger's most appealing product from the tour of 1797.

The Castle of Ballynafad, Barony of Tirerill Co. of Sligo.

provided us with the signed view of the castle in 2122 TX(105) in the National Library which bears his original number 20 and which is perhaps the most attractive picture of his that we have from the whole trip (*Fig. 83*). It shows a rider with an attendant holding the horse's reins in front of the tall-chimneyed castle, but it is left to our imagination to work out which member of the party may have been the horseman.

The visit to Markree Castle, the seat of the Right Hon. Joseph Cooper, was in the company of Colonel Irwin and, according to Wilde (54), they were well received, and there they dined, supped and spent the night, before heading off the following morning for the north-west of Sligo, which is the subject of the next chapter.

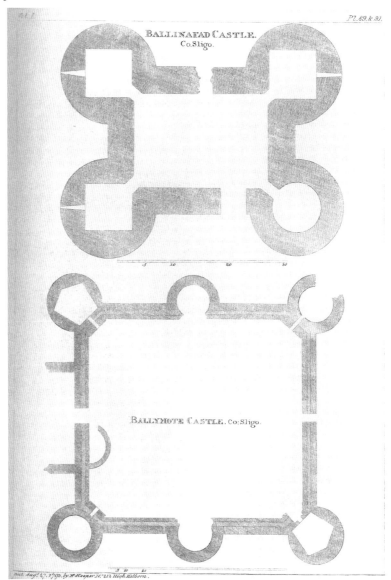

Fig. 84
The plans of Ballinafad and Ballymote castles, Co. Sligo, form plates 89 and 91 respectively of vol. 1 of Grose's *Antiquities of Ireland.*

5. THE NORTH-WEST COAST OF SLIGO

On 4 July, three years to the day after the American Declaration of Independence, Beranger and Bigari departed from Mercrea (Markree) Castle near Collooney in the company of their genial and attentive Sligo host, Col. Lewis Irwin, who made them welcome at his home, Tanrego House, near Beltra (*Fig. 10*). But before reaching it, he must have sidetracked them to go across Traecuchullin to

> draw a plan and view of Cuchullin's tomb, a circle of stones, 27 feet in diameter, but much covered by the sand which the waves carry on it [Wilde, 54].

This comment, which Wilde abstracted from the Diary, was expanded upon somewhat by Beranger in MS 4162, p. 14:

> Cuchullin's Tomb is situated on the strand of Tanrego bay which, from this monument, is called in Irish Traecuchullin, i.e. Cuchullin's Strand, it is a circle of large and small stones, choaked up with sand which the sea washes upon it, so that only the tops of the stones are seen. It measures 27 feet in diameter. See drawing and plan No 21.

According to p. 192 of Wood-Martin's *Rude stone monuments of Sligo* (1888), this tomb had disappeared by 1858 — perhaps covered in by sand which may still preserve it. But, if not, we can content ourselves with Beranger's lost plan and drawing of it as copied by J. S. C(ooper) on 14 October 1794, and now preserved as MS 3.C.42, sheet 12, right, in the Royal Irish Academy (*Fig. 85*). The view makes it look like a stone circle, but the raised centre would argue for its having belonged to the type of megalithic tombs known as passage graves. At this juncture in the Diary, Wilde (54) remarks that Beranger quotes MacPherson's *Ossian*:

> 'By the dark rolling waves of Lego they raised the hero's tomb'

and Beranger comments on this further:

> Sligo was formerly called Slego, in our historical writers; take off the S, and we will have Lego. Antiquarians have more than once twisted and curtailed names more than this; and Mr. MacPherson said, in one of his notes, that 'Cuchullin was killed somewhere in Connaught,

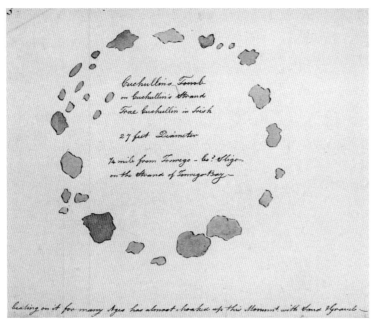

Fig. 85
'CuChullin's Tomb', a megalithic structure formerly visible on Tanrego Bay, Co. Sligo, in drawings by J.S. C(ooper) of 14 October 1794. Copied from lost originals by Beranger, both plan and view now form part of sheet 12 of the Royal Irish Academy's manuscript 3.C.42.

which must have been near Lough Gill, in the vicinity of the town of Sligo, upon the tract of land between Tanrego Bay and Lough Gill, there being only three or four miles' distance from the verge of one to the strand of the other' [Wilde, 54].

Beranger, too, should be allowed his bit of speculation!

The 'tourists', as Wilde called them, spent a couple of days with Colonel Irwin at Tanrego, during which he showed them (when the tide was out)

two islands, which, when the tide is in, are not accessible but by a boat, on which cattle were grazing; the foundation of which islands are oyster shells, with about six inches of earth over them. Walked round them, and was amazed at the sight. The oysters are so plentiful at Tanrego, that they are got by cars full, only paying the carriage [Wilde, 54],

to which Beranger added ruefully that the oysters were not in season at the time. In between working at their drawings and walking about in the evenings,

the Colonel procured an old man in the neighbourhood who sung to us in Irish the feats of the old hero Cuchullin [Wilde, 55]

whereupon Beranger ordered the interpreter to write it down and add it to the other MSS of his writing.

Clogh Glass

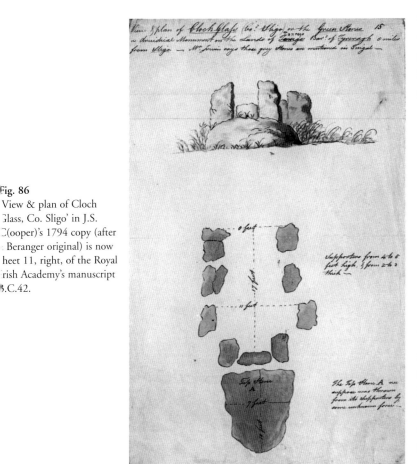

Fig. 86
View & plan of Cloch Glass, Co. Sligo' in J.S. C(ooper)'s 1794 copy (after Beranger original) is now sheet 11, right, of the Royal Irish Academy's manuscript 3.C.42.

On 6 July they all set out for Tubberpatrick, the seat of Captain Jones, and on the way drew a 'cromlegh, called Clogh Glass, i.e. the Green Stones' (Wilde, 55), which Beranger described further in MS 4162, p. 14:

This cromliagh is sit: in a field on the lands of Tanrego, Barony of Tyreragh, 8 miles from Sligo. It consisted of 11 suporters from 4 to 5 feet high & 2 and 3 feet thick. They contain an aria 17 feet by 11. A stone lying near it and shewn as the top stone is 10 feet by seven, so that it is clear this stone could never have covered the suporters, but in part. See drawing No 22.

This is almost certainly the megalith northeast of Beltra Post Office in what were once the grounds of Tanrego House. The illustration we have of it is, like that of Cuchullin's tomb, a copy by J.S.C(ooper), dated 14 October 1794, of a lost original by Beranger, whose initials GB are given in the

Fig. 87
This megalith near Beltra in County Sligo is very likely to be the same as that called 'Cloch Glass' by Beranger.

bottom left-hand corner. It is now preserved in the Royal Irish Academy, where its accession number is 3.C.42, sheet 11, right. The drawing (*Fig. 86*) gives a plan of the megalith, with fallen capstone at the bottom and, beneath the caption on top, an end view looking across the capstone. The plan does not quite match the present configuration of stones (*Fig. 87*), but is near enough to make it highly likely that what survives today is the same Cloch Glass of the drawing which states that the capstone 'was thrown from it's supporters by some unknown force' and that 'Mr Irwin says those grey stones are mentioned in Fingal' (MacPherson's *Ossian*).

This drawing was one of a number executed by J.S.C. — or S.C., presumably Austin Cooper's cousin Samuel — over a span of four days in the middle of October 1794, and we should be very grateful to him for his activity because the Beranger originals on which he based his pictures have, sadly, since been lost.

Cloch-Morkit, Hill of Skrine

The next megalith to come to our attention is a drawing that shows not one but two monuments of interest (*Fig. 88*), and is now preserved as 3.C.42, sheet 5, right, in the Royal Irish Academy. The centrepiece is, as the caption states, 'Cloch-morkit or the riding Stone — a Druidical Rocking Stone on the Hill of Skrine — Co.^{y} Sligo'. On p. 15 of MS 4162, Beranger expands the description:

> This rocking stone is sit: on the foot of the hill of Skrine is of circular form 6½ feet thick and 23 feet in girth. It stands on a natural rock on which it was formerly rocking, but has lost its equilibrium & is at present immovable. See Drawing 23, Letter C.

Beranger once copied a drawing of another example in Dalkey, Co. Dublin, and, although the object of some considerable interest in the later eighteenth and early nineteenth centuries as examples of human ingenuity, such rocking stones were, almost certainly, Ice Age glacial erratics, of which there are many in the region. But definitely man-made is the second monument — a stone fort best viewed from near where the road from Carrowneden joins the one that goes northwards around Red Hill (Beranger's Hill of Skrine), on the top of which stands the somewhat dilapidated stone fort (*Fig. 89*). In MS 4162, p. 15, Beranger gives a useful description of it as it was two centuries ago:

> This fort is a circle of 104 feet diameter built of flat stones, the walls are 8 feet thick and at present from 4 to 5 feet high. no mortar has been employed in its structure. it is situated on the top of the hill of Skrine, Barony of Tireragh, Co of Sligo. See Drawing 23 Letter A.

Fig. 88
'Cloch-morkit or the riding stone' and a stone fort on top of the Hill of Skrine, Co. Sligo, as copied on 15 October 1794 by S.C(ooper) from a Beranger original, and now preserved as sheet 5, right, of manuscript 3.C.42 in the Royal Irish Academy.

Fig. 89
Could the large boulder in
the field in the foreground
be the Cloch-morkit 'riding
stone' of Beranger's drawing
(*Fig. 88*), with the stone
fort on the top of the Hill
of Skreen visible in the
background?

The reason why it was Beranger who was doing the drawings of Cloch Glass and Cloch-Morkit on 7 July was because 'Mr. Bigary had protested against all ridings' and Beranger had to go it alone with Colonel Irwin to draw the 'Cromleaghs and a circular fort of dry stones on the hill of Skryne, or Skreen' (Wilde, 55). However, on the same day, the artists must have reunited and continued their tour (together with the ever-helpful Colonel Irwin) to Fortland, the seat of Robert Brown near Easky Bridge, now partially demolished. There, according to the Journal, they

> walked about the concerns, and under a fine shade of trees, along a rivulet, which was very comfortable in the extreme warm weather we had, Mr. Bigary protesting it was as warm as in Italy [Wilde, 55].

Knockmallagrish

In the Diary, Beranger also noted that, on the north-east coast of Sligo,

> there are an immensity of round raths, or forts, or mounds, or barrows, or tumuli, with each their fosse; — some at musket shot, some half-quarter of a mile from one another, from which this place is called in Irish Lishagan — Fortland. They are of various dimensions. We took the plan and section of the largest amongst them [Wilde, 55].

This example, visited on 8 July, Beranger identifies by name on p. 15 of MS 4162 as Knockmallagrish, where he describes it as the largest of the raths with which the coast is covered, which has given that part the name of Lishagan, in English Fortland. They are in the Barony of Tyreragh. This one is very considerable, having two fosses and their parapet in the area at the top is a round elevation representing a little mount. For Dimensions see Plan and Secn No 24.

Despite the detailed description of what sounds like a raised rath, this is the only monument on the whole tour — other than the vanished Cuchullin's Tomb mentioned above and Leaba Yearmaid near Cong (*Fig. 140*) — that I did not succeed in locating. Nor was my quest helped by the absence of any surviving plan or section, original or copied — one of the very few instances where no material has survived from a site visit on the tour.

Finn MacCool's Griddle

The next monument is yet another where we owe the drawing (*Fig. 90*) to the copying activity of (J) S. C(ooper), dated 18 October 1794; it was included in the material recently returned by the Department of Archaeology in University College Dublin to the Royal Irish Academy, where its accession number is 3.C.42, sheet 11, left. The subject of the drawing is a megalith called 'Fin(n)macCool's Griddle' (*Fig. 91*), an imaginative description, the first word derived from the famous Irish hero beloved of medieval storytellers, the second offering a visual comparison from the sphere of domestic baking, using a word that is applied to a number of megaliths in the area — but apparently nowhere else in the country. Beranger's descriptive captions on the drawing are augmented by further comments of his for 8 July in MS 4162, pp 15–16:

> This cromliagh is sit: on a little hill in a bog of one hundred thousand acres, very difficult of access by help of guides. Barony of Tyreragh and lands of Glenask 24 miles from Sligo. The top stone 11½ feet long, 6½ feet broad and 3½ thick stands or has under it (for it does not bear on all) 7 suporters from 5 to 6 feet high & from 2 to 3 thick. it rests only upon 3 points. No 2. Solid supporter & 1 & 3 round paving stones serving like props to make the top stone even. No 3 has a long stone under it to make still rise to equallity with No 1 which stands solid on one of the suporters. on one of the sides of the Cromliagh is a recess 7 feet square composed of stones like flaggs of same hight but thinner, whether these had a top stone or not we could not learn. See Drawing No 25.

Bigari once more funked going to the monument, which was just as well for him, because it turned out to be the most frightening experience of the whole tour for Beranger, as he explains in detail in the Diary:

> June 9th. Set out with Colonel Irwin, interpreter, and servants on horseback, to draw a famous

Cromlegh, called Finmacool's Griddle, situated in a bog ten miles long, and about three broad. Took two guides on the verge of said bog. Went by various windings, until arrived at a small hill, on which this old monument is fixed. Drew a plan; but Mr. Irwin, looking at his watch, and seeing dinner-time approach, asked our guides for a short cut to go to Fortland, which he knew there was. They seemed ignorant of it, but undertook to try and find it out. We followed, when, all of a sudden, my horse sank under me in the bog. This stopped us; and, as he could not get out, the guides were sent for assistance and spades to dig him out. We left our interpreter and servants on the spot; and the Colonel, trusting to his memory, undertook to guide me, and we set forwards on foot, making many zigzags on the worst ground I ever trod on, sinking at every step halfway of my boots, and being obliged to walk, or rather run, pretty fast, for fear of sinking. After an hour's travelling, we could see nothing but the heaven and the bog, and the ground became softer and wetter, so that we could not advance without sinking in it. We tried to the right, then to the left, and twined and twined so much that we knew not which way to go, the Colonel having lost sight of his landmark. We continued moving on, as the Colonel told me that we should be lost if we ceased moving one moment. I confess here that I thought it my last day. The anxiety of the mind, the fatigue of the body, the insufferable heat of the day, and

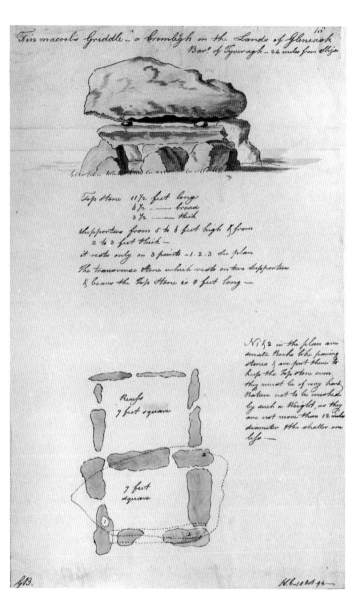

Fig. 90
View and plan of 'Finnmacool's Griddle — a Cromlegh on the lands of Gleneask', Co. Sligo, as drawn by J.S. C(ooper) on 18 October 1794, after a Beranger original, and now preserved as sheet 11, left, of the manuscript 3.C.42 in the library of the Royal Irish Academy.

Fig. 91
'Finnmacool's Griddle', in a vast bog in north-west Sligo, is now much more accessible than it was in 1779.

the intolerable thirst I felt, made me almost unable to proceed; but remembering that to stop a moment was instant death, I followed Mr. Irwin, putting my foot from where he withdrew his, as nearly as I could on this ground, which was now quite liquid, and appeared a lough to me. Two hours more were we in this situation, when Mr. Irwin got sight of some other mark, which gave me new courage; and little by little the ground grew firmer, and we made for some stacks of turf, and so forth on firm ground unto Fortland, where we arrived at seven, having been since three o'clock wandering in this horrid wilderness. We found the family alarmed (as our horses were arrived some hours before), and [they] had sent men to find us out in the bog. I threw myself on a chair, not being able to stir; could not eat, but only drink wine and water, which, being warmed out of precaution, did not quench my thirst. Mr. Bigari was all this time capering about the room, and felicitating himself that he had not been of the party. As for the Colonel, he was but little fatigued, and eat his dinner whilst I went to bed dinner and supperless [Wilde, 55–6].

By curious coincidence, Wood-Martin experienced similar difficulties almost 100 years later on visiting the same monument, as he relates on pp 25–6 of *Rude stone monuments of Ireland* (1888). Today the megalith (*Fig. 91*) is fortunately more easily reachable by a series of bog-roads which bring the traveller to within a few hundred yards of 'the Griddle'.

Vol. I.   Pl. 103.

ROSS LEE CASTLE. Co. Sligo.

Fig. 92
The 1792 engraving of
Rosslee Castle, Co. Sligo,
on plate 103 of the first
volume of Grose's
Antiquities was ultimately
based on a lost original by
Bigari.

Fig. 93
The hills forming the
background in the
eighteenth-century view of
Rosslee Castle, Co. Sligo
(*Fig. 92*), simply do not
exist, as Josephine Shields's
photo shows.

Rosslee Castle

On 10 July our pair of artists visited Rosslee Castle on the Atlantic shore just north of Easkey. Two views of it survive — the first a watercolour, by an unidentified artist, being p. 33 of the Royal Irish Academy's manuscript 3.C.29 (*Pl. 11*), which was prepared for the making of the second one, the engraving plate 103 in the first of Grose's two volumes of *Antiquities* (*Fig. 92*). Both curiously manage to create hills behind the castle where there is nothing but ocean (*Fig. 93*). The tall tower still exists, though repointed in the meantime, but the extension with doorway further to the right has disappeared, and the plan engraved on plate 104 (*Fig. 94*) shows steps leading up to the east wall of the tower, traces of which can still be made out. What have also disappeared are the wall fragments extending outwards towards the sea, as visible in the upper part of the same plan. The letterpress for vol. 1 of Grose's *Antiquities* ascribes the original of the engraved view to Bigari, and Beranger gave his description of the castle as follows in MS 4162, p. 16:

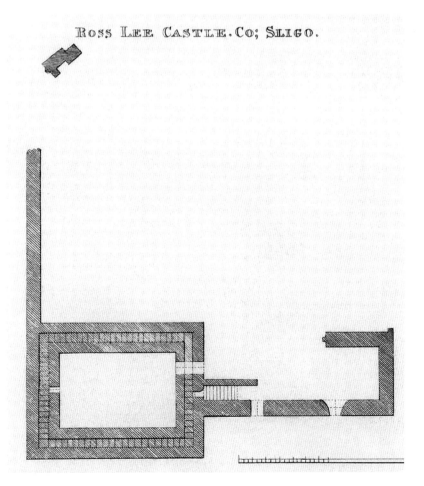

ROSS LEE CASTLE. CO; SLIGO.

Fig. 94
Plan of Rosslee Castle, engraved as plate 104 of vol. 1 of Grose's *Antiquities of Ireland,* shows that a hall once existed on the eastern side of the castle.

Rosslee Castle stands on the seashore of the Antlatick occean, Barony of Tyreragh. Seems of indiferent workmanship of black stone. It was larger formerly. That part which remains has stairs in the thickness of the wall all round. It is near a rivulet in which tradition says there was a wire to catch salmon, the door of which had a bell corresponding in the kitchen by which they had notice when a salmon was catched. See Drawg No 26.

The Diary, as excerpted by Wilde (56), tells the same fish story in greater detail, and notes that it was also told of Cong Abbey (see below). Carrick Castle on the Boyne, near Slane, was another location for the story.

Rathmulcah

On the morning of 11 July, Beranger and Bigari departed from Fortland and headed for Mayo, visiting on the way their last Sligo monument in the form of an earthwork whose fame far outstrips its importance. This is the large rath or ringfort known as Rathmulcah (*Fig. 95*), with a very deep ditch particularly on its southern side, and a souterrain in the centre, now blocked up. Its fame rests on a description by one Mylo Symner of the opening up of the souterrain in the 1640s, and a subsequent reference to it and a plan in Ware's *Antiquities*, which Beranger did not think very accurate, as he commented in his Diary:

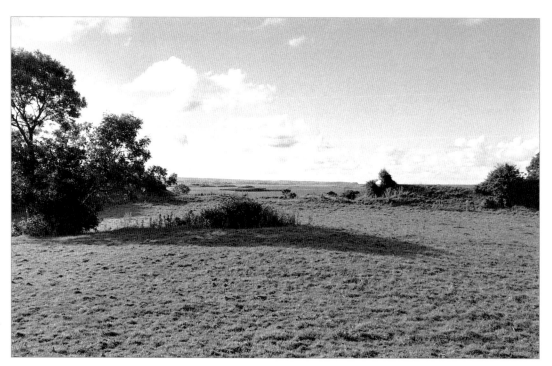

Fig. 95
The old fort at Rathmulcah, Co. Sligo, was the scene of jollification in 1779 when the two artists emerged from the souterrain at the centre of this picture.

Stopped near Castle Connor, to visit a subterraneaous cave under a rath, called Rathmullan; got candles, went in, and planned. Ware is greatly mistaken in the description of this cave in his vol. 11 of 'Antiquities', p. 138, and in the plan and section, Plate I, No. 5, as it is a zigzag, which comes much nearer the figure he gives in same Plate, No. 6, and I think it may be a mistake of the number [Wilde, 56].

In MS 4162, pp 16–17, Beranger gives a description of his experiences in the 'cave':

This rath is sitd on the lands of Runroe, parish of Castle Connor, Bar^y of Tyreragh, the cave is a long narrow winding gallery of bad masonry in which one must sometimes creep and sometimes walk bended down. What the usage of it was we could not guess, except it was a covered way to sally out thro a hole A (in plan No 27) which is in the center of the fort, this place is all damp wet and dirty at present, it was exedingly cold in it, no light but under the hole. I did not see the end of it as I fell down at the first angle extinguished the candle & hurted my leg and before I was recovered could not see Mr. Irwin and Bigary, and could hardly creep back to the entrance by the great pain I felt.

Nollaig Ó Muraíle kindly informs me that, in addition, Rathmulcah was mentioned not only by Dubhaltach Mac Firbisigh in his *Genealogies* written in the 1650s but also in the 1684 description of County Sligo by Downings, who claims it to have been a place of worship where 'stone urnes were found, as is said'. We know from Beranger's notes quoted above that he did a plan of the rath, but it is, sadly, another example of a monument where neither his original nor a copy has come down to us.

But before leaving the site — and County Sligo — our artists had an unexpected treat in store for them, as the Diary relates:

On coming out of the cave we found all the inhabitants of both sexes gathered on the rath, and amongst them two beautiful young women, who attracted our sight, and whom we could not cease to admire. The Colonel bid them all welcome, and ordered a gallon of whiskey to be brought; invited them all to sit down on the grass. The whiskey went about; we embraced all the females, the two beauties included; repeated it several times; made, at our example, the men do the same; were very merry, and quitted them after they had bestowed many blessings on us [Wilde, 57].

6. COUNTY MAYO

On crossing the River Moy into County Mayo late in the afternoon of 11 July, Beranger and Bigari's first stop was at

> Ardnaree, seat of Mr. Jones, County of Mayo, where we dined, and were told that Colonel Cuffe was waiting for us, and should join us after dinner, which he did [Wilde, 57].

Beranger, Bigari and Colonel Irwin do not seem to have tarried long at Ardnaree and, with Colonel Cuffe, they continued on to Newtown Gore. This was a large house, three storeys over basement, that is now a mere ivied shell about two and a half miles south-west of Ballina, a town which was, as they noted, 'famous for its salmon fishery'. In his Journal Beranger noted that

> this seat is an old castle, which has been modernized. The rooms are large and spacious, environed by a grove and gardens. It is situated near Lough Conn, a branch of which runs by the garden, along a thick, shady walk, which afforded us a cool shelter, and where we resorted in the height of the heat. It is the property of the Earl of Arran [Wilde, 57].

Killala round tower

Newtown Gore was obviously used as a base for visiting antiquities farther to the north, of which the first was the round tower at Killala (*Fig. 97*), visited on 13 July. In the Diary, Beranger wrote:

> Arrived at Killala; were presented to the Bishop by Colonel Cuffe; took part of a collation of fruits and wine; went with Messrs Hutchinson, the Bishop's sons, to see the Round Tower; drew it, and a skull of a whale which came on shore there; returned to the Palace; took our leave, and set out. The palace has a small court before it; looks like a farmer's house, only two stories high; in the dining room floor you are under the eaves, which are seen, and the rooms there are appropriated for bed chambers [Wilde, 57].

The drawing of the whale skull does not survive, but we have at least a copy of the drawing of the round tower, with a detail of the doorway (*Fig. 96*), executed by Austin Cooper, which is now p. 55 of the second album of his drawings preserved as 2122 TX(2) in the National Library and which can

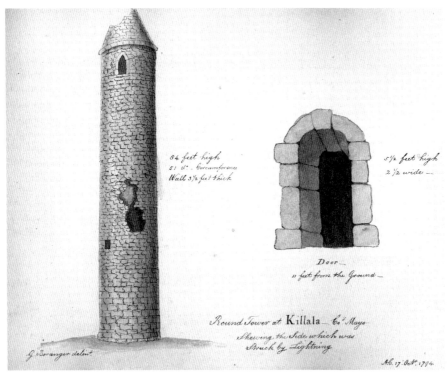

84 feet high
51 d°. Circumference
Wall 3½ feet thick

5½ feet high
2½ wide —

Door
11 feet from the Ground —

Round Tower at Killala Co. Mayo
Shewing the Side which was
Struck by Lightning

G. Beranger delint.

AC. 17 Oct. 1794

Fig. 96
Killala round tower once had a gaping hole, seen in this 1794 Austin Cooper copy (of a Beranger original) that is now p. 55 of the album 2122 TX(2) in the National Library.

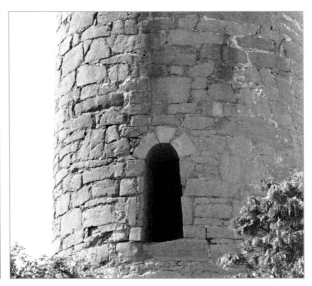

Fig. 97 (left and below)
The round tower at Killala, Co. Mayo, shows traces of the 1841 repair to a gaping hole halfway up which Beranger drew in 1779. The doorway (below) is on the other side.

be seen to be a fairly accurate representation (compare *Fig. 97*). It is signed with Cooper's initials and dated 17 October 1794 — the same week that his cousin Samuel had re-drawn the Beranger originals of the monuments on the north Sligo coast, so the Cooper family would seem to have had a veritable feast of copying that week. The defective roof of the tower and the hole caused by lightning in the north-eastern side, both seen in the illustration, may have been repaired by a later dean in 1841, according to Lennox Barrow's book *The round towers of Ireland* (1979).

On p. 17 of the National Library's MS 4162, Beranger describes the tower as follows:

> The Tower of Killala seems wel built. The roof damaged, it is 84 feet high 51 in circumference and the walls 3½ feet thick. There is a hole in it towards the middle of the hight which was made by lightning. the door is plain, 5½ feet high by 2⅓ wide and 11 feet from the ground. See drawing No 28.

Moyne Abbey

The Killala tower belonged to an old Irish monastery supposed to have been founded by St Patrick, but the artists' next port of call was to a very much later, medieval abbey, namely Moyne (*Fig. 98*),

> on the wide part of the River Moy, near the Bay, about two miles from Killala. Drew and plan. Eat here the largest cockles I ever had seen — as big as eggs, and drank some wine Colonel Cuffe had taken in his chariot, with some loaves; a tomb served as a table [Wilde, 57–8].

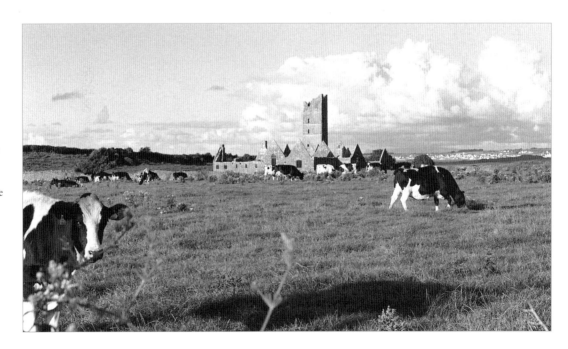

Fig. 98
Moyne Abbey in County Mayo is one of the few monuments of which no drawings survive from the antiquarian visitation of 1779.

Sadly neither the drawing nor the plan just referred to in the Diary survive — another of the rare instances in the whole tour where we have no visual record of any kind of the artists' activities, and even Beranger's description is meagre:

> The Abbey of Moyne is situated on the wide part of the river Moy where it disembogues it self in the Bay of Killala, 1½ miles from that town. It is of good workmanship and blueish stone [Nat. Lib. MS 4162, p. 17].

Rosserk Abbey

It is surprising, too, that Grose's *Antiquities* has no engraving of Moyne Friary, founded by the de Burgos around the middle of the fifteenth century for the Franciscans. For that, however, Grose vol. 1, plate 65, has — under the name Rosserick — an attractive engraving of the neighbouring 'abbey' at Rosserk (*Fig. 99*), which is beautifully situated right beside the shore. This was founded before 1441 for the Third Order of Franciscans, which included friars who were part of the community yet were married and living at home, and — though roofless — it is otherwise the only fully preserved house of the order to come down to us intact in Ireland. Grose's letterpress acknowledges Bigari as the author

Fig. 99 (far left)
Rosserk ('Rosserick') Abbey Co. Mayo, in a 1792 engraving, after a Bigari original, published as plate 65 in the first volume of Grose's *Antiquities of Ireland.*

Fig. 100 (left)
An unsigned drawing of Rosserk Abbey, Co. Mayo, 2122 TX(78) in the National Library, is ascribed on the back to Barralet (who was not on the tour) — but doubtless erroneously, as the masonry shows characteristics of Bigari's style.

Fig. 101
The interior of Rosserk
Abbey has changed little
since visited by Bigari and
Beranger in 1779.

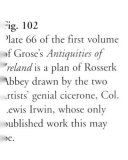

Fig. 102
Plate 66 of the first volume
of Grose's *Antiquities of
Ireland* is a plan of Rosserk
Abbey drawn by the two
artists' genial cicerone, Col.
Lewis Irwin, whose only
published work this may
be.

ROSSERICK MONASTREY, Co.MAYO.

of the original drawing, and this has been preserved for us as 2122 TX(78) in the National Library (*Fig. 100*), where it is wrongly ascribed to Barralet on the reverse. It is an interior view, little different from today (*Fig. 101*), with the masonry shown in typical Bigari style; it looks back from underneath the south window of the side-chapel towards the tower, and features the characteristic triple arcade above the arch. Curiously, Beranger's brief text in MS 4162, p. 18 —

The Abbey of Roserk is situated on the River Moy 3½ miles from Killala, it is well built of a blueish stone

— makes no reference to any drawings, though the Diary (Wilde, 58) does say that he did draw and 'plan' there. Perhaps even more curious is that the plan, as reproduced in plate 66 of vol. 1 of Grose's *Antiquities* (*Fig. 102*), is attributed to neither Beranger nor Bigari but to the faithful Lewis F. Irwin, Esq., and, if executed on the occasion of their combined visit there, shows Irwin to have been a valuable team member and a talented surveyor, whose only published work this plan may have been.

Perhaps Lewis Irwin's preoccupation with making the plan allowed Beranger more time to concentrate on details, preserved for us in yet another October 1799 Austin Cooper copy, this time as p. 7 of the National Library's manuscript drawing 2122 TX(4). The drawing (*Fig. 103*) shows the left half of the west doorway, with its unusual plain pinnacles rising from the sides, though omitting the

Fig. 104
The west doorway of
Rosserk Abbey, Co. Mayo.

Fig. 103 (above left)
Details of halves of the west doorway and south chapel
window of Rosserk Abbey, Co. Mayo, as drawn by Austin
Cooper in October 1799 and now p. 7 of 2122 TX(4) in
the National Library. Plate 126 of the second volume of
Grose's *Antiquities of Ireland* (*Fig. 14*) reproduced these
drawings of the Beranger originals.

Fig. 105 (left)
The window of the south chapel in Rosserk Abbey, Co.
Mayo.

foliage on the outermost moulding of the arch and
the details of the culminating crocket (*Fig. 104*). It
also provides us with a detail of the fine window
tracery still surviving in the south side-chapel (*Fig.
105*). Both items are reproduced as nos 22 and 24
on plate 126 of the second volume of Grose's
Antiquities (*Fig. 14*).

Nephin Mountain

According to Wilde (58), the two artists spent the next day — 14 July, precisely ten years before the fall of the Bastille — working at their sketches at Newtown Gore. While there, Beranger did a watercolour, later copied into p. 5 of the Royal Irish Academy album 3.C.31 (*Pl. 12*), which, as he noted in a description at the back of the manuscript, was a

> view of the mountain of Nephin, County of Mayo, and Province of Connaught, about 120 miles from Dublin, taken from Newtown Gore, 4 miles distant. This high mountain, who rears its lofty head above those in the neighbourhood, has a spring of water on its sumit, which, after rain, forms a furious torrant, which has dug for itself a bed in the mountain (tho' composed of white marble), and, running down, spreads itself at the foot, forming a lake. This bed I took for a highroad, at the distance, untill I was informed of the contrary, and told what it was.

However, it is difficult to square the view of Nephin as seen from the now-ruined Newtown Gore with what Beranger depicts in his small postcard-sized watercolour. Most local experts would agree that the view is not that from Newtown Gore but are puzzled about the artist's exact location when he painted the scene, Michael O'Sullivan of Westport suggesting that it may have been taken from the south-west side of Nephin, so that the sheet of water visible at the foot of the mountain would not be Lough Conn but Lough Beltra. If the watercolour in the Academy album is a copy of the view which Beranger says he 'took' at Newtown Gore, then the jury is still out as to where he took it from.

Having taken leave of Colonel Cuffe, our two artists proceeded to Foxford, also on the Moy, which Beranger — being somewhat of a gourmet — notes in his diary for 15 July

> is famous for abounding with Lampreys in the river, which nobody there will eat; got four large ones for 6d., and got them packed in grass. As it was a market day, went to walk about the place (whilst the horses baited); the place looks poor. I observed all the countrywomen who came to market having their aprons about their necks, instead of cloaks; but, on being amongst them in the market, we were surprised to find that to be their only upper covering, having neither gown nor shift, which we supposed was owing to the excessive heat of the weather [Wilde, 58–9].

Ballylaghan Castle

They then proceeded on their way towards Castlebar, taking in on the way three important Mayo antiquities — Ballylaghan, Strade and Turlough. Ballylaghan is one of the smaller Norman castles of the thirteenth century in Ireland, and also one of the most north-westerly, though of its history almost nothing is known.

Castle of Ballylaghan, Co. Mayo.

Fig. 106
The unsigned drawing of Ballylaghan Castle, Co. Mayo, p. 16 of 2122 TX(3) in the National Library, shows Bigari's characteristic style of depicting masonry.

BALLYLAGHAN CASTLE, Co. Carlow.

Fig. 107
The mighty gate-towers and the now-vanished vaulted entrance to Ballylaghan Castle, Co. Mayo, were engraved in 1792 after Bigari's original as plate 3 of the second volume of Grose's *Antiquities of Ireland* (where it was erroneously located in County Carlow).

Fig. 108
The remnants of
Ballylaghan Castle, Co.
Mayo, give little indication
of the former strength of its
entrance gate.

Of the surviving parts of the outer wall, that in the north-western quadrant is very angular in plan, suggesting provision for cross-firing, but the main surviving defence is the double-towered gateway in the south-eastern quadrant, which is the subject of Bigari's drawing — No. 2122 TX(3), p. 16, in the National Library (*Fig. 106*), bearing the original number 32 on the top right. This later formed the basis for the watercolour on p. 54 of the Royal Irish Academy's MS 3.C.29 (*Pl. 13*) before being engraved as plate 3 (*Fig. 107*) in the second volume of Grose's *Antiquities* (where it is mistakenly entered under County Carlow!). It fits the dramatic style of Bigari, who makes a splendid stage set out of it, showing arches appearing to stretch far back into the interior of the castle, and with tall walls behind. What survives of the entrance today (*Fig. 108*) leaves a question mark over whether Bigari was doing a bit of tentative reconstruction, though that would seem to be refuted by the details of the plan preserved in one copy (*Fig. 109*) in the National Library manuscript 671 (which came from Burton Conyngham via the Phillipps Collection), and also in another initialled by Austin Cooper, dated October 1799, and preserved in the National Library as 2122 TX(4), p. 24. Here we are shown the vaulting above the entrance passage, both flanking towers much more intact than they are today, and a stretch of wall heading north-eastwards from the gateway — all of which, on plan, correspond well with the drawing, though much less intact today. That the walls were much better preserved in Bigari's day than they are now is suggested by Beranger's difficulty in obtaining access to the interior because of blocked-up doors, as we can read in his description of the castle preserved in Nat. Lib. MS

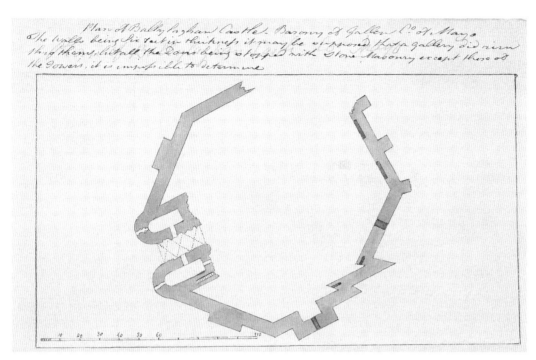

Fig. 109
The plan of Ballylaghan
Castle, Co. Mayo, in the
National Library's
manuscript 671, was
prepared for use in Grose's
Antiquities but rejected in
the final selection. It shows
the former presence of
triple ogival vaults spanning
the entrance passage.

4162, p. 19, after his visit on 15 July:

> The castle of Ballylaghan is situated on the road from Strade [*recte* Foxford] to Castlebar in the Barony of Gallen, two towers remain, & a part of the wall which notwithstanding various angles seems to have formed a kind of Octogon, is still remaining. The wall is 6 feet thick and it may be suposed to have contained a gallery or covered way, but all the doors being stopped with masonry we could not enquire or look into it. The principal entrance is between the towers, but other doors at present stoped up are in some other parts of the sides. The whole is of blackish stones and good workmanship. See plan etc. No 32.

It would look, therefore, on the whole, as if Bigari is indeed giving us a much better idea of the original appearance of this castle than we gain today from what survives.

Strade Abbey

The next stop was only a few miles down the road — the abbey at Strade, now behind the Michael Davitt Museum. Strade was originally a Franciscan foundation but, at the insistence of Basilia, daughter-in-law of the founder, Jordan of Exeter, it subsequently became Dominican in 1252. It was burned down two years later, and at least the chancel of the present church is likely to have been built

Fig. 110
The fine canopied
fifteenth-century tomb in
Strade Abbey.

shortly afterwards. But the north side-chapel is probably a fifteenth-century addition, as is the fine tomb inserted in the north wall of the choir (*Fig. 110*). Beranger gives us his views on this and other details of the abbey in his description in MS 4162, p. 18:

This abbey is situated in ye village of same name, seems to have been of more extend, is of tolerable workmanship of a blueish stone. The tower is down and only part of the arch remaining, it is very much in ruin, the great altar was magnificent in its time, and loaded with carvings of which some remain. There is a monument said to be ancient of curious workmanship which have some saints in base relief on it, of which we took a drawing. It is situated about 7 miles from Castlebar in the Barony of Gallen. See plan Drawings and parts No. 31.

Fig. 111
The sheet numbered 2122
TX(100) in the National
Library has two distinct
illustrations of Strade: on
the left is half of the
ornamental fifteenth-
century tomb, probably
drawn by Bigari because the
scale is in Italian, while the
right-hand half is occupied
by a plan of the abbey on
which he, uniquely, marked
the spot from where he
drew his view.

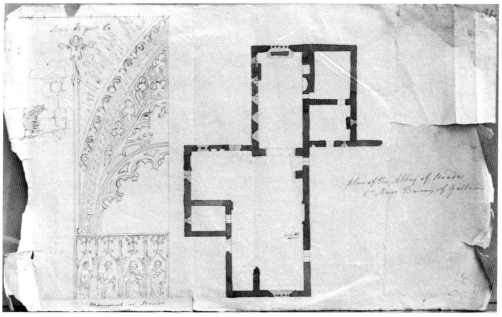

On a sheet numbered 2122 TX(100) in the National Library, an original drawing (*Fig. 111*) by Bigari (scale given in Italian as *scala di piedi*) shows us the left-hand side of that tomb, with the Three Kings bearing gifts in the three left-hand niches, suggesting a pilgrimage to Cologne (where their relics are enshrined in the Cathedral), and Christ showing the five wounds on the right, all arched over by a splendid piece of flamboyant tracery.

The accompanying plan — of which MS 671 in the National Library preserves another version — is reasonably accurate, except that the number of windows in the north wall of the choir should have been increased by two. With the words *punto della veduta* Bigari marked the spot from whence he took his view, preserved only in the engraving on the plate numbered 57 in the second volume of Grose's *Antiquities* (*Fig. 112*). Even if Grose had not acknowledged the authorship of the original from which the engraving was made, we could have guessed that it was Bigari because of the depth given to the choir in comparison to what we see today (*Fig. 113*). Through the arch inserted in the fifteenth century we can notice the narrow, two-light, half-blocked east window, beneath which the beautiful carved altar can be glimpsed in Bigari's gloomy shadow. Details of the window in the east wall of the side-chapel — where the sun seems to shine unexpectedly from the north — differ from what we see reconstructed today (*Fig. 113*), and the small building seen to the west of it on the plan was converted into the family vault of the O'Donnells of Tyrconnell only fourteen years after Bigari made his drawing.

One man who had travelled in Ireland only four years before the artists' visit, and whose account was so uncomplimentary that he got the nickname of 'lying Dick Twiss', now comes into our narrative again (see above, p. 13) because, as Beranger relates in his Diary,

> Whilst we were surveying the Abbey, we were accosted by two genteel dressed ladies who came to view us, having been told that Mr. Twiss was in our company. Our greatest anxiety was immediately to convince them that the report was false, and thoroughly to acquaint them of our business. As soon as they were assured of their mistake, they inveighed against Twiss for his slandering that province.

Richard Twiss's *Tour in Ireland in 1775* made him so unpopular, not only in Connacht but throughout the whole country, that an enterprising Dublin manufacturer produced chamber-pots bearing a portrait of Twiss accompanied by the following verse, attributed to Anne Whaley, later Lady Clare:

> Here you may behold a liar,
> Well deserving of hell-fire:
> Everyone who likes may P—
> Upon the learned Doctor T—.

Our two artists joined heartily in their condemnation of Twiss, but refused the ladies' offers of refreshments

STRADE ABBEY, Co.Mayo.

Fig. 112
Based on a Bigari original, the 1794 engraving of Strade Abbey, Co. Mayo, on plate 57 of the second volume of Grose's *Antiquities of Ireland* suggests that, in Mayo, the sun shines from the north.

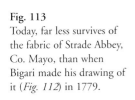

Fig. 113
Today, far less survives of the fabric of Strade Abbey, Co. Mayo, than when Bigari made his drawing of it (*Fig. 112*) in 1779.

as the day was advanced, and we intended to be early at Castlebar; but the real cause of our quick departure was, the fear that the neighbourhood might think like them, and that we might be insulted by the country people [Wilde, 59–60].

Their hopes of getting early to Castlebar cannot have been too high because the state of the roads leading to the town did not compare with what the motorist finds today. They had had, as Beranger's Diary remarked,

a most horrid stony road, the rocks being like trees laid across the way. We did not go at the rate of a mile an hour, and were afraid of our carriages breaking down, which at last happened to Mr. Irwin's cabriole, the fore axle-tree snapping at Strade, where he left it under the care of a servant to be mended; and, after having drawn the Abbey, he mounted the led horses with his son [Wilde, 59].

Turlough round tower and church

Another reason why the party was not destined to get to Castlebar as early as they might have liked was the necessity to draw the church and round tower some miles down the road at Turlough, on a raised site now overlooking the Folklife section of the National Museum. The tower may have formed part of an early monastery, said to have been founded by St Patrick, though in all likelihood it probably served as a stopping-off point for pilgrims *en route* to Croagh Patrick, who would have been able to see its conical top from afar as a landmark. Though one of the stumpier examples of its kind, the tower is slightly taller in relationship to its width than Bigari makes it out to be in his signed drawing 2122 TX(3), p. 17, in the National Library (*Fig. 114*) — bearing the original number 33 and with the spelling Turlagh — and the doorway which he includes at about the correct height on the right should, in fact, have been omitted, as it is not visible from where the artist drew his picture. Artistic licence!

Fig. 114
Bigari's signed view of the round tower at Turlough, Co. Mayo, is preserved in the National Library as p. 17 of 2122 TX(3).

Round Tower at Turlagh

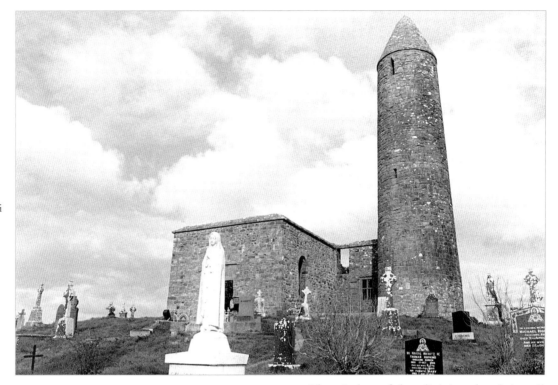

Fig. 115
The church at Turlough,
Co. Mayo, is a different
one to that drawn by Bigari
in 1779.

Fig. 115
The church at Turlough,
Co. Mayo, is a different
one to that drawn by Bigari
in 1779.

ROUND TOWER at TURLOGH Co.Mayo.

Fig. 116
We are fortunate in the case
of Turlough, Co. Mayo,
that we can follow the three
stages in the development
of an engraving — the
original drawing by Bigari
(*Fig. 114*), the album
watercolour prepared for
the engraver (*Pl. 14*), and
finally the engraving itself,
shown here from plate 67
of the first volume of
Grose's *Antiquities of
Ireland* — each showing a
different number of figures
acting as the supporting
cast.

The window of the adjoining church is well
rendered, and Bigari even includes the detail of
the small and charming Crucifixion plaque of
1625 beside it. But the larger ecclesiastical ruins
on the left in Bigari's view have been largely
swept away to make room for the very block-like
— presumably late eighteenth-century — church
that we see today (*Fig. 115*). The drawing, which
has two men conversing far apart, was made into
a watercolour (showing four figures) that is now
p. 20 in the Royal Irish Academy's manuscript
3.C.29 (*Pl. 14*), intended to be handed over to
the engraver of plate 67 of vol. 1 of Grose's
Antiquities (*Fig. 116*), who compromises by
presenting us with three men, two together and
one apart. The letterpress in Grose must have
been based on comments by Beranger, as it
repeats many (but also manages to get wrong
some) of the details given in p. 19 of MS 4162,

which is as follows:

> This tower is 70 feet high and exceeds in Diamr the generallity of this kind of buildings, since the diameter within is 9 feet, the walls 5 feet thus the whole diameter 19 feet, the door is 14 feet from the ground & out of reach for measuring, the church seems more modern and has the date of 1625 on it. It is built touching the tower, both of a brownish stone. It lies in the Barony of Carra, 4 miles from Castlebar.

The original number 33 on the top right of the sheet of Bigari's drawing is almost certainly Beranger's enumeration, as it corresponds to the numerical order of drawings listed in MS 4162, though the number 33 is not specifically assigned to Turlough round tower. Colonel Irwin, Beranger and Bigari finally reached Castlebar about half past eight in the evening, eating their lampreys, among other things, for supper (Wilde, 59). The town, Beranger noted in his Diary,

> looks decent enough. The church is new, and the steeple composed of squares, octagons and circular figures, which gives it an odd look at the distance. It has this inscription: 'This church was built at Castlebar in the year — :'

and, in a note, Beranger adds:

> one of the troopers newly arrived in this garrison read the inscription and answered, 'and where the devil else could it have been built?' but still that inscription remained when I was there, notwithstanding its absurdity. At the end of the town is the seat of Lord Lucan, in which are thick groves, which afforded us comfortable walks under their shades [Wilde, 60].

On 16 July the party travelled to what Beranger called Newport-Prat, where, as the Notebook informs us,

> The bridge being broke down by the floods, we forded the river with some difficulty; set up at the inn, and a very good one, where we were well entertained; sent notice of our arrival to the Earl of Altamont, at Westport; received an answer before ten, that he should be glad to see us. Here Mr. Irwin got a touch of the gout [Wilde, 60].

Burrishoole Abbey

On the following day, 17 July, the two artists probably left poor Colonel Irwin behind in some considerable pain in Newport as they set off for the enchantingly located abbey of Burrishool(e), built for the Dominicans around 1469 by Richard de Burgo of Turlough. Beranger's comments about it on pp 19–20 of MS 4162 are comparatively brief:

Vol. 1.   Pl. 63.

Pub. Apr.l.s.1793.by H.Hooper N.e12.High Holborn.   J.Pass sculp.

ABBEY OF BURYSHOOL, CO. MAYO.

Fig. 117
A lost Bigari original served as the basis for this 1793 engraving of 'Buryshool Abbey', Co. Mayo, which was published as plate 63 of the first volume of Grose's *Antiquities of Ireland*.

Fig. 118
With the exception of the back wall, the abbey at Burrishoole, Co. Mayo, is much as it was when Beranger and Bigari visited it in 1779.

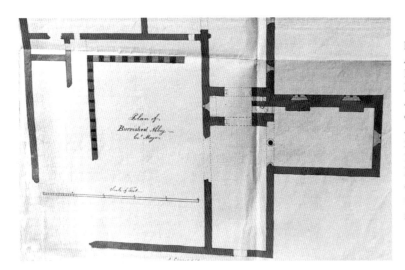

Fig. 119
A copy of a plan of
Burrishoole Abbey, Co.
Mayo, drawn and signed by
Austin Cooper as a Fellow
of the Society of
Antiquaries, is preserved as
2122 TX(3), p. 35, in the
National Library. The
layout of domestic quarters
on the top left is clearer in
the drawing than on the
ground today.

The Abbey of Burrishool is situated near the sea 1½ mile from Newportprat, on the road
leading to Erris, it is of plain, strong workmanship, rather clumsy, part of the steeple remains,
which is upon an arch. Two sides also remain of the cloysters, the arches of which are of
different structure, but massy and rather clumsy, the whole is of blackish stone. The regularity
of the building seem to mark the extend of the abbey which I believe never was larger. It may
be ranked among the small kind. See drawings No 34.

No original artwork survives from the site visit, but we know what Bigari drew through plate 63 of
the first volume of Grose's *Antiquities,* which acknowledges him to be the author of the original on
which the engraving (*Fig. 117*) was based. Comparing it with the view today (*Fig. 118*), it can be seen
that there are no major changes, except for an obviously more recent north wall which blocks out the
view of the cloister arcade forming the background of the engraving. That the wall was not there at
the time, and that the now-disappeared northern tract of the cloister arcade was, is demonstrated by
the plan made by 'Austin Cooper F.S.A.' (though possibly based on a Beranger or Bigari original) that
is now 2122 TX(3), p. 35, in the National Library (*Fig. 119*). It shows that some of the north-eastern
corner of the domestic buildings has vanished and how much repair work has been done in the
meantime by the Office of Public Works.

As the pair were drawing and 'planning' the abbey, the ghost of their Clones experience once more
raised its ugly head, as we learn from the Diary:

> We were surrounded by a vast number of people, amongst whom we observed some
> uncommon whisperings, and goings and comings. Mr. Bigari thought that their intention was
> to rob us; and we came off safe, and returned to Newport [Wilde, 60].

The Castle of Slane.

Pl. 1
Watercolour view of Slane Castle as it was before the alterations of the early 1780s. The watercolour, now in a Dublin private collection, was executed by Gabriel Beranger after an original by Thomas Roberts (1748–78).

O.Rourk's Hall at Drumahair, Co. of Leitrim.

Pl. 2
Coloured drawing of 'ORourk's Hall at Drumahair, Co. of Leitrim', signed by A.M. Bigari and now 2122 TX(66) in the National Library.

Pl. 3
Watercolour by an
unidentified artist of an
exterior view of
'Dromahair Abbey',
prepared for engraving
in Grose's *Antiquities of
Ireland* and now p. 14 of
the Royal Irish
Academy's MS 3.C.29.

Pl. 4
The interior of
'Dramahair Abbey' in a
watercolour by an
unknown hand,
prepared, but finally
rejected, for engraving in
Grose's *Antiquities of
Ireland*. It is now 1976
TX(61) in the Prints and
Drawings Department
of the National Library.

Pl. 5
J. T(urner)'s 1799
watercolour view of
Tomb 7 of the
megalithic cemetery at
Carrowmore, Co. Sligo,
after an original by
Beranger and now on
sheet 12 of MS 3.C.42
in the library of the
Royal Irish Academy.

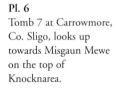

Pl. 6
Tomb 7 at Carrowmore,
Co. Sligo, looks up
towards Misgaun Mewe
on the top of
Knocknarea.

Pl. 7
Watercolour by an
unidentified hand of the
church of
'Ennismacreeny' on
Church Island in Lough
Key, now forming p. 48
of the Royal Irish
Academy's manuscript
3.C.29 (compare Figs
59–60).

Pl. 8
Watercolour of
McDermott's Castle on
Lough Key, Co.
Roscommon, prepared
by an unidentified hand
for engraving in Grose's
Antiquities of Ireland
(*Fig. 64*) and now
preserved as p. 47 of MS
3.C.29 in the Royal Irish
Academy. The name
Beranger is written on
the back.

Pl. 9
The medieval
McDermott castle on an
island in Lough Key
drawn on the 1779 tour
(*Pl. 8*) was replaced by a
folly early in the
following century.

Pl. 10
Watercolour (artist
unknown) of Court
Abbey, Co. Sligo, forms
p. 28 of the Royal Irish
Academy's manuscript
3.C.29, and was
probably the immediate
model for the engraving
of the same subject in
Grose's *Antiquities* (*Fig.
78*).

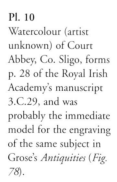

Pl. 11
This watercolour by an unidentified artist of Rosslee Castle, near Easky in County Sligo, which now forms p. 33 of the manuscript 3.C.29 in the Royal Irish Academy, acted as a model for the engraving in Grose's *Antiquities of Ireland* shown in Fig. 92.

Pl. 12
It is difficult to know precisely where Beranger stood when he drew this view of Nephin Mountain, Co. Mayo, which he later copied into the watercolour album 3.C.31 in the Royal Irish Academy.

Pl. 13
The watercolour of Ballylaghan Castle, Co. Mayo, by an unknown artist is on p. 54 of the Royal Irish Academy's manuscript 3.C.29, and was used as a basis for the engraving of the same subject in the second volume of Grose's *Antiquities* (*Fig. 107*).

Pl. 14
The watercolour of Turlough, Co. Mayo, by an unknown artist, as preserved on p. 20 of the manuscript 3.C.29 in the Royal Irish Academy, was used as a basis for the engraving of the round tower in the first volume of Grose's *Antiquities of Ireland* (*Fig. 116*).

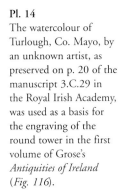

Pl. 15
Beranger's watercolour 'View of Croagh Patrick in County Mayo', on p. 6 of the Royal Irish Academy's postcard-size album 3.C.31, is a copy made around 1791 of one he executed while staying at Westport House in 1779.

Pl. 16
Beranger's watercolour of Clew Bay, on p. 7 of the Royal Irish Academy's manuscript 3.C.31, shows a wall on the left where the Westport Quay was subsequently developed by 1783, though this copy may date from as late as 1791.

Pl. 17
The anonymous
watercolour of Murrisk
Abbey, Co. Mayo, on p.
19 of the Royal Irish
Academy's manuscript
3.C.29 closely follows
Bigari's original (*Fig.
123*), and was used as
the basis for the
engraving in Grose's
Antiquities (*Fig. 125*).

Pl. 18
The coloured drawing
numbered PD 1495 TA
in the National Library
illustrating Ballintubber
Abbey, Co. Mayo, was
probably the final draft
for the engraving of the
abbey in Grose's
Antiquities (*Fig. 129*).

Pl. 19
The unknown artist of the watercolour of Claddagh Castle, Co. Galway, on p. 36 of the Royal Irish Academy's MS 3.C.29 has added two figures to Bigari's original (*Fig. 158*), who obligingly reappear in Grose's engraving (*Fig. 159*).

Pl. 20
The unknown artist's view of Athenry Abbey, Co. Galway, on p. 34 of the Royal Irish Academy's MS 3.C.29 was the basis for an engraving in Grose's *Antiquities of Ireland* (*Fig. 163*).

Rath Cruaghan or Croghan, County of Roscommon, on which the Ancient Kings 79 of Connaught, were inaugurated, and on which, they kept their Provincial Assemblies it is an artificial mount, made of Earth of a Circular form, all covered with grass, and in very good order, it Stands in a Large field and has a gentle Slope of an easy ascent all round it

The diameter at The Top is 400 feet, and at bottom 450 being 1350 in Circumf.y the Slope is 33 feet. it has in The Center of the Top, a Small mount whose Top has only 6 Feet diameter, on which it is Supposed The King had his Station. There is no Sign of remains of any Stone buildings on the whole Spot of ground

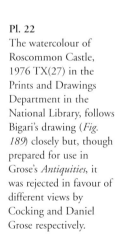

Pl. 21
The long, low outline of the great mound at Rathcroghan, Co. Roscommon, is well depicted in this watercolour which Beranger painted for p. 79 of his album MS 3.C.30 in the Royal Irish Academy, perhaps using his cicerone, Charles O'Conor of Belanagare, as a human scale.

Pl. 22
The watercolour of Roscommon Castle, 1976 TX(27) in the Prints and Drawings Department in the National Library, follows Bigari's drawing (*Fig. 189*) closely but, though prepared for use in Grose's *Antiquities*, it was rejected in favour of different views by Cocking and Daniel Grose respectively.

Pl. 23
The anonymous watercolour of Multyfarnham Abbey, Co. Westmeath, on p. 49 of MS 3.C.29 in the Royal Irish Academy, copied from a Bigari original, was later turned into an engraving in Grose's *Antiquities* shown in Fig. 212.

Pl. 24
The interior of St Mary's Church, Inishmurray, with the hills of north Sligo in the background.

Westport

Fig. 120
The portrait of Peter
Browne, second earl of
Altamont, hangs in
Westport House, which he
enlarged the year before he
played host to Bigari and
Beranger.

On the afternoon of 17 July, Beranger and Bigari travelled to Westport, where their host was Lord Altamont. This was Peter Browne, the second earl, whose portrait (*Fig. 120*) still hangs in the portrait gallery in Westport House. He had married Elizabeth, a daughter of Denis Kelly, the Chief Justice of Jamaica, and through this advantageous union much money flowed into Westport from the sugar plantations, with the help of which the town expanded and was made more beautiful. The house where he had grown up can be seen in two interesting views painted by George Moore in 1760, both of which now hang in the stairway of the house. The eastern façade (*Fig. 121*) remains much the same, but the western side was altered by a considerable addition probably in 1778, the date inscribed on the pediment of the south side. Thus half of the mansion to which our artists came the following year was brand-new, so that there must have been ample room for their quarters. Because they had had to leave Colonel Irwin confined at Newport with the gout, Lord Altamont sent him an express invitation to come to Westport House.

> After dinner, his Lordship showed us his wolf-dogs, three in number; they are amazing large, white, with black spots, but of the make and shape of the greyhound, only the head and neck somewhat larger in proportion. We had here at supper the largest shrimps I had ever seen, being almost as big as prawns [Wilde, 60].

In his Diary, Beranger informs us that on the following day, 18 July, the artists

> Stayed and worked at our drawings; took a walk after dinner with my Lord to a large circle of stones, having a cromlegh in the centre, situated on his Lordship's ground on the sea-side; told him my notion, that they were burial places, and not temples, and proposed to get it opened, to which he consented and fixed next morning for the operation; took a view and sketch of the famous Croagh Patrick, which could then be fairly seen.
> See Plate [Wilde, 60–1].

Fig. 121
George Moore's 1760 painting of and in Westport House, where Beranger and Bigari stayed and worked in 1779, and which nowadays opens its doors to the public in summer.

Beranger worked up the view and sketch of Croagh Patrick into a pair of watercolours, Nos 6 and 7 respectively in the postcard-size album MS 3.C.31 in the Royal Irish Academy (*Pls 15–16*), to which he appended the following extended captions at the back of the album:

> No. 6. 'View of Croagh Patrick, in the County of Mayo, and province of Connaught about 129 miles from Dublin, taken from the sea shore near Westport'. This mountain, one of the highest in Ireland, is famous for the residence St. Patrick made there, and from whence he expelled all venimous reptiles (as history tells us in vide Sir James Ware). The view from the summit is most extensive and delightfull, having before one, Clue Bay and its 400 islands, and for a background the mountains of the baronies of Erris and Tirawly. On the right Westport and Lord Altamont's domain; on the left the Islands of Achill, with the Island of Clara [Clare], and in the rear the wild and romantic Joyces Country. This mountain forms the southern shore of Clue Bay, which the foot entirely occupys, being a distance of near eight miles, as I was told; the summit, in the form of a cone, is generally enveloped by clouds; and though it appears

pointy, has a large area at its top, where there is a stone altar built, on which mass is said on the saint's day. I believe it to have been formerly a volcano — at least it has very much the look of one. As may be seen by the drawing.

No. 7. View of Clue Bay, taken from the rear of the house of ye earl of Altamont, showing Croagh Patrick, the high island of Clara, on which, I was told, the inhabitants are about 1500 in number, the extremity of Lord Altamonts park. All the points and headlands seen in this view are part of the numerous islands this bay contains, which are said to be 400 in number. They are of various extent and height. Some are cultivated; some have trees and grass, others are mixed with rocks, others bare rocks (on which sea monsters [seals] lay basking in the sun, of which I saw many whilst I was sailing from Westport to Croagh Patrick). I thought to reckon them from the top of the mountain, but found it impossible — some appearing like a single island, when in fact they were separated by small channels, and others partly hid behind the high ones, so as to be half covered by the hill, and prevented the eye to distinguish whether they were joined or detach'd from it: beside, the whole is so confusingly arranged that one is bewildered, and I am certain it is impossible to count them from that eminence. At the left of the drawing is represented a wall, which was building; and since, I hear, a quay and custom house has been erected there, to serve the town of Westport.

The view of 'Clue Bay' must have been taken from near the bridge beside the sea near the entrance to Westport House, but the copy from the Academy album reproduced here (*Pl. 16*) is likely to have been painted after 1783, the date formerly on a building on the quay which Beranger reported as having already been built when he wrote his caption.

On 19 July, the day dawned for what was to be one of the first recorded archaeological excavations in the country, which, using methods rather different from today's, Beranger describes in his Diary as follows:

After breakfast we set out with his Lordship and a large company of labourers, with all the tools required to blast and remove large stones. The top stone of the cromleagh was broke, and removed also its pillars or supporters; but, as the work went on slowly, the men working unwillingly, murmuring, and saying it was a sin to disturb the dead, his Lordship made them observe that the person buried there was not a Christian but a heathen, which, being d—d, it was no sin to dig up his bones; to which they agreed, and fell to work with alacrity. At about four feet deep was found a kind of circle of paving stones, in the centre of which were bones which had been burned, some of them being sound in one end, but of a brown colour, and the other end like charcoal. The skull, though broke, was found, and, near it, a ball as round and of the size of a billiard ball, which, being washed and cleaned, appeared to us to be marble, which his Lordship kept. There were smaller bones found, and the jaw bones of an animal with tusks, which we supposed was his favourite dog. The circle of stones which contained these

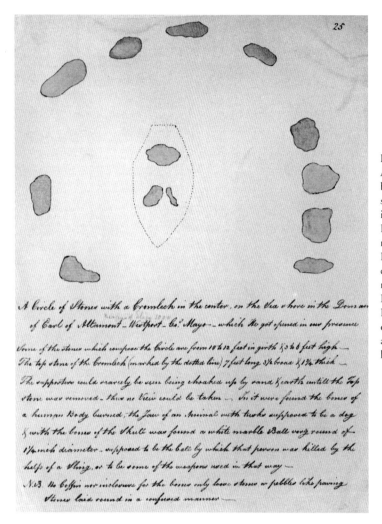

Fig. 122
A 1790s drawing, probably by Austin Cooper, of a stone circle with cromlech in the grounds of Westport House. This is now sheet 7, right, of MS 3.C.42 in the Royal Irish Academy. The excavation of the monument, supervised by Lord Altamont at Beranger's request, was one of the earliest recorded archaeological 'digs' of its kind in Ireland.

bones was about two feet diameter. Having thus assured ourselves that this monument was a mausoleum, and not a temple, we got the bones re-interred, and the grave covered, and one of the fragments of stone put over it [Wilde, 62].

In a marginal note, Beranger showed himself pleased that he had proved wrong O'Halloran's contention that these were temples, and added that

I know it answers his purpose, but still it is an error, and a rash assertion, of which I am obliged to take notice [Wilde, 62].

A serious-minded scientist, Beranger would have fitted well into the world of archaeology today!

In his Diary, according to Wilde (62), Beranger gave a ground-plan of the circle of pebbles or paving stones, which was two feet in diameter, but this is not present on the only plan we have — a copy, probably by Austin Cooper of the 1790s, of what was almost certainly a Beranger original (now lost). This is preserved among the drawings recently returned by the Department of Archaeology in University College Dublin to the Royal Irish Academy, where it now has the accession number 3.C.42, sheet 7, right (*Fig. 122*). This shows an incomplete circle of stones with an apparent dolmen in the middle (like that at Carrowmore illustrated on *Pl. 5*), and is, therefore, a megalithic tomb, the location of which has sadly been lost. The long text accompanying the drawing follows very closely Beranger's text on p. 20 in MS 4162, which adds little to it except to note that the stones supporting the capstone that was blasted measured four to five feet in their whole length when lying on the ground. The 'plan No 35' at the end of the text refers presumably to the original of Cooper's copy and, to judge by the extended caption, no general view was taken of the monument.

After a hard, and obviously satisfying, day's work, the party returned to Westport House, where the mysterious whisperings of two days earlier were clarified, as Beranger explains in the Diary:

> Dined at my Lord's in company with his brother the honble John Brown, collector of Newport, who told us that we were near being seized by the people of Burryshool, who had taken us for spies; that they had applied to him for an order to lodge us in jail, but that he had charged them at their peril not to molest us, as he knew our business — which accounted for their uncommon behaviour whilst we were amongst them. Settled our journey for next day to Murrisk or Morrisk Abbey, at the foot of Croagh Patrick, Mr Brown having ordered the Revenue barge and crew to be ready for next morning early [Wilde, 63].

Murrisk Abbey and Croagh Patrick

The barge may well be the sailing-boat seen at anchor in Clew Bay in both of the Westport watercolours (*Pls 15–16*) described above. The Diary continues:

> July 20th. — Set out in the barge with Mr. Bigari; hoisted sail, navigated through Clew Bay, an Archipelago of near 400 islands, of various sizes, some wooded, some cultivated, and some bare rocks. We were delighted with the scene, and could not cease to admire that variety of objects. We had for guide his Lordship's sportsman, who was an excellent player on the German flute, and regaled us with music, which he now and then interrupted to fire at the sea monsters swimming about us; a heavy shower of rain interrupted our sport. We arrived at Murrisk, drew the Abbey and plan [Wilde, 63].

Attractively sited beside the seashore near the foot of Croagh Patrick, the 'abbey' of Murrisk was founded by the O'Malleys sometime around 1456 for the Augustinian friars from Banada (see p. 92),

The Abbey of Murrisk County of Mayo.

Fig. 123
Though unsigned, this drawing of Murrisk Abbey in County Mayo is almost certainly the work of Bigari and is now p. 18 of the album 2122 TX(3) in the National Library.

Fig. 124
With the exception of the entrance porch in the angle of the cloister, Murrisk shows little apparent change in the last 200 years, though parts of its masonry may have undergone some alterations.

Fig. 125
In addition to Bigari's original drawing (*Fig. 123*) and its copy in watercolour (*Pl. 17*), we also have this engraving of Murrisk Abbey, Co. Mayo, on plate 64 of the first volume of Grose's *Antiquities of Ireland.*

MORISK ABBEY. Co. Mayo.

and was frequently used as a base for pilgrims who came to climb Croagh Patrick. Beranger gives a description of it in MS 4162, p. 21:

> The Abbey of Morisk or Murrisk is situated on the shore of Clue Bay in the Barony of Morisk at the foot of Croagh Patrick Mountain. It is not & seems not to have been of large extent and may have been a single church, as no appearance of cloysters are to be seen. There are battlements on one side or south of the building, it is well built of a redish stone; the steeple is down and the bare walls of the building remaining. A note of Chs O Connor Esqr says it was built by the O Mailies the year not yet discovered. See drawings No 36.

The same number 36 is still present on the back of the original Bigari drawing, 2122 TX(3), p. 18, in the National Library (*Fig. 123*), with preliminary pencil sketch on the reverse. With the exception of a few minor details, the drawing gives a faithful representation of what still survives (*Fig. 124*). One man relaxes inside a wall where a portico supporting a tower once stood at the western end, and he is conversing with another, outside, resting on a stick. An arch, now largely blocked up, leads into the church beyond, which has some fine ashlar masonry on the south side though it is otherwise not quite as regular as that shown by Bigari. This drawing formed the basis of an attractive watercolour on p. 19 of the Royal Irish Academy's manuscript 3.C.29 (*Pl. 17*), which was, in turn, to act as a basis for the engraving on plate 64 of vol. 1 of Grose's *Antiquities* (*Fig. 125*). In October 1799 Austin Cooper copied a plan (*Fig. 126*) — after a lost original, probably by Beranger — on a sheet now MS 2122

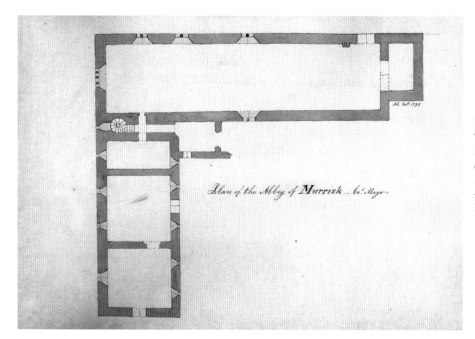

Fig. 126
The plan of 'The Abbey of Murrisk', Co. Mayo, executed by Austin Cooper in October 1799, is now p. 4 of 2122 TX(4) in the National Library.

TX(4), p. 4, where the windows on the west side of the domestic buildings give the impression that much of this wall has been rebuilt in the meantime.

When the artists had completed the drawing and the plan, the rain came down, as it is wont to do, so they

> took refuge in the house of Mr. Garvey, who insisted on our dining with him; dined heartily; rain continued heavily; were obliged to pass the night here; were very merry with the family, had the music of the German flute, and our crew singing and drinking in the kitchen.
>
> After supper, about ten, Mr. Bigary and I were surprised with a sudden and thundering noise, which made us think that Croagh Patrick was tumbling down, and going to bury us under its ruins; the company perceived our surprise, and told us that the noise we heard was occasioned by the torrents running down the mountain, dragging and carrying rocks and stones before them. Mr. Garvey offered to give us a sight of them, which we accepted, as the weather was fair. One of the torrents was running just by the side of the avenue, and even overflowed part of it. It would require the pen of a poet to describe the awful scene that presented itself to us. The thundering noise and roarings of torrents at various distances, heightened by the stillness of the night; the moon covered with clouds, which, gliding over it now and then, afforded us a sight of the immense region of Croagh Patrick, filled us with a kind of horror, which made us quake, though we were sure that there was no danger. We staid for some time looking and listening, and lost in contemplation, and returned home, the mind filled with the grand objects we had seen, which made us grave the whole evening.

July 21st. — Got up early, and under the guidance of Mr. Garvey we ascended Cro. Pat. to the foot of the reek; there, turning about, we had a most glorious view, having before us Clew Bay and all its islands, and for back ground the mountains of Erris and Tyrawley. To the right Westport, and to the left the Islands of Achill, with the high island of Clara, and in the rear Joyce's Country. Mr. Bigary proposed mounting up the Reek; but, as it was enveloped in clouds, which would have obstructed the view of any object, and would have wet our clothes, we over-ruled him, and descended the hill, having got a good appetite for our breakfast. Croagh Patrick is situated in the Joyce's Country, and forms the southern entrance of Clew Bay; it is very rocky, and affords some pasture for sheep. The Reek is composed of rock, which seemed to me divided in small stones, &c.; though the summit seems to terminate in a point, our interpreter (who went there to gain indulgences) told us that it is pretty flat, and forms a plain somewhat hollowed, where there is built a stone altar to say mass on the saint's day…Eat our breakfast, and walked about until 10, when our vessel was afloat. Took leave of the good family who had entertained us so well. Embarked and set sail, and arrived at Westport at 12; where to our great joy, we found Mr. Irwin and his son arrived [Wilde, 63–4].

Their joy, however, was comparatively short-lived, as Colonel Irwin had to leave them there, but they cannot have been too much displeased when, as Wilde (64) puts it, with true Irish liberality he informed them that their portion of the account had been lost! However, because Beranger's Diary has also been lost, we do not know what it had to say about Westport and its hospitable House, but we have his valuable account of the barony of Erris, derived from local information. He was told that there were no antiquities there, and says

that if we intended to try it on uncertainty, we must leave our carriage, take horses and provisions, and penetrate into a vast tract of wilderness, composed of mountains and bogs, without town, village, or hamlet; where we would not even see a tree; that our lodgings must be in one of the cottages which we chanced to meet, there being now and then an odd one found where chance had left an arable spot; that wherever we found a cabin we must take a guide to the next one, and so on; that without this precaution we should be lost amongst the mountains and bogs, and that we should hasten our journey to the Mullet, the most western part of the barony, and the only one inhabited. That summer was the only time to undertake this journey, which in autumn and winter was impracticable. In regard to the inhabitants, we were told they were very hospitable, never shutting the doors of their cabins; that any poor stranger gone astray, or travelling along, might freely come in whether by night or day, and take his share of what the house afforded. All these difficulties made us lay aside the intention of penetrating in that country, since we were uncertain to find any antiquities there [Wilde, 64].

Ballintubber Abbey

Rain on 22 July kept the artists inside and working at their drawings. On the following day, 23 July, rather than facing such uncertainty on a trip to the Mullet, they took leave of Lord Altamont and headed southwards for Ballinrobe, where they had letters for Mr Gallagher, sub-sheriff to Lord Westport, eldest son of Lord Altamont. However, before getting there, they deviated to visit and draw Ballintubber Abbey, one of the most famous foundations of its kind in Connacht and, like Murrisk, a place long associated with pilgrimage to Croagh Patrick. Beranger gives his own description of it in MS 4162, pp 21–2:

> This Abbey is situate on the road leading from Westport to Ballinrobe at 7 miles from the last mentioned town, this was a noble structure of exellent workmanship and finishing, it was of much larger extent than it is at present but could not trace more then is shown in ye plan; the chancell part is covered also two chapels on each side, the groining remain intire in the chancel and spring from consoles of a particular shape adorned with carvings, the east window is composed of 3 openings or rather windows under which is the great altar. There are also altars in the little chappels. The tower is quite down but the noble arch which suported it remains and is equal in hight to that of Boyle being above 45 feet, the principal door was also beautifull being an pointed arch suported by 5 colums with capitals adorned with carvings at present defaced. See plans, views and parts No 37.

In the Diary, Wilde noted Beranger's interest in encountering

> a schoolmaster in the abbey with a parcel of children; his desk was a large monument, and the children sat on stones arranged. Joy of our interpreter on finding a person of his [own] profession [Wilde, 65].

No trace of either master or pupils is to be found in Bigari's original drawing (*Fig. 127*) — 2122 TX(3), p. 19, in the National Library — which bears Beranger's quoted number 37 in the top right-hand corner, demonstrating how the original drawings tie in with the contents of MS 4162. In his own inimitable style, Bigari has added great depth to the chancel by the trick of making it one bay longer than it actually is, and has made his two human scale models slightly less than life-size so that the vaulted ceiling will seem to be taller than it is in reality (*Fig. 128*). One noteworthy feature is the altar with sculptures under a series of arches mentioned by Beranger, and the question may well be posed as to whether this is an altar that has since disappeared, or — as seems more likely — the tomb-frontal of Tiobóid na Long de Burgo (died 1629), with its seven 'weeper' apostles, before it was moved to its present position in the sacristy. An attractive watercolour version of this drawing (*Pl. 18*) is preserved as PD 1495 TA in the National Library and, though with stronger colours than those used in the Royal Irish Academy's manuscript 3.C.29, it may have served as a final version prepared for the

Fig. 127
Bigari's signed drawing of
Ballintubber Abbey, Co.
Mayo, adding a fourth bay
in the choir arcade to create
the illusion of extra depth,
is now p. 19 of 2122 TX(3)
in the National Library.

Fig. 128
Ballintubber Abbey was
enhancingly restored and
re-roofed in 1966.

BALLINTUBBER ABBEY, Co Mayo.

Fig. 129 (left)
The engraving on plate 61 of the first volume of Grose's *Antiquities* brings out very clearly the fourth bay that Bigari added to the actual three in the choir of Ballintubber Abbey.

Fig. 130 (above)
Austin Cooper's 1799 copy of lost Beranger drawings of the chapter house doorway, a horizontal profile of its mouldings, as well as a console and one of the east windows of Ballintubber Abbey, Co. Mayo, is on p. 1 of 2122 TX(4) in the National Library. These were reproduced as nos 8–9 and 11 of plate 126 of the second volume of Grose's *Antiquities* (*Fig. 14*).

engraver of plate 61 of vol. 1 of Grose's *Antiquities* (*Fig. 129*), the letterpress for which betrays the use of one version or another of Beranger's account quoted above.

The abbey proudly claims to have been sufficiently unaffected by the consequences of the Reformation to have always provided a location for the saying of Mass since its foundation for the Augustinians by Cathal Crobhdearg, king of Connacht, in 1216. Its restoration was completed for the 750th anniversary in 1966 under the direction of the late Percy Le Clerc, who restored the sober dignity of the interior by providing a new wood-supported slate roof for the nave. The white limewash background brought out details of carvings on the consoles, two of which Beranger drew. One of these is no. 10 on plate 126 of the second volume of Grose's *Antiquities* (*Fig. 14*), presumably copying a lost Beranger original of which not a trace survives. The other we know from a copy made by Austin Cooper in 1799 (*Fig. 130*), though it is difficult to be certain which of the partially abraded examples it was that he actually drew. The same sheet — part of 2122 TX(4), p. 1, in the National Library — also copied lost Beranger drawings of the chapter house doorway (as if seen from below, to judge by the alignment of the capital abaci) together with a cross-section and an exterior view of one — probably the central — of the east windows. All of these details were also reproduced from the lost originals in the engraved plate 126 of vol. 2 of Grose's *Antiquities* (*Fig. 14*).

Cong Abbey

At this juncture, we can now take up Wilde's own narrative, which probably gives a précis of what Beranger had written in the lost Diary:

> Sigr. Bigari stayed at the inn, finishing some sketches during the morning, and then they both proceeded to the Neale, to see Sir John Browne, who politely invited the artists to take up their quarters there. They then passed on to Cong, where they were entertained by Mr. Ireland, who … acted as their guide to the antiquities in that celebrated locality. Under the name of the 'Priest's Hole', now known as the 'Pigeon Hole', he describes that remarkable cavern and subterranean river, with its 'blessed trouts' &c. [Wilde, 65].

The fine abbey of Cong goes back to a foundation of St Fechin in the seventh century, but most of what survives can scarcely date from much earlier than the death of Rory O'Connor, king of Connacht and last high king of Ireland, who was buried here in 1198. After his visit on 24 July Beranger described the abbey as follows in MS 4162, p. 22:

> The Abbey of Cong sit: in the Town of that name, County of Mayo, was once magnificent, which one must judge by the work bestowed on the finishing of the doors, from whence alone it can be inferred to have been a noble building; All the rest what remains are bare walls, no covering, arch nor tower, remaining, we were at a loss where to take the view, nothing but bare walls being to be seen, and since this could not be remedied, Mr. Bigari determined to show the wall that has the doors, which is in the aria which we suppose contained ye cloysters. See plan, view and parts No 38.

Bigari's view of 'the wall that has the doors' — p. 13 of 2122 TX(4) in the National Library (*Fig. 131*) — employs a much weaker ink than he normally uses, which could give rise to a query as to whether it is an original or a copy, as is the much better and bolder version engraved as plate 55 of vol. 2 of Grose's *Antiquities* (*Fig. 133*). It is, however, likely to be an original. What is remarkable here is the view through the central doorway to the wall and windows beyond. These no longer exist (compare *Fig. 132*), but the wall is entire in the plan by Bigari copied by Austin Cooper in 1799 and again in 1800 (2122 TX(4), pp 6 and 31 respectively) and also present among the plans in the portfolio MS 671 in the National Library, which came from Burton Conyngham via the Phillipps Collection (*Fig. 134*). This plan also gives details of the internal divisions of the eastern side of the domestic buildings, some of which are not otherwise easy to discern on the ground today. But Beranger also occupied himself with sketching architectural details of one half of the two highly decorative doorways, as seen in the copy made by Austin Cooper in October 1799 and now preserved as p. 14 of 2122 TX(4) in the National Library (*Fig. 135*). In addition, Beranger provided cross-sections and mouldings, together with a drawing of capitals from the doorways — all reproduced as nos 2–7 on plate 126 of

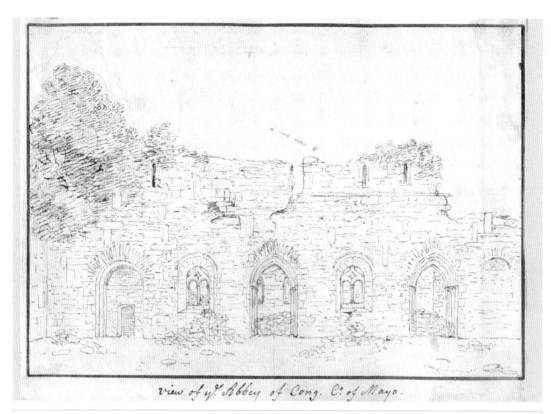

view of y.ͤ Abbey of Cong. C.º of Mayo.

Fig. 131
A probable Bigari original of Cong Abbey's 'wall that has the doors' on p. 13 of 2122 TX(4) in the National Library.

Fig. 132
The modern view of Cong Abbey shows that the wall with window visible through the central doorway in the probable Bigari drawing (*Fig. 131*) no longer exists.

Vol.2.   Pl.55.

Publish'd March 22 1794 by M. Hooper Nth. high Holborn   J. Newton Sculp.

ABBEY of CONG, Co.Mayo.

Fig. 133
The 1794 engraving of Bigari's drawing of 'the wall with the doors' at Cong, Co. Mayo, is plate 55 of the second volume of Grose's *Antiquities of Ireland*, and shows clearly another wall behind it which has since been reduced to its foundations.

vol. 2 of Grose's *Antiquities* (*Fig. 14*). These doorways and capitals are among the finest carved by the West of Ireland school of masons in the early thirteenth century (*Figs 136–139*).

Beranger's narrative in the Diary, as quoted by Wilde (66), continues with an interesting description of the unorthodox method of their host, Sir John Browne, in taming a limestone landscape to make a garden:

> The ground of the concerns at the Neale are of the same composition; and walking over it, it seemed to us a good ground covered with grass, until Sir John Browne told us that he had been at the expense to dig and blast some of them to make a pond for water, which was a commodity not found formerly at the Neale. And those blasted rocks he got broke, and the crevices stopped with them, and gravel mixed, after which he covered it with six inches of earth, which formed the lawns and fields before us. But the most remarkable circumstance is, that those rocks, which are about four or five feet thick, lie upon a rock so perfectly even that it appears to be one single flag, which composes the bottom of the large pond under the windows of the mansion house, in the centre of which he preserved rock enough to form an island which is now covered with some shrubs, in which the vast quantity of foreign waterfowl which he feeds on it breed quiet and undisturbed. On telling us that he had begun another pond some

hundred yards further, we went to it, and were surprised to find an even flag without joint or fissure, and of such an enormous size. We measured as far as the digging and blasting had gone on, and found it to be 100 feet long, by 48 broad. It has the effect, to the eye, of a pond on which the water is frozen. Sir John told us that he verily believes that it extends thus under the whole estate, of which I make no doubt; Mr. Bigari danced a Minuet with Miss Browne upon this curious floor. Sir John told us that, before he had made the pond of water, this element was so scarce there, and in the whole neighbourhood, that, if some visitors arrived there unexpected, they were often obliged to leave a bottle of white wine in their rooms to wash their hands in the morning, the little water which might be in the house being wanted for breakfast [Wilde, 66].

Sir John had yet another surprise up his sleeve for the visitors:

A singular bird of the waterfowl kind appears in the pond every Sunday, eats and swims the whole day familiarly amongst the tame fowls, and disappears before morning. He has never been seen on any other day, but comes regularly on Sundays. This afforded us many speculations in conjecturing where he could be on the other six days, &c.; how or why he should only come on Sunday; as we were there on that day, we went to the pond before breakfast, and had the pleasure to see him pretty close, having taken oats to feed the fowl, close to the edge of the pond. He seems to be the size of a teal, as black as jet, and in shape nearly of a wild duck, only the beak seems more sharp and pointed [Wilde, 66–7].

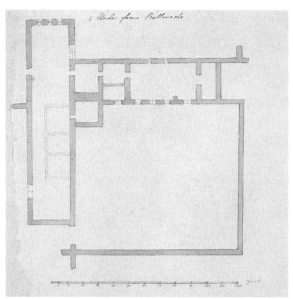

Fig. 134
The plan of Cong Abbey that was presumably in the Burton Conyngham, Cooper and Phillipps collections before becoming MS 671 in the National Library was probably prepared for use in Grose's *Antiquities*, but discarded.

Fig. 135
Beranger's details of halves of two doorways at Cong, together with horizontal cross-sections and details of a capital, were copied in 1799 by Austin Cooper in drawings now preserved as p. 14 of 2122 TX(4) in the National Library. They were reproduced as nos 2–6 on Plate 126 of the second volume of Grose's *Antiquities of Ireland* (*Fig. 14*).

Fig. 136 (right)
The central doorway of the claustral buildings at Cong, dating from the early thirteenth century.

Fig. 137 (far right)
The south doorway of the claustral buildings at Cong has richly decorated capitals and arches.

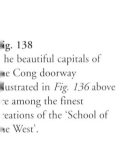

Fig. 138
The beautiful capitals of the Cong doorway illustrated in *Fig. 136* above are among the finest creations of the 'School of the West'.

Sir John was a man who must have kept himself well informed of the latest fads and fashions in the capital, being a very good friend of the progressive and enlightened Lord Charlemont. Cosmopolitan taste must have been reflected in his estate at the Neale, with the erection of temples, urns and statues, as well as a

> miniature model of one of the pyramids of Egypt from a plan and drawing given him by his brother-in-law, the Earl of Charlemont, who has travelled in Egypt, and other parts of Africa and Asia [Wilde, 67].

The pyramid still survives, minus the statue of Apollo that crowned it, which had disappeared even in Wilde's day.

Fig. 139
A capital with interlocking foliage on the south side of the south claustral doorway at Cong, Co. Mayo.

Leaba Dhiarmaid, Ballinchalla

The two artists must have dined well at the Neale, receiving 'a dish of venison every day', as Sir John had 200 brace of deer in his deer-park. But duty called again on 26 July, when their genial host took them in a coach and four to visit

> Leabbie Diarmuid, i.e. Dermott's bed, at Ballinchalla, near Lough Mask, which is a cavern containing a river, said to communicate with the one in the Priest's Hole, a mile from Cong, distant five or six miles from one another. Sir John told us that he had once this river plum'd on the edge where we were standing, and found forty feet depth; that he had put on the river where we were a plank or board, on which he had got six candles fastened, and put it adrift, which said board was found in the subterraneous river near Cong [Wilde, 67].

Wilde rightly remarked that it is very unusual to have a cave named after Dermot, who, together with his lover Gráinne, with whom he eloped, is normally associated with dolmens. But he did not know of the existence of a very atmospheric illustration of it, presumably by Austin Cooper and now preserved in 2122 TX(3), p. 44, in the National Library (*Fig. 140*), which is probably based on an original by Bigari as the whole appears overdramatised to look like the stage setting for an opera. It is

Fig. 140
A copy, probably by Austin
Cooper, of a likely Bigari
original makes the cave of
Leabbie Yearmaid
(Dhiarmaid) at Ballinchalla,
Co. Mayo, look like a stage
setting for an opera. It is
now p. 44 of the National
Library's album 2122
TX(3).

interesting to note that this is one of the very few sites (Abbeyknockmoy being another) mentioned in the Diary as having been visited but which gets no entry in the catalogue MS 4162, though the text surrounding two sides of the copy drawing reflect very accurately what Beranger noted in his Diary, as quoted above.

Killemanain / Inishmaine Abbey

On the same day, 26 July, Sir John brought the artists to two monuments on the shore of Lough Mask, which lay only about four miles to the north-west of his home at the Neale. The first of these was what Beranger calls the Abbey of Killemanain and which he gives as being on the island of Ballinchalla, but — probably owing to the lowering of the level of the lake in the 1850s — it is now very much part of the mainland. It is normally called Inishmaine, and was probably an old Irish monastic foundation going back to the seventh century, but its high-quality stonework may be explained by one of its thirteenth-century priors being probably closely connected with the O'Connor kings of Connacht. Beranger's description of it on p. 22 of MS 4162 is as follows:

Fig. 141
Bigari's interior view of Killemanain *alias* Inishmaine Abbey, Co. Mayo, on p. 16 of the Royal Irish Academy's MS 12.T.16 makes the building look much larger than it is by using the trick of reducing to dwarf proportions the two well-dressed figures on the bottom left (Sir John and Lady Browne?).

Fig. 142
Killemanain, or Inishmaine, Abbey is on a comparatively small scale, and combines an early-looking doorway on the left with fine 'School of the West' columns and windows of the early thirteenth century.

The Abbey of Killemanain was I believe only a church as it seems to be almost a regular figure nearly representing a cross, it is of good workmanship, the arch going in to the chancell was composed of pillars, in the taste of those of the doors of Cong, one side only remains, this is as yet the only place where the base of the colums are to be seen. The windows also imitate those of Ballintubber. See plans etc. No 39.

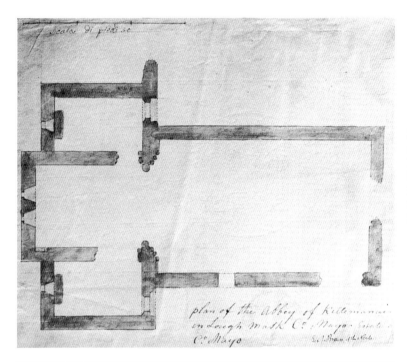

Fig. 143
A plan of the abbey of Killemanain, or Inishmaine, probably by Bigari and preserved on p. 15 of MS 12.T.16 in the Royal Irish Academy.

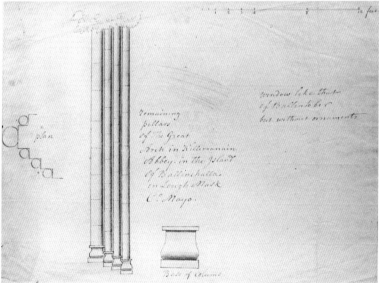

Fig. 144
Beranger's original drawing of architectural details of the abbey of Killemanain, otherwise Inishmaine, in County Mayo, preserved as number 10/25 in the Royal Irish Academy's manuscript 3.D.4. It features the base of a column, because this was the only place where Beranger had been able to see one exposed.

Fig. 145
The National Library's 2122 TX(107) is a 1799 copy by Austin Cooper of a Beranger original showing a gate-tower at Killemanain, Co. Mayo (here called Ballinchalla), which must once have controlled access to an enclosure containing the convent church with twin-windowed wall on the right. The Gothic doorway and turreted wall on the left were added by Sir John Browne of the Neale. This drawing, of a larger size than usual, appeared on the art market in 1999, and could belong to a set of the same dimensions of which others may yet remain to be found.

Fig. 146
Gone is Sir John Browne of the Neale's Gothic addition to the left of the low tower that guarded the entrance to the church of Inishmain nunnery, seen in the background to its right. As the element *Inish* in the name indicates, the eight-acre convent enclosure was once an island, before the level of Lough Mask was lowered about a century and a half ago.

Beranger would appear to have been the first person to note down the close link in architectural detail between buildings such as Inishmaine, Cong and Ballintubber, which Harold G. Leask was to group together under the name 'School of the West' more than 150 years later and which has been the subject of a recent study by Britta Kalkreuter.

Page 16 of the Royal Irish Academy's MS 12.T.16 contains a vigorous depiction (*Fig. 141*) of the church interior by Bigari, which makes the chancel and its arch very much more monumental than it is in reality (*Fig. 142*) by portraying the elegantly dressed tourists (Sir John and his wife?) at little more than the size of dwarfs. Page 34 of the same institution's MS 3.C.33 preserves a copy of this drawing, dated October 1799, which is of unusually good quality for its often mediocre artist, the Rev. J. Turner. The following page (35) consists of the same draughtsman's plan of the monument, which also contains a cross-section of the pillars together with the base of one column — items which are spread over two separate sheets of original drawings from the tour, also in the Royal Irish Academy. The first of these is the plan (*Fig. 143*) on p. 15 of MS 12.T.16, which may be by Bigari because of the scale of feet being given in Italian, *scala di piedi*. Missing parts of the caption on the bottom right suggest that the sheet of paper on which it is written must have extended farther to the right and included the name of the estate-owner as Sir John Browne of the Neale, which a secondary hand has written in at the bottom right-hand corner.

The second original drawing on which Cooper based his 1799 copy bears the number 10/25 in the Royal Irish Academy's MS 3.D.4 (*Fig. 144*) and still has Beranger's original number 39 C marked on the back. His drawing shows the right-hand pillars of the chancel arch, together with a cross-section (which he calls a 'plan') and a detail of one of the bases. To the right there is repetition of the statement quoted above from MS 4162 to the effect that 'The window is like that at Ballintober', and adding the further comment 'but without ornament'.

This charming little church can be seen in the background of a drawing entitled 'Castle in Ballinchalla Island in Lough Mask — Co.ʸ Mayo', signed by A(ustin) C(ooper) on 18 October 1799, and stating it to be after a Beranger original (*Fig. 145*). It was offered for sale at a Dublin auction late in 1999, and subsequently bought from a dealer by the National Library, where its accession number is 2122 TX(107). Where it was before it came into the possession of the man whose widow sold it in 1999 we simply do not know, and this leaves open the question of whether other, similar, loose leaves from the same source may yet surface on the art market.

What Beranger called the 'Castle of Ballinchalla' he describes in slightly more detail in MS 4162, p. 23, as follows:

> One small tower only remains of this castle, which seems of good workmanship of a blueish stone. The little turret with battlements & the small gothick door have been built by Sir John Brown of ye Neale (part of whose estate this island is) as he told us. See draws No 39, Letter D.

Perhaps his word 'tower' is a better description of the monument (*Fig. 146*), as it may well have been a fifteenth- or sixteenth-century gate-tower of an enclosure for a community of nuns in a convent which seems to have been active here at Inishmaine from the thirteenth to the sixteenth century. The staircase to the upper floors, still partially preserved, is shown in a small plan on the upper right-hand corner. The area to the left of the building is the same kind of flat expanse of limestone that Beranger described above as being present at the Neale.

Druidical monument, Ennishowen

The last monument on the shores of Lough Mask visited by the two artists is also perhaps the most intriguing. Today it is a mound with surrounding ditch, both almost entirely covered in scrub, trees and undergrowth (*Fig. 147*). In a letter on p. 95 of MS 1415 in the National Library, Beranger stated his belief that it was a temple and not a burial place, and it certainly looked different when he made the original of the drawing (*Fig. 148*) which only recently came to light in the unexpected circumstances outlined at the end of Chapter 2 (p. 23). His description on p. 23 of MS 4162 of what he called the 'Druidical monument in Ennishowen, Lough Mask' is as follows:

> This monument is a circle of large flaggs errect from 5.6 to 8 feet high above ye ground and from 1 to 3 feet broad, and about 4 inches thick. The greatest part are perforated with smooth round holes which admit one's finger, whether these were made by art or insects we could not decide. Part of the flags are down and these are marked by the dotted lines on the plan. The diameter of the monument is 64 feet. It has a ditch round it and some trees, see plan, sectn etc. No 40.

Fig. 147
'The Druids Temple' at Ennishowen is now visually enlarged by the great amount of scrub and bush that engulfs it.

Fig. 148
'View of the Druids Temple in the Island of Ennishowen, County of Mayo' was twice initialled by Beranger. The monument is likely to be a passage grave surmounted by upright stones, of which only a few remain standing. The only Beranger picture known to bear the date 1784, this loose sheet was looted from a Belgian castle at the end of the First World War. Are there others of similar size and date out there somewhere?

By a further piece of good fortune, the drawings recently returned by the Department of Archaeology in University College Dublin to the Royal Irish Academy (see p. 22) contained a copy of a plan and cross-section of the same monument, now numbered 3.C.42, Sheet 10, right (*Fig. 149*), signed by (J.) S. Cooper on 20 October 1784. The original of the cross-section has been lost, but that of the plan, initialled by Beranger, is preserved on the left of the same sheet in the Royal Irish Academy. The accompanying text partially repeats the Beranger description given above, and describes it as a

> Plan of a Druids Temple on an artificial mount surrounded by a ditch and grove of trees in the Island of Ennishowen, in Lough Mask Estate of Sir Jn. Browne of the Neal — Co.y Mayo … it must be called the Irish Stonehenge & is the only one of its kind we have heard of.

The cross-section beneath the plan gives the width and depth of the ditch around the mound, and also shows how the upright stones stood on the very edge of the mound. In his *Lough Corrib, its shores and islands, with notices of Lough Mask*, first published in 1867, Sir William Wilde noted that the ditch was overgrown with bushes in his day and that some of the stones were perforated; he described it as an 'entrenched fort' which he associated with the First Battle of Moytura between the Tuatha de Danann and the Firbolgs.

The Eoghan after whom the island was named remains something of an obscure mythical figure, but we would be better seeing the monument on his island not as a rath but as a passage grave, as is probably also the case with Eochy's cairn, another stone mound not far away which also gets its name from a mythical personage. But if the identification as a passage grave is correct, what makes it unique is the deep ditch surrounding it and, above all, the stones with perforations which stood around the perimeter — nineteen in Beranger's day, reduced to thirteen when Wilde described it, even fewer when sketched by Mrs L. Piggins of Westport around 1970, and down to four when examined recently by the Mayo antiquarians Noel O'Neill and Gerry Bracken. Beranger's view, plan and section, when illustrated together here, help bring to life an important Connacht monument which has suffered such sad neglect and decay in recent centuries.

At this point, Beranger's Diary refers briefly to the Partry Mountains on the opposite (western) shore of Lough Mask

> which look like wildernesses. Sir John told us that he had 15,000 acres in these mountains, which brought him only £50 per annum. This Lough is famous for producing the Gilleroe trout, which has a gizzard like a goose, of which a devil is made, and has no different taste; but though Sir John offered half a crown, which set them all afishing, they could not catch one, the weather being too calm, since they are seldom caught but when the wind ruffles the surface of the lake [Wilde, 68].

The entry for 27 July tells us that Beranger and Bigari

> took leave of Sir John and Lady Brown, Mr. Cromie and family. Took up some money from Sir John on my draught on Colonel Burton, and set out from the Neal at 12 o'clock, passed through Kilmaine and Ballyndangan in different villages and arrived through a flat country at Dunmore, Co. Galway, at half past after five [Wilde, 69].

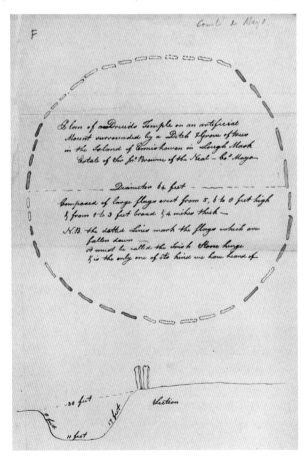

Fig. 149
Beranger's plan and cross-section of the 'Druids Temple' on the Island of Ennishowen (Inishowen) overlooking Lough Mask as seen in a copy by (J.) S. C(ooper) of October 1794, preserved as 3.C.42, sheet 10, right, in the Royal Irish Academy. Because the monument was 'the only one of its kind we have heard of', Beranger commented in the long caption that 'it must be called the Irish Stonehenge'.

7 . COUNTY GALWAY

The two artists' first host in County Galway was Ralph Ousley, member of a remarkable Connacht family related to one of Wilde's ancestors. Ralph, something of an antiquarian himself, lived at Dunmore Castle where presumably Beranger and Bigari stayed — and doubtless met the young son of the family, Gore, then aged nine, who was later to become a famous orientalist and His Majesty's Ambassador Extraordinary and Minister Plenipotentiary to the court of Persia. Three years after their visit, in 1782, Austin Cooper was to copy a drawing of the castle made in the same year by William Ouseley (which made attractive end-papers for my book on Cooper), but it is strange that neither Beranger nor Bigari drew the renovated thirteenth-century castle where they were guests. Certainly, no reference is made to it in MS 4162, nor, it would appear, was it mentioned in Beranger's Diary, where he expressed his disappointment at the comparatively flat country they walked during the days that he used Dunmore as his base:

> During this tour we had no hills to walk over — rolling over an even flat country, mostly pasture ground. We regretted the mountainous counties, where every hill afforded some new and charming scene, and we would willingly have undergone the same fatigues to enjoy some like prospects, variety having its charms, which uniformity cannot afford [Wilde, 71].

Dunmore Abbey

After breakfast on the morning after their arrival, 28 July, they

> took a draft and plan of Dunmore Abbey, the chancell of which has been roofed, and serves for a church [Wilde, 71].

The drawing they made of 'a coat of arms and inscription over the door of the abbey in the town' (Wilde, 70) does not survive, but the 'draft and plan' do. The former is 2122 TX(3), p. 20, in the National Library (*Fig. 150*), and, though unsigned, the view is undoubtedly by Bigari and is acknowledged as such in the letterpress attached to its engraved version on plate 34 of vol. 1 of Grose's *Antiquities* (*Fig. 151*). It shows the abbey church founded for the Augustinian friars by Walter de Bermingham in 1425, and built shortly afterwards close to what is now the centre of the town. As Beranger noted, the choir was roofed in his day to serve as the local Protestant parish church, and the

The Abbey of Dunmore C.º of Galway

Fig. 150
The gentry are seen parading in front of Dunmore Abbey in County Galway in this original unsigned drawing by Bigari on p. 20 of 2122 TX(3) in the National Library.

Vol.I.   Pl. 34.

Pub. May 3: 1793 by M. Hooper.   Sparrow sc.

DUNMORE ABBEY, Co.Galway.

Fig. 151
Bigari's view of Dunmore Abbey, Co. Galway (*Fig. 150*), differs from the engraving published as plate 34 in the first volume of Grose's *Antiquities of Ireland* only in the personnel strolling in front of the church.

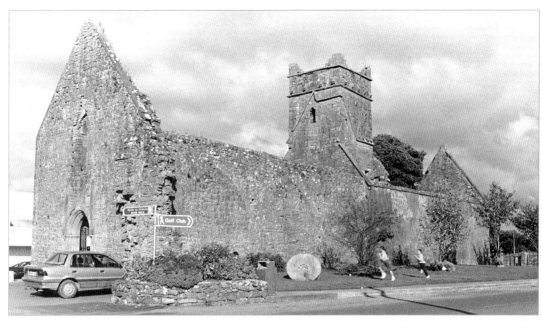

Fig. 152
Major changes to the church in the centre of Dunmore, Co. Galway, include the blocking up of the nave-aisle arches and the removal of the roof of the chancel, which was in use as a Protestant church in 1779.

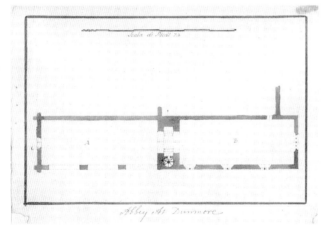

Fig. 153
The plan of the Dunmore Abbey church, Co. Galway, 2122 TX(91) in the National Library, is probably by Beranger, though the scale is given in Bigari's own language — scala di piedi.

nave originally had aisles accessible through arches which have since been built up (*Fig. 152*).

The plan of the church, preserved as 2122 TX(91) in the National Library (*Fig. 153*), is also unsigned but can be ascribed to Beranger on the basis of an attribution in J.S. Cooper's copy on p. 49 of the National Library's album 2122 TX(2). It brings out clearly the long, hall-like nature of this church, only interrupted halfway along its length by a tower with internal staircase which still survives. The letters on the plan are explained in Beranger's description of the church in MS 4162, p. 23:

This Abbey is in the town of Dunmore, and I believe was much larger, but cannot be traced as the ground is level and no ruins about it being a kind of market. The part A on the plan is a waste, the arches built up, and B is converted in a parish church, where service is performed. Over ye door C are arms and inscription which I coppied. See Drawgs No 41

The original Beranger number 41 still survives on the back of the plan.

Abbeyknockmoy

Although Wilde (70) says that it was after a couple of days, it is more likely that it was on the same day that Ralph Ousley set out with them for the great Cistercian abbey of Knockmoy — without, surprisingly, stopping and sketching in the town of Tuam, which is so rich in antiquities. However, a breakdown they had with the chaise that day may have prevented them. Why Abbeyknockmoy is omitted from

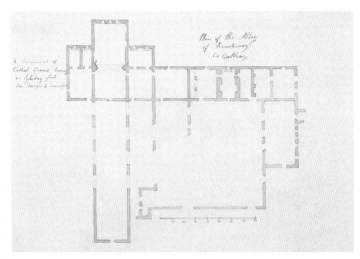

Fig. 154
The plan of the abbey of Knockmoy, Co. Galway, marking the location of the alleged monument of 'Cathal Crowe Darrag or Bloody fist' is preserved in the National Library's manuscript 671. It was found among Grose drawings, according to the Phillipps Collection catalogue, and must have been prepared for use in his *Antiquities of Ireland* but rejected.

the list of sites visited and described in MS 4162 is difficult to know, but we are fortunate that there is quite a detailed discussion about it — particularly because of its frescos — in the Diary, which Wilde (70) quotes:

> We drew the Abbey, and plan, and Fresco painting on the wall, and found an inscription on the monument of Cathal Cruive Diarrag, King of Connaught, and founder of the Abbey,

KNOCKMOY ABBEY. Co, Galway.

Fig. 155
Bigari's view of Knockmoy Abbey, Co. Galway, is preserved only in the form of this 1792 engraving that was published as plate 18 in the second volume of Grose's *Antiquities of Ireland*.

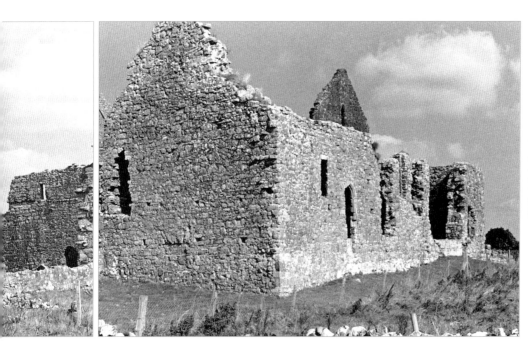

Fig. 156
By comparison, the standpoint of the modern photographer demonstrates how Bigari was able to compress a large panorama into a small picture (*Fig. 155*).

which our interpreter could not read, nor even know the letters, which I was obliged to design, and took up an hour. We had heard much of these ancient Fresco paintings, and on inspection were much disappointed, as they are bare black outlines. Mr. Bigari, who possesses the art of Fresco painter, and has done great works of this kind abroad, assured us, after a nice inspection, that they had never been coloured, and that the spots of various hues were occasioned by time and damps, since the same colour extended farther than the outlines; and supposing the coats had been green, the same colour went through the face and hands, which shows it to be the effect of the inclemency of the weather. So that they may be called Fresco drawings.

These famous fresco paintings, which Beranger, in a letter to Burton Conyngham of 3 August (Nat. Lib. MS 1415, p. 100), compared to 'figures drawn on an alehouse wall with charcoal', were engraved for Ledwich's *Antiquities of Ireland* after drawings made in 1784 by W.L., whom the Austin Cooper drawings (Nat. Lib. 2122 TX(1) p. 79) identify as the architect William Leeson, a man who had been involved in the design and layout of the town of Westport in 1767. They depict what is normally taken to be the story of St Sebastian killed by arrows (and identified by Beranger as such), together with the Morality Play figures of the Three Live Kings and the Three Dead Kings. The inscription accompanying the kings, which reads — in so many words — 'We were as you are, you will be as we are', was finally deciphered by Henry S. Crawford with the help of R.A.S. Macalister in 1919, when the discovery was published in the *Journal of the Royal Society of Antiquaries of Ireland*. The frescos, of *c.* 1550, were carefully conserved in 1989 by experts who described them technically as 'line-paintings' and revealed a considerable amount of colouring, which has now been protected from the elements to prevent further deterioration.

It is a pity that none of the artists' original drawings of Knockmoy and its frescos have been preserved, though a copy of the plan of the abbey survives in the portfolio numbered as MS 671 in the National Library (*Fig. 154*), which came from the Burton Conyngham and Phillipps Collections. With the exception of minor details, it corresponds fairly well to that published by Cochrane in the *Journal of the Royal Society of Antiquaries* of 1904. But, at least, one view has been preserved for us in the form of an engraving (*Fig. 155*), plate 18 of the second volume of Grose's *Antiquities,* where Bigari is acknowledged as the artist. It shows the south nave arcade in a complete state, and also gives details of the refectory on the southern side of the cloister arcade. Further parts were uncovered during excavations carried out by David Sweetman in 1982–3, and published four years later in the *Proceedings of the Royal Irish Academy*. The most curious aspect of the engraving is the large traceried window in the wall of the south transept which, if correct, would suggest that the upper floor of the eastern side of the claustral range was not in use around the fifteenth century, when such window styles were in vogue. The abbey itself dates from the early thirteenth century and is one of the best preserved of the medieval Irish Cistercian foundations (*Fig. 156*), built, as Roger Stalley remarked, more in a Romanesque than a Gothic style.

Claddagh Castle

ig. 157
osephine Shields's
hotograph of Claddagh
Castle in County Galway
nows it in a parlous
ondition, a fate shared by
nany other late medieval
rivately owned tower-
ouses in Ireland.

ig. 158
igari's only surviving
rawing of a tower-house is
nat of Claddagh, four
niles from Dunmore in
County Galway, which is
ow preserved on p. 21 of
122 TX(3) in the National
ibrary.

"The Castle of Claddagh 4 miles from Dunmore, C.º Galway"

That night Beranger and Bigari must have returned to Ousley hospitality at Dunmore, with their chaise presumably restored to working order. According to Wilde, they were supplied next day (29 July) with a guide by Mr Ousley, and their first stop was only a few miles to the south at Claddagh Castle (not to be confused with the area of the same name in Galway City). Beranger described it on p. 24 of MS 4162 as a square tower which

> seems not to have been more extensive, it is well built of a pale of brown stone. It is sit: 4 miles from Dunmore. See Dr. No. 43

In contrast to the much more important Knockmoy Abbey, for which no original drawings survive, this obscure tower-house — now so ruined (*Fig. 157*) — has a whole array of a view, a watercolour, an engraving and a plan to document it. The view — 2122 TX(3), p. 21, in the National Library (*Fig. 158*) — is clearly by Bigari, and shows a tall and seemingly well-built tower with a remarkable batter around the base into which the entrance doorway is recessed. To this the watercolour (*Pl. 19*), preserved as p. 36 in the Royal Irish Academy's manuscript 3.C.29, and the engraving, which is plate 31 of the first volume of Grose's *Antiquities* (*Fig. 159*), add two figures, one lying on the ground looking up at the other. The

CLADDAGH CASTLE. Co. Galway.

Fig. 159 (above)
For such an out-of-the-way monument, Claddagh Castle is well documented by material surviving from the 1779 tour — a Bigari original (*Fig. 158*), a plan (*Fig. 160*) and a watercolour (*Pl. 19*) which was prepared for the making of this engraving, which was published as plate 31 of vol. 1 of Grose's *Antiquities of Ireland*.

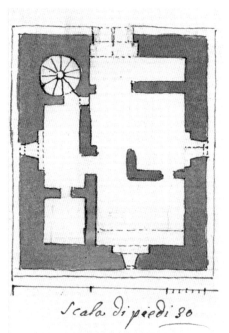

Scala di piedi 80

Fig. 160
The scale of feet, written in Italian in a hand that is not Beranger's, suggests that it was Bigari who made the plan of Claddagh Castle, Co. Galway, which is preserved as 2122 TX(94) in the National Library.

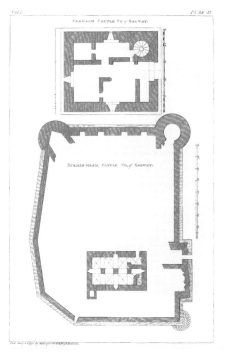

Fig. 161
The plans of Claddagh and Birmingham (Athenry) castles in County Galway were reproduced as plates 29 and 32 in the first volume of Grose's *Antiquities of Ireland*.

plan, on a small strip of paper, is probably by Bigari, as it is accompanied by the words *scala di piedi* in Bigari's native tongue, and is preserved as 2122 TX(94) in the National Library (*Fig. 160*). Bearing the number 42, and not 43 as one would have expected from Nat. Lib. MS 4162, it was engraved as plate 29 of the first volume of Grose's *Antiquities* (*Fig. 161*).

Athenry Abbey and Castle

The main focus of the day's activities was, however, the town of Athenry, which Beranger in his Diary described as

> an ancient town of the Co. of Galway situate 91½ miles west from Dublin, and 22 south of Dunmore, said to have been built by King John — part of the old wall and the ruins of some turrets and gates are still seen. There is a barrack close to the Abbey, which Abbey has much suffered from the neighbourhood of those children of Mars, who, not satisfied with breaking down all the ancient tombs (the marbles of which are still scattered over the ground, …) [Wilde, 70–1],

had still further desecrated the church — which, Beranger continues, obliged them to take 'more snuff there than in all the other Abbeys we had seen'. On p. 24 of MS 4162 Beranger tells us a bit more about this 'odour of sanctity':

> This abbey was formerly much larger & part of it was destroyed to built the barraks anexed, whose yard may probably have contained the cloysters, it is well built of blueish stone. The tower is larger below then above for ½ its hight. The east window is bold and good workmanship. It contained quantity of mausoleums, against which it seems the soldiers declared war, and demolished every one, the floor of the church being covered of their fragmenths, and not satisfied with this, they have made the church their common necessary, so

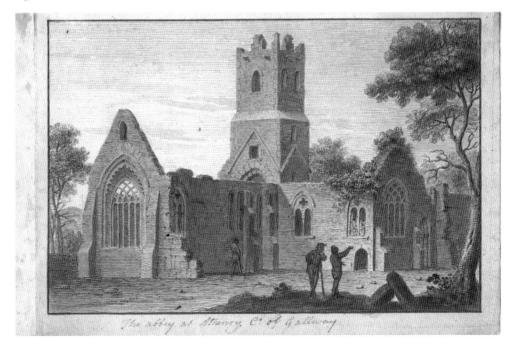

Fig. 162
Though unsigned, this drawing of Athenry Abbey is by Bigari, and is now 2122 TX(3), p. 22, in the National Library.

ATHENRY   ABBEY. Co.Galway.

Fig. 163
The 1792 engraving of Athenry Abbey, Co. Galway, that is plate 27 of vol. 1 of Grose's *Antiquities* follows closely the watercolour version (*Pl. 20*) which was prepared as a model for it.

Fig. 164
Through the collapse of its lofty tower shown in the previous illustration, Athenry Abbey, Co. Galway, has lost in both stature and dignity.

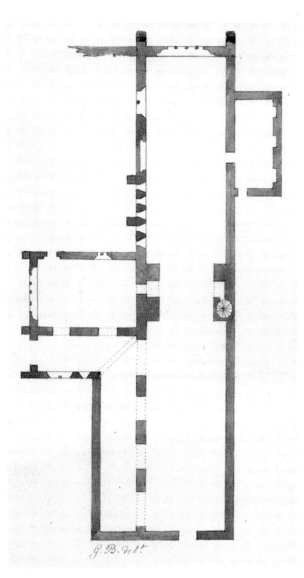

Fig. 165
While Bigari was occupied
in sketching his view of
Athenry Abbey, Co. Galway
(Fig. 162), Beranger busied
himself in preparing this
plan, which survives in an
original bearing his own
initials that is now 2122
TX(92) in the National
Library.

that the filth and smell was intollerable during our survey. See Drawg and plan No. 44. Letters A.B.C.

These comments no doubt explain why Bigari stood well back from the abbey to execute his fine view, which is preserved as 2122 TX(3), p. 22, in the National Library (*Fig. 162*), with the original Beranger number 44 on the top right. The watercolour version of it, Royal Irish Academy MS 3.C.29, p. 34 (*Pl. 20*), was engraved as plate 27 in the first volume of Grose's *Antiquities* (*Fig. 163*). Bigari went to great trouble in detailing the various features of the friary building, and particularly the tracery of the windows (which, however, differs from certain elements visible today — *Fig. 164* — thus raising the question of the extent of subsequent restoration), but the most valuable feature of the drawing is the two-tiered tower which now only survives to the level of the chancel wall, and which is a considerable loss to the overall appearance of the building. But even if the tower had totally disappeared, we would still have been able to reconstruct its presence on the basis of a plan signed with Beranger's initials and bearing his original number 44. This is now 2122 TX(92) in the National Library (*Fig. 165*), where we can see clearly the southern side-aisle and transept added in 1324, at the same time that the eastern end of the chancel with its lancet windows was added as an extension of the choir. The friary, however, had been founded in 1241 for the Dominicans by Milo de Bermingham, and was probably completed in time to bury within its walls its initial benefactor when he died in 1252.

He it was who also built the castle in Athenry which Beranger and Bigari took a plan and view of after they had dined on 29 July, before working during the remainder of the evening on their sketches. The castle consists of a tall hall-tower (with first-floor entrance) standing off-centre in a roughly D-shaped protecting wall with one well-preserved round bastion at the south-eastern corner and another

BIRMINGHAM CASTLE, Co. Galway.

Fig. 166
The 1793 engraving of Birmingham, *alias* Athenry Castle, Co. Galway, published as plate 28 of vol. 1 of Grose's *Antiquities of Ireland* is after a lost Bigari original probably taken from the west, though it is not easy to reconcile it with the plan shown on Fig. 161.

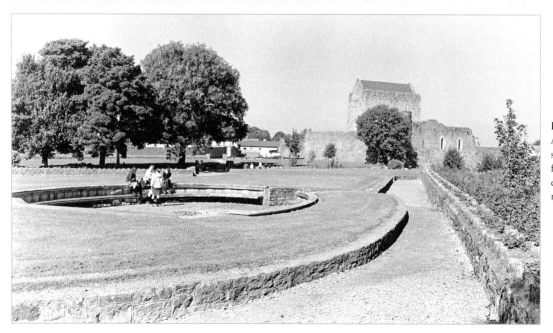

Fig. 167
Athenry Castle, seen from a somewhat different angle from that in Grose's engraving, shows the roof reconstructed by Dúchas.

KILCONNEL ABBEY, Co. Galway.

Fig. 168
Bigari's view of Kilconnell
Abbey, Co. Galway,
survives only through the
1793 engraving published
as plate 35 of vol. 1 of
Grose's *Antiquities of
Ireland*.

Fig. 169
The noble Franciscan friary
at Kilconnell, Co. Galway,
has come through the last
223 years almost unscathed.

more fragmentary tower in the north-eastern corner, as can be seen in the plan presented on plate 32 of the first volume of Grose's *Antiquities* (*Fig. 161*). Plate 28 provides us with an engraving (*Fig. 166*) of what it calls 'Birmingham Castle', which was based on what the letterpress confirms to have been an original by Bigari. The engraving, which does not entirely tally with the plan, would seem to have been taken from the west, and things look different now with the restoration of the roof by Dúchas, which has officially opened the castle to the public (*Fig. 167*). On p. 24 of MS 4162 Beranger provides us with a description of the castle as it was in his day:

> This castle consist in a square tower, well built of brownish stone, it stands in a large area surrounded by a wall of irregular figure composing a sort of Hexagon flanked on one of the faces by 2 towers, there is a projection at the entrance, and a walk and parapet on the wall; in which we discovered one embrasure. I supose there is more, but being thick overgrown with ivy we could not see them. See drawing and plan No 44 Letters D.E.

Kilconnell Abbey

The only monument visited on 30 July was one a mere fourteen miles away towards Ballinasloe, namely the well-preserved 'abbey' at Kilconnell, deserving more than the frugal description of being 'well built of blueish stone' which is all that Beranger has to say about it on p. 25 of MS 4162. One of the best preserved of its kind, it was founded for the Franciscan friars in 1414 by William O'Kelly, lord of Uí Maine, and Bigari's view, engraved from a lost original as plate 35 of vol. 1 of Grose's *Antiquities* (*Fig. 168*), shows it to be much as it is today (*Fig. 169*), though the arch capitals are not

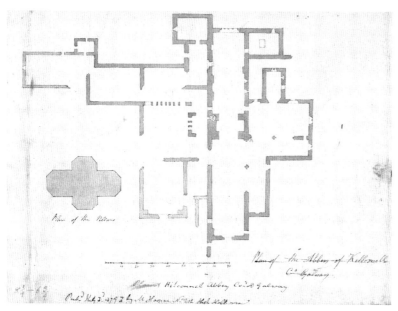

Fig. 170
The plan of Kilconnell Abbey, Co. Galway, preserved as 1976 TX(72) in the Prints and Drawings Department of the National Library, was used as the basis for that published in Grose's *Antiquities*. It probably belonged to the collection of drawings that now forms Number 671 in the Manuscripts Department of the same institution.

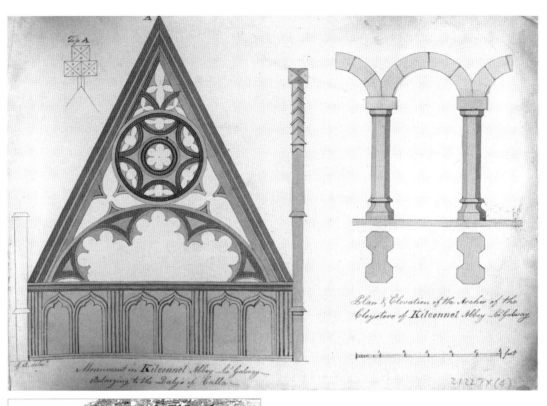

Fig. 171
Page 2 of 2122 TX(4) in the National Library preserves what we may take to be Austin Cooper copies of lost Beranger originals showing a fifteenth-century tomb and section of the cloister of Kilconnell Abbey, Co. Galway. Compare the number of cusped arches in Beranger's drawing with those in the photo reproduced here beneath it.

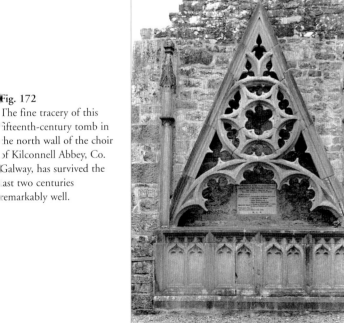

Fig. 172
The fine tracery of this fifteenth-century tomb in the north wall of the choir of Kilconnell Abbey, Co. Galway, has survived the last two centuries remarkably well.

right and the south window on the extreme right seems rather different. The extensive plan engraved as plate 36 of vol. 1 of Grose's *Antiquities,* in all likelihood based directly on the wash drawing 1976 TX(72) in the National Library (*Fig. 170*), demonstrates the presence of a square cloister area to the north of the tower, and one of its typical arcades (*Fig. 173*) was featured in a lost Beranger original, as seen copied by Austin Cooper in 2122 TX(4), p. 2 (*Fig. 171*). To the left, beside it, is a drawing of a fine fifteenth-century tomb with flamboyant tracery in the north wall of the choir — still well preserved (*Fig. 172*) and now bearing within it a plaque of the Daly family of Raford.

Having finished their work at Kilconnell, the artists returned via 'Newtown-Bellew, alias Mylough', to Dunmore apparently, as Wilde (71) put it, for the purpose of correcting their drawings

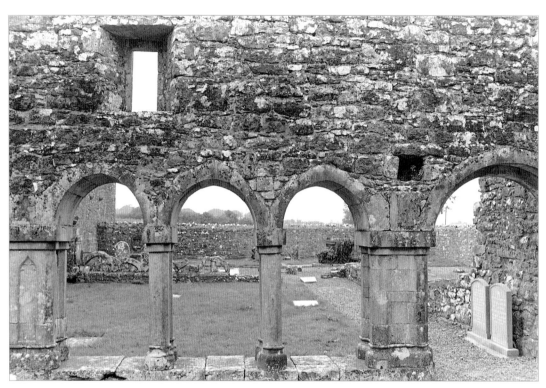

Fig. 173
The cloister at Kilconnell
Abbey, Co. Galway, shows
how accurate Beranger's
rendering of it was in Fig.
171.

and again enjoying the society of Mr Ousley. He was the source of the information which Beranger wrote in his Diary about the County Galway before he and Bigari took their departure from it:

County of Galway; — the second largest county in the kingdom, is in general a warm limestone soil, producing excellent pasture, and of late a considerable deal of tillage; is mostly an open champaign country, interspersed with a few hills, which lie mostly to the west, in that part called Connamarra, which is divided from the rest by Lough Corrib, and contains a large tract of mountains, and the best kelp shores in Ireland. It has several lakes, and abundance of bogs; it is rather bare of wood, but abounds with game; it produces the best wool, remarkable for its fineness [Wilde, 71].

8 . RETURN TO ROSCOMMON

arly August saw our artists returning once again to County Roscommon, which they had left just over a month previously, but the county boundary was not to separate them from the company of Ralph Ousley, who accompanied them for a further day. He cannot, however, have been too happy when the party's progress was halted because a bridge over the River Suck had collapsed, but they finally succeeded in getting themselves, their chaise and their baggage across, as Wilde (71) tells us in his commentary.

Ballintober Castle

Shortly afterwards, they took their leave of Mr Ousley, and 2 August saw them all reaching Ballintober Castle, which Beranger described in MS 4162, p. 25, as follows:

> This castle all in ruins, is of large extent of a square figure, somewhat in the manner of that of Ballymote, but flanked only by four towers of various forms as may be seen in the plan, the walls are not so thick as at balymote, and the habitations, were close to the walls, leaving an area or Bawn in the center; the entrance was defended by a kind of tower of peculiar make, hardly determinable, in its present situation but different of any thing we have yet seen. The materials are a blackish stone and the workmanship very good, tho in an odd manner of architecture as may be seen in the figures of the towers on the plan. See Drawings No 46.

The number 46 is found on the top right of the original Bigari drawing, preserved as p. 23 of 2122 TX(3) in the National Library (*Fig. 174*), which was not engraved in Grose's *Antiquities*. It portrays two figures in front of the — even then — much ruined towers of the gatehouse guarding the entrance on the south-western side. The buildings in the background show that Bigari's aggrandising tendencies were not required to indicate the considerable extent of this castle. What he has done is to contract the length of the side with the entrance to get most of it into the picture without going back too far, as a comparison with the present situation will make clear (*Fig. 175*). The castle itself forms almost a square, each side measuring well over 200 feet in length, with angular bastions at each corner, some of which were converted into tower-houses around 1627.

It has long been debated whether the castle was built by the Norman de Burgos or the Irish O'Connor kings, but historical likelihood rather than hard factual evidence — and Ballintober's

The Castle of Ballintober

Fig. 174
Bigari's original drawing of
Ballintober Castle, Co.
Roscommon, now 2122
TX(3), p. 23, in the
National Library, was not
subsequently engraved in
Grose's *Antiquities of
Ireland*, but shows the
extent of this impressive
fortification.

Fig. 175
The camera today finds it
difficult to provide the
panorama offered in Bigari's
drawing of 1779 in the
previous illustration.

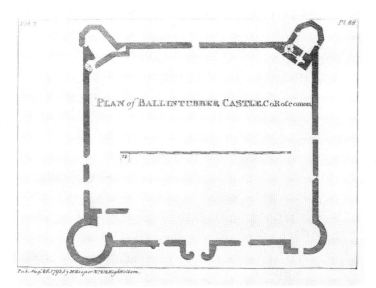

Fig. 176
The plan of Ballintober Castle, Co. Roscommon, published as plate 88 in the second volume of Grose's *Antiquities,* makes the fortification appear to be more of a rectangle than it actually is.

comparative similarity to Roscommon Castle (to be encountered shortly) — would favour the former. The fact that the layout is not entirely rectangular is not made clear in the plan published as plate 88 in the second volume of Grose's *Antiquities* (*Fig. 176*).

Though Ousley parted from our pair at Ballintober, he did provide them with a guide to bring them to their next host, though the journey was not without its hazards, as Beranger's Diary relates:

We set forwards under the direction of our guide, who brought us through ways where never chair [chaise] went since the creation, through meadows, fields, gaps of ditches, boggy grounds; we cursed him a hundred times through means of our interpreter (for the fellow spoke only Irish). At last we arrived at a lake, as we thought; but asking him which way we were to turn, were ready to beat him heartily when he pointed to this sheet of water. After a long altercation he rid [rode] in the water, and we sailed after him like a boat, having water to the axle-tree. The ground was well enough, it being some overflowed meadows; but we were tumbling all the way, expecting to be drowned, until we arrived at a new road, yet unfinished, which, not being gravelled, was so softened by the heavy rain of the day before, that our wheels sunk in it, and the chair could not go on. Here we certainly had knocked him down, if our interpreter had not interfered. We alighted to ease the horse, and walked for two miles, sinking halfway boot at every step. At last we found a good road, and a rivulet, where we washed our boots [Wilde, 72].

They went on, the Journal continues, and

arrived at Belinagar, the residence of Charles O'Connor, Esq. (descendant of the ancient kings of Connaught, and well-known in the literary world by his literary publications concerning Ireland), past 7 o'clock. He had just sat down to dinner, having given over seeing us that day. We were in a good mood to help him to despatch it, and eat as heartily as we had yet done during our tour [Wilde, 72].

Charles O'Conor (1710–91) was, indeed, one of the best-known figures in the field of Gaelic scholarship during the eighteenth century, which is doubtless why Burton Conyngham invited him to join the select band of members forming the Hibernian Antiquarian Society — a distinction which, as the only Catholic in a very élite Protestant group, he very much savoured (see pp 2–3). He was a great collector of Irish manuscripts, and a member of the Royal Irish Academy, where his portrait (*Fig. 2*) hangs in the Members' Room. He had already been the squire of Belanagare for 40 years when he entertained our two artists — and their Irish interpreter, in whom O'Conor showed a great interest when he found out that the latter belonged to the well-known McGuire family of Fermanagh.

Cloonshanville Abbey

On the morning after their arrival, that is on 3 August, the two artists were brought by Charles O'Conor and his son Denis to Frenchpark, where they were welcomed by Arthur French, Esq., and used the house as a base to visit Cloonshanville. As Beranger put it in his Diary:

> We were well received, a large company being there of both sexes; we all mounted, and went to see the deerpark, being in all eighteen, besides the servants; every gentleman picked up a lady; fine cavalcade. Were shown here five large red deer, some enormous large bulls of English breed, and a flock of small black Welsh sheep, having some 1, others 2, 3, 4 and 5 horns each [Wilde, 72–3].

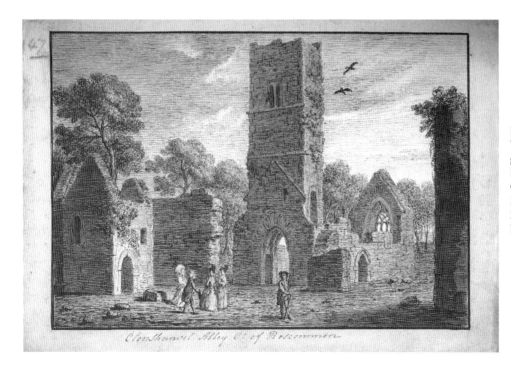

Fig. 177
Well-dressed ladies and gentlemen add elegance to Bigari's view of Cloonshanville Abbey, Co. Roscommon, preserved as 2122 TX(3), p. 34, in the National Library of Ireland.

Fig. 178
Though prepared for use in Grose's *Antiquities*, this watercolour of Cloonshanville Abbey, Co. Roscommon, 1976 TX 46 in the Prints and Drawings Department of the National Library, was rejected in favour of views by Cocking and Daniel Grose respectively. (See dust-jacket.)

Fig. 179
The tower of Cloonshanville is the only lofty feature to survive from the better-preserved complex of buildings shown in Bigari's view seen in the previous illustration.

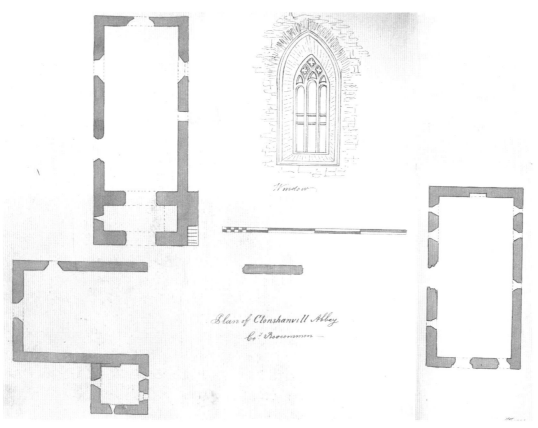

Window

Plan of Clonshanvill Abbey
Co. Roscommon —

Fig. 180
The plan and detail of the now-vanished east window of Cloonshanville Abbey, Co. Roscommon, were signed by J.T. in 1794 and are now preserved on p. 85 of 2122 TX(2) in the National Library. The building on the right no longer exists.

This probably helps to explain why there are more 'society' ladies and gentlemen depicted on the Cloonshanville drawing by Bigari than in any other of his pictures surviving from this trip (*Fig. 177*). One of the local ladies, a Mrs Davis, whose family had rented the lands earlier in the century, even helped Beranger to measure the ruins for his plan (*Fig. 180*) preserved — along with a drawing of the east window — in a 1794 copy by J.T(urner) on p. 85 of the National Library's album 2122 TX(2). The plan, however, is not specifically mentioned in Beranger's description on p. 26 of MS 4162:

> Clonshanville Abby is composed at present of three distinct parts, which may formerly have made but one building, it is much ruined and seems good workmanship of blueish Stone. Part of the tower is yet standing upon its arch. The rest is bare walls. The easwindow is neat and entire, no remains of cloysters, nor any sign of the place where they stood, the tower has ofsetts and is 60 feet high. See Drawings etc. No. 47.

The monastery was the Dominican Priory of the Holy Cross, founded probably by Mac Dermot Roe around 1385, and Bigari's view — preserved as p. 34 of 2122 TX(3) in the National Library (*Fig. 177*)

— shows its tall, slender tower with the south wall of the choir joining it to the east gable with traceried window. The later building seen on the left, now occupied by the traditional burial place of the French family, could, therefore, possibly be interpreted as having been an unusual two-storey mausoleum. Today it is of one storey only, restored in 1994, so that the tower and a section of the north side-chapel are the only meaningful parts of the old priory still remaining (*Fig. 179*). With the accession number of 1976 TX 46, the National Library possesses a fine watercolour version (*Fig. 178*), rightly acknowledging Bigari as its artist, but the comment made on top to the effect that it was 'engraved from another view' shows that this was prepared for a London engraver for use in Grose's *Antiquities* but rejected in favour of two others (by T. Cocking and Daniel Grose respectively).

After their work — and play — the party 'returned to Frenchpark, dined, and spent the day agreeably' (Wilde, 73), before going back to Belanagare, and there Charles O'Conor conducted the two artists to his library where, as Beranger noted in his Diary,

> amongst a vast number of Irish manuscripts, he showed me the Annals of Connaught. Worked at our sketches, Mr. O'Connor writing under those of Connaught, and some others, the names of the founders, and dates of their foundation [Wilde, 73].

Because, with the apparent exception of Misgaun Mewe (*Fig. 29*) and the O'Connor tomb at Roscommon to be mentioned below (p. 186), no original drawings survive with such information on them, we come to realise with sadness that almost all of the original field drawings on which the worked-up views illustrated here were based have presumably perished.

Rathcroghan

On the following day, 4 August, the two artists set out with Charles O'Conor to investigate the remains of Rathcroghan, that remarkable collection of mysterious earthworks spanning many centuries and spread out over a wide area in the plains of Roscommon. It has been associated with the legendary Queen Maeve and the opening scene of the great Irish epic, the *Táin Bó Cuailnge*. There, Beranger reports in his Diary, they

> were met by Charles O'Conor's son and some other gentlemen; went to Rathcroghan, an artificial mound, where the ancient kings of Ireland were inaugurated, and also kept their provincial assemblies, 400 feet in diameter at the top. Drew and section [Wilde, 74].

In his commentary, Wilde corrects Beranger by saying that the inauguration site of the kings of Connacht was not at Rathcroghan but at Carnfree, a few miles away, and also points out that Beranger appears to have taken the unusual step of inserting a pen and ink sketch of Rathcroghan in the Diary, which probably formed the basis for the watercolour (*Pl. 21*) preserved on p. 79 of the large Beranger album, MS 3.C.30, in the Royal Irish Academy. It shows the long, low mound already mentioned, and described in some greater detail on p. 26 of MS 4162:

> this is a round artificial mount 400 feet diameter at the top, it is made of sods covered with grass, and in a very good preservation, it is situated in a field, in the barony of Balintober, 4 miles from Belinagar. Here the kings of Conaught were inaugurated, and kept their Provincial assemblies, assembling at the top and encamping round about. Not far from this mount is the burial place, but so confused that no drawing could be made, having formerly only been surrounded with a ditch now confounded with that of the field, and some confused rough stones scatered here and there, by which one may pass often, without taking any notice if not warned so to do. See Drawg and plan No 48.

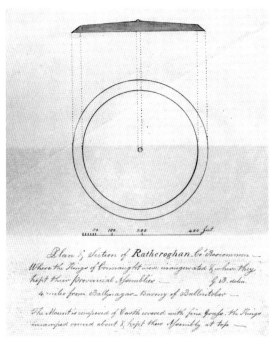

Fig. 181
It was from a Beranger original that Austin Cooper copied this plan of the mound at Rathcroghan, Co. Roscommon, now p. 16 of 2122 TX(4) in the National Library.

The plan referred to is preserved, together with a cross-section, in a copy on p. 16 of 2122 TX(4) in the National Library (*Fig. 181*) — unsigned, but almost certainly by Austin Cooper and executed not before 1796, the date of the watermark. It attributes the original to Beranger, and the accompanying text repeats some of Beranger's comments already quoted above. The scale which the plan provides reinforces the measurements of the mound as given in the Diary, according to Wilde (74–5), namely '1350 feet in circumference at the bottom, the slope to the top 33; and the circular elevation in the centre 6 feet above the surface'. The caption at the bottom of the watercolour view adds that 'There is no sign of remains of any stone buildings on the whole spot of ground'.

Rathcroghan also brought forth effusions from Beranger the writer, who shows how well read he was on Irish antiquarian matters in the following extract from his Diary, where he criticises the exaggerations of certain historians, including O'Halloran in his *An introduction to the study of the history and antiquities of Ireland* (1772):

> Here, Mr. O'Halloran (Chapter IX.) says, was a superb edifice raised for the Kings of Connaught, but I can assure the reader that, not even the least trace of such a building is to be seen. It seems strange that at this day Greek and Roman antiquities are found in various parts of Europe, which proves the grandeur of those nations, and that no traces remain of the grandeur of the ancient Irish, which we are pressed to believe without proofs, except some

manuscripts, which very few can read, and which I do not know if sufficiently authenticated, and out of which the Irish historian picks what suits him, hides what is fabulous and absurd. I think the shortest way to satisfy the unbelievers would be to give the world a true translation of those Manuscripts, Psalters, and Leabhars, as they are, that we may from thence form an idea of their history, and judge ourselves of their merit and truth. Some of these are written, Mr. McCurtin tells us, by St. Benignus. Query, what materials had he — was he inspired? I cannot read ancient Irish, and must I believe, because an honest Irishman, enthusiastick and fired by the love of his country, sees through a magnifying glass, and believes? We are told by Irish historians (McCurtain, Walsh, O'Conor, O'Halloran), that the zeal of your primitive Christians in Ireland destroyed the Heathen manuscripts, and that the Danes finished most of those that had escaped the first Christians' fury; but still, that enough remains to make up a complete Irish history. My answer is, that this is very lucky, and I wish to see a true translation of them; I am not to believe in hearsay, except what is told me by an inspired writer; but was St. Benignus one? I am afraid a manuscript older than his cannot be found. Where, then, has he got his materials? [Wilde, 75]

Having finished the sketch of the long, low rath, the artists were brought to a nearby 'cave', called at the time the 'Hellmouth door of Ireland' but now better known as Owey na gCat, 'the cave of the cats', which tradition associates with Queen Maeve and sees as a special residence of the fairies in that district (Wilde, 76). There, as the Diary relates,

we found some men waiting for us; and having lighted some candles we descended first on all-fours through a narrow gallery, which for the length of 12 or 14 feet is the work of man, being masonry said to be done by the Druids, who performed here some of their secret rites. (See O'Conor's Dissertations, p.178). A yard or two farther we could walk erect, the cave being 7 or 8 feet high, and about 4 feet broad; the walls and roof (work of nature), of a brownish colour, smooth and shining, as if varnished, the ground of solid rock, like the rest, smooth, always descending; but the unevenness not unlike steps, favouring our descent and preventing us from slipping. We went about the length of 150 yards, when we found our career to be at an end, the cave going no further. We examined closely, but solid rock was everywhere — no door, window, nor crevice where the woman and her calf could pass [referring to the tale related above on p. 78 about Keshcorran]. We commented on the story, and joked the country people on their belief; but the answer was, that the devil had stopped it up, and this statement we could not contradict conveniently [Wilde, 76].

Their work completed at Rathcroghan, the party adjourned to Mount Druid, the home of Charles O'Conor's son, Denis, and then walked back home across the fields to Belanagare, a mere half a mile away.

Fig. 182
The initials AB on the bottom left of this illustration of Tulsk Abbey, Co. Roscommon, stand for Angelo Bigari, whose view is now preserved as p. 25 of 2122 TX(3) in the National Library.

Fig. 183
The south chapel on the left that was added to the main church is so covered with ivy that much of the masonry of Tulsk Abbey in County Roscommon is now obscured.

Tulsk Abbey

On the following day, 5 August, Beranger records in his Diary

> Set out, Mr. O'Conor and Mr. Bigari in the chaise (I riding Mr. O'Conor's horse); arrived at Tulsk, a borough of the County Roscommon, which sends two members to parliament, etc. Drew the Abbey and plan [Wilde, 80].

Close to an important crossroads, the abbey was founded for the Dominicans around 1448, probably by one of the McDowell family. On p. 27 of MS 4162, Beranger says of it

> The Abbey of Tulsk, sit: in the town or village of that name 6 miles from Belinagar, is of a blueish stone well built but so ruined that nothing but walls remain, and one strong plain pillar of stones of various sizes masoned together suporting the ends of two arches, which give entrance to a chappel, if the building was much larger is not possible to ascertain, but that there was more of it, is certain by the fragments of walls, see Drawing No. 49.

Bigari's drawing, preserved on p. 25 of 2122 TX(3) in the National Library (*Fig. 182*) and signed simply 'AB', lacks humans as a scale, yet he does not try to make it seem larger than it is (*Fig. 183*), showing us a now heavily ivied window on the left and a view through two arches to the vanished west wall in the background — though building up of the north wall of the choir in the meantime obliterates the view of the pillar supporting the arches. The tower-house on the right is still standing, though not to the same height, and out of sight from the artist's stance are the much later Grace and Taaffe mausolea of 1868 and 1872 respectively (one of which featured in Maurice and Michael Craig's lovely book *Mausolea Hibernica*). The plan of the buildings (*Fig. 184*) on p. 48 of the second Cooper album in the National Library — 2122 TX(2) — indicates neither draughtsman nor progenitor, but we may take it as a copy of a product of the 1779 tour, showing little change from the ground-plan that exists today.

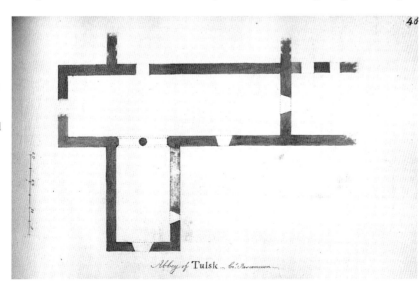

Fig. 184
The unsigned plan of Tulsk Abbey, Co. Roscommon, now p. 48 of the album 2122 TX(2) in the National Library, is probably by Austin Cooper, who is likely to have copied it from one that was produced during the Connacht tour of 1779.

Roscommon Abbey and Castle

It would have been in the afternoon that the party

> set forward, and arrived at Roscommon, the shire town of the county, situate sixty-nine miles south-west (!) from Dublin. It is a long, poor-looking town, has a barrack for one troop of horse, and sends two members to Parliament [Wilde, 80].

> August 6th, went to the Abbey, drew and plan, also the tomb of Roderick O'Conor, last King of Connaught, and one of the ancestors of Mr. O'Conor, to ascertain the dress of the Gallowglasses, or guards, of which the figures are carved round the monument [Wilde, 80].

This brief account is both augmented and corrected in MS 4162, p. 27, as follows:

> This Abbey is sit: in the town of Roscommon. It was well built of blackish stone, is much in ruin, as is the tower, it was occupied by Dominicans. It was formerly larger but could not be traced being in a garden belonging to the Rector of the Parish. It is famous for having in it the tomb of its founder Fedlim O Connor, king of Connaught, on which are in basso relievo (of bad design) seven figures of Gallowglasses, or warriors, in as many compartments, one with a sword, an[d] another with an ax alternately. This monarch died in 1225 according to Mr. Chs O'Connor. See Drawing and parts No 50.

The number 50 is visible on the top right — and the number 50 C on the back — of a sheet with the accession number 2122 TX(9) in the National Library, which shows the monarch's tomb in a Gothic niche with his effigy on top of the tomb-front with some of the gallowglasses drawn in, and a detail of one of them at a larger scale on the right (*Fig. 185*). The accompanying text is almost certainly in Beranger's own hand, except for the words 'who died in A.D.: 1225', which are in a script that is probably that of Charles O'Conor, as in the Nat. Lib. MS 1415, pp 135–9. There is a drawing of the effigy on p. 11 of 2122 TX(4) in the National Library, which could conceivably have been copied from another original drawing by Beranger but, as it is placed

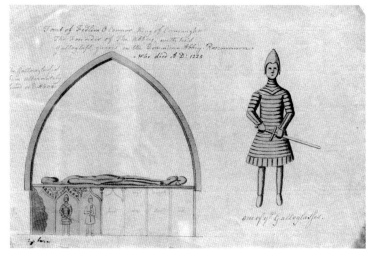

Fig. 185
Beranger's handwriting features on this drawing of the tomb of 'Fedlim O'Connor' in Roscommon Abbey which, together with a detail of a gallowglass on the tomb-front beneath the supine effigy, is preserved as 2122 TX(9) in the National Library of Ireland.

Fig. 186
Bigari's initials 'AB' are
found at the bottom left-
hand corner of this view of
Roscommon Abbey on p.
27 of 2122 TX(3) in the
National Library.

above a somewhat gauche drawing of the gallowglasses copied from one signed by William Ousley, it may not have been a product of the 1779 tour and is therefore not illustrated here.

The number 50 is also found on the upper right-hand corner of Bigari's signed view of the abbey, preserved as p. 27 of 2122 TX(3) in the National Library (*Fig. 186*), which was well engraved as plate 97 of the second volume of Grose's *Antiquities* (*Fig. 187*). As at Tulsk, it shows no admiring or conversing humans, but comparison of the drawing with today's view taken from the same angle (*Fig. 188*) makes us aware of how much the appearance of the abbey has diminished owing to the collapse of the nave arcade and the tower, which was 'much in ruin' even in Beranger's day.

The artists must have been out drawing early in the morning of 6 August, for afterwards Beranger records in the Diary:

> returned to the inn; were met there by the Rev. John O'Conor, D.D.; breakfasted; went after to the Castle, where access had been refused to us by the surly owner, who by means of Rev. Mr. O'Conor was now become polite; drew and plan [Wilde, 82].

Beranger gives a more detailed description of this castle on the outskirts of Roscommon town in pp 27–8 of MS 4162 as follows:

> This castle stands in a field at the back of the town of Roscommon, is much ruined having

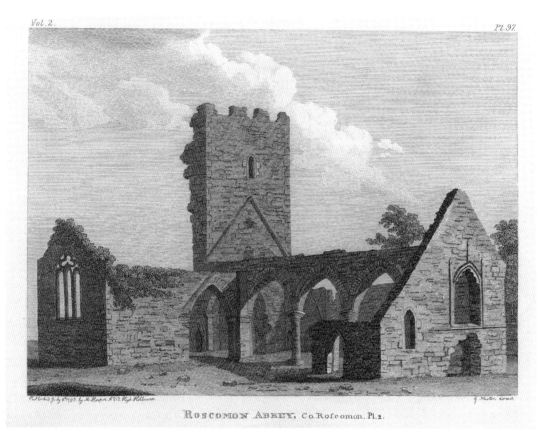

Vol. 2.   *Pl. 97.*

ROSCOMON ABBEY, Co. Rofcomon. Pl. 2.

Fig. 187
The engraver who worked on plate 97 of the second volume of Grose's *Antiquities of Ireland* gave a curious tilt to the nave arcade capitals of Roscommon Abbey, Co. Roscommon. Is it any wonder that they subsequently fell?

Fig. 188
Roscommon Abbey looks poorer in appearance for having lost its central tower, which was already 'much in ruin' when Bigari sketched it in 1779 (*Fig. 186*).

been battered down by cannon by Cromwell. It was nearly a square flanked by 4 towers. The great entrance has lesser towers to deffend it. There is also an issue at the back, which was strongly fortified. Two thick walls remaining which contained a staircase on one side. the towers of the corners contained also staircases in the thickness of their walls, one of which is still practicable and leads to the top which is an arch, the habitation we suposed to have been in the towers and over the entrance, leaving a spacious area in the center, it is of excellent workmanship of a reddish stone. See drawings No. 51.

The same number 51 is also to be found in the top right (and 51 C on the back) of Bigari's signed drawing, preserved as 2122 TX(63) in the National Library (*Fig. 189*). The watercolour also there (*Pl. 22*), but with the accession number 1976 TX(27), shows that Bigari's drawing was regarded as a possibility for inclusion in Grose's *Antiquities* but, as a note on the top left remarks, the castle was 'engraved from another view'. This formidable castle was founded in 1269 by Robert de Ufford but, after its capture and wholesale destruction in 1272, King Edward I gave it its present form around 1280. It was, therefore, a royal castle, so well built that much of it remains as it was (*Fig. 190*), with the postern near the left, and late sixteenth-century alterations visible in the form of windows in the upper floors of the gatehouse behind the two figures on the east side. The plan engraved as plate 82 of vol. 1 of Grose's *Antiquities* (*Fig. 191*), and probably based on one by Beranger, gives a good idea of the layout of the castle, with its rounded bastion at each corner and massively deep gatehouse on the east side (on top, on the plan), though the exterior and interior shapes of the bastions are somewhat schematic.

Having finished their work at the castle, the two artists, as the Diary tells us,

took leave of Messrs. O'Conors, set forwards, and arrived at Mount Talbot, the seat of William Talbot, Esq. Met in the avenue Mr. Talbot, Jun., with Denis Kelly of Castle Kelly, County Gallway, Esq., which last gentleman invited us at dinner at his house for the Sunday following, with the family of Mount Talbot. We were introduced by Mr. Talbot, Jun., to Lady Ann Talbot, his lady, and to Lady Theodosia, and Lady Arabella Crosbie, her sisters, to Mr. Talbot, Sen., and other gentlemen and ladies then residing there on a visit. After refreshing ourselves for some time, we went with Mr. Talbot, Sen., to see the concerns, which are a continued wood, and occupying near 800 acres, through which are walks adorned with rural seats, temples, and hermitages; and vistas are cut through the wood, — all terminated by the river Suck, which meanders through the estate, and separates the counties of Roscommon and Galway. If these concerns were situated on unequal ground, and not on a level as they are, they might be ranked amongst the finest in the kingdom. The town of Mount Talbot is yet in its infancy, and may in time become a decent town; but its church, situated on the north side of it, built by Mr. Talbot, is one of the prettyest country churches I have ever seen, being finished in the Gothick style, somewhat in the manner of the chappels in Westminster Abbey, the seats and organ elegant, and the whole adorned with nice stucco ornaments, the ground of which, being

Fig. 189
Bigari signed his name and initials to this view of Roscommon Castle, Co. Roscommon, which is 2122 TX(63) in the National Library.

Fig. 190
With walls as massive as this, it is not surprising that Roscommon Castle has not deteriorated greatly since Bigari's day.

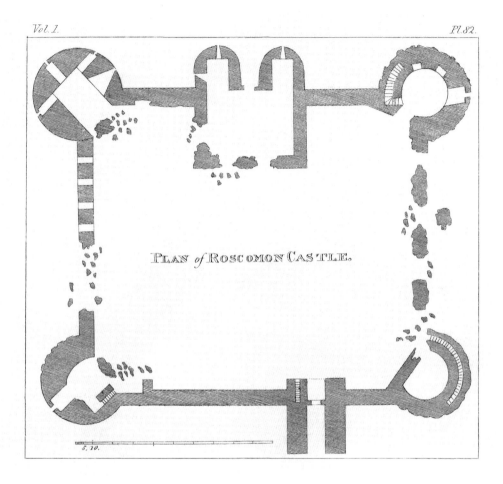

Fig. 191
The plan of Roscommon
Castle forming plate 82 of
vol. 1 of Grose's *Antiquities
of Ireland,* though
schematic in places, gives a
good idea of the layout of
this impressive fortification.

coloured differently, makes said ornaments more conspicuous. The very pulpit is adorned with raised stucco; and when the east window is finished (which is to be of stained glass), it will certainly be a curiosity worth visiting by travellers [Wilde, 82].

Sadly, the church is no longer with us, having already been demolished before the days of Wilde, who mourned its disappearance.

At this stage in the tour, our two heroes must have been getting somewhat exhausted, having been on the go for a full eight weeks, and so they probably welcomed the respite and entertainment offered by their visits to the Kelly and Talbot houses in Roscommon and east Galway, as detailed in the following extract from Beranger's Diary:

We dined with the family and visitors in a rural temple on the banks of the river Suck, and in the evening walked to another, in which we drank tea. Towards 9 o'clock we all embarked in a

barge, and went home by water,

August 7th. Got up at six o'clock, worked at our drawings; I went after breakfast with Mr. Talbot, Junior, on horseback, to Castle Kelly; returned by 12 o'clock; found at Mount Talbot, Captain Sandys, formerly of the Carabineers (an old acquaintance), who took up there his quarters; went in the evening with the company to walk; came home before dark, and were treated by the ladies with a concert before supper.

August 8th. Worked until 3 o'clock; set out with the family and visitors (two coaches, our chaise, and gentlemen and servants on horseback, forming a large caravan), for Castle Kelly, Co. Gallway, distance two miles from Mount Talbot; arrived, and were elegantly entertained at dinner, being thirty in number. I left the gentlemen at their bottle, and escaped to the ladies, but was soon after joined by them all at tea, after which Mr. Bigari (an excellent dancer) danced with Miss Kelly and some other ladies. Returned home at 10, and found supper ready.

August 9th. Mr. Talbot, Junior, obliged to go abroad, left the company to the care of Lady Anne. Worked at our drawings, walked about, paid a visit to Castle Kelly, and got a concert before supper [Wilde, 82–3].

Rinndoon Castle

On the following day, 10 August, the pair of artists reached yet another important castle at Rinndoon, near the end of a peninsula jutting out into the western side of Lough Ree. Beranger, who called it St John's Castle, had little to say of it on p. 78 of MS 4162:

> This castle is sit: on a peninsula on that wide part of the Shannon called Lough Ree. It is the most irregular figure the plan forming a letter not unlike a P.

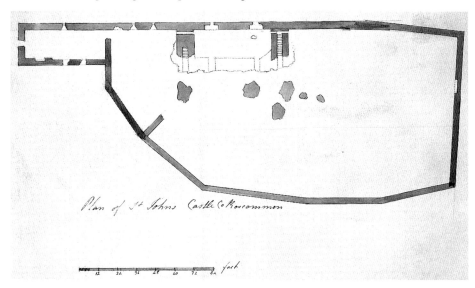

Plan of St Johns Castle Co Roscommon

Fig. 192
The curious P-shaped plan of Rinndoon ('St John's') Castle, Co. Roscommon, forming part of MS 671 in the Manuscripts Department of the National Library, was prepared for use in Grose's *Antiquities* but rejected in the final selection of illustrations.

Fig. 193
Bigari twisted and compressed Rinndoon Castle, Co. Roscommon, in his drawing, which survives only in the 1793 engraving published as plate 93 of the second volume of Grose's *Antiquities*.

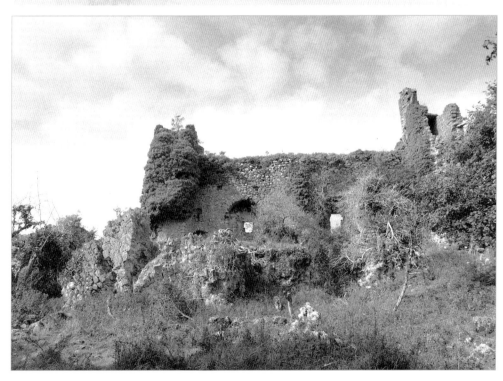

Fig. 194
The modern photographer finds it difficult to harmonise his view with that 'invented' by Bigari in Rinndoon Castle, Co. Roscommon, as the outside wall still obscures much of the view of the interior.

The configuration like the letter P — perhaps a butcher's cleaver is a better comparison — can best be seen on the plan preserved in the National Library's manuscript 671 (*Fig. 192*), which came originally from the Burton Conyngham collection. North is to the right, and the handle is a two-storey building just to the south of the entrance, which is scarcely marked on the plan for some strange reason. Inside the centre of the west wall is the keep, indicated by the two stairways, and further fragments to the east. The curving wall farther to the east is not very accurately surveyed, and it is across that wall that Bigari made his drawing of the keep that is preserved only in its engraved form as plate 93 of the second volume of Grose's *Antiquities* (*Fig. 193*), the accompanying letterpress mistakenly placing the castle beside 'Loughkee'. But Bigari had to 'think away' the upper portions of that wall in order to get his view of the keep, which he delineates fairly accurately with the two flanking stair towers. Today, the wall — and the growth on it — hinders us from seeing the view he presented (*Fig. 194*).

9. BACK EAST OF THE SHANNON AGAIN
— AND OFF HOME

On the afternoon of 10 August the travellers arrived at Athlone on the Shannon to take up their quarters at the sign of The Three Blackmores, which the late Billy English thought was probably in Connaught Street. They had hoped, in vain, to meet up with Burton Conyngham here (Nat. Lib. MS 1415, pp 100–1), and they were also disappointed to find that Mr Willis and all the other people to whom they had letters of introduction were out of town; so, having spent a whole day in their fruitless search, they decided to set out on the next morning, 12 August, for Clonmacnois.

Clonmacnois

This magnetic monastery, which once stood at the crossroads of Ireland, was founded by St Ciarán in the 540s and, for much of the earlier Middle Ages, was an important centre for art and learning. Their trip thither, and their two-day sojourn there, is described in Beranger's Diary as follows:

> Set out at 5 in the morning, in a long narrow boat, with Mr. Bigari and our interpreter; this vessel was so narrow that the seats held but one person, so that we were sitting behind one another, with order of the conductor not to lean to right or left, or that if we did we should be overset and drowned, which not choosing, we kept in an erect posture, having got only leave to move our head to admire the Shannon and its pleasing banks. Tedious as this posture was, we continued strictly to observe it; but being tired of it, we landed on an island, spread the cloth upon the grass, and eat a cold fowl, which we washed down with wine and water; went in our vehicle with great care, and arrived at Clonmacnoise, ten miles from Athlone, which voyage took up three good hours, though the vessel (by its structure) went fast, one man making it go by two oars or paddles; staid here the whole day, working and finishing everything, very hungry, and nothing to eat, there being nothing to be found in the few miserable cabins but sour ale, and smoked whiskey. Clonmacnoise, or the Seven Churches, is described by Sir James Ware, in his Antiquities; it is situated on an uneven rising ground on the banks of the Shannon, in the King's County, ten miles of Athlone, where the river is rather narrow. We left this place rather late, and returned to Athlone by moonlight [Wilde, 83–4].

Wilde says that Beranger's Diary entry about Clonmacnoise was rather meagre, and, as he quotes instead the relevant passage from pp 28–9 of MS 4162, we could do worse than do the same:

> August 12th and 13th. Clonmacnois or the Seven churches as it is called is situated on the borders of the Shannon, 10 miles from Athlone on a high ground composed of various little hillocks, on part of which some of the buildings stand and others at the foot in hollows, the plan of Ware coppied from his Antiquities, was exact for what remains of it what is since destroyed we marked on his plan, adding the distances of the buildings from each other from which Mr. Bigary has intention to make a plan of its present state which is begun. The principal antiquities are two Round Towers elegantly finished in hewn stone. The largest marked B on the plan is 62 feet high wanting its roof, and has 56 feet in circumference the walls are 3f 8 thick. The other marked A is 7 feet Diamr within and the walls 3 feet thick, hight 56 feet including its roof which is standing, the dimentions of the door and their figure are marked on drawing No 53, letter F. The next considerable building is the Cathedrall which has an inscription within. See Draw: 53 Letter G, the doors of this building is exact in Ware, but still made Drawings of them, they are very richly adorned the rest of the buildings are small chappels, one of which is made a parish church and locked up. An other by the inscription Dr: 53 letter G markes that it was built in 1689, as it is impossible for me to give a name to the various parts not knowing the terms of architecture, I took care to represent them on paper with their plans, from which an architect can name and describe them, those that are no more extand are marked on the plan. See various Drawings No 53 with ye explanations on them.

Further comments by Beranger, some of which help to expand on the above, are contained in a letter he wrote from Athlone presumably to Burton Conyngham (and not to Col. Vallencey as I had suggested in the *Journal of the Old Athlone Society*, vol. 1, no. 3), preserved on pp 103–6 of MS 1415 in the National Library, from which the following is excerpted:

> Sir
>
> We have been at Clonmacnois full of hopes of finding great antiquities, but were mistaken and found nothing equal to our expectations, except two round towers, who undoubtedly are like those of their kind of unknown creation. They are exedingly well built of hewn stone but not of the highest kind, one being 56 feet high including its cap or Piramidal roof & the other without cap 62, the other buildings afforded nothing extraordinary above a common wall, an inscription, in the largest upon a wall is as follows, in Roman characters on a large flagg inlaid in the wall with a molding
>
> Carolus Coughlanus, vicarius Generalis Cluanmacnose proprys impendys hanc Dirutam Eclesiam Restauravit Anno Dom 1647

And on another of the churches was the following English inscription on a large flagg under a Coat of Arms in the front of the building over the entrance ·

> M. Edmund Dowling of Clondalare who built this chappel to the greater glory of God and use of his posterity 1689

I believe that there was formerly some building or other of antiquity, as the large church which they call the Cathedral, and which has the above Latin inscription, seems to be built of cut mountain stone, the corners of which stones are worn away & look roundish & filled up with morter, which makes me believe they were old materials employed to rebuilt this church, you shall be more able to determine on seeing the drawings. It was a tedious job, as Clonmacnois is 12 miles from this place by land & 10 by water, Mr Kelly of Castle Kelly had given us letters for Mr Moony within 5 miles of Clonmacnois, but on our arrival he was abroad & the house so full of compny: that his Lady was sorry she could not spare us a bed, she invited us at diner, which we declined & sett out for Clonmacnois where we spend the whole day & came here to diner at 9. next day we sett of with day light by water "to save our horse", taking our dinner with us, & arrived there in three hours, we worked hard, & took various views & plans, I inquired for the Anchorites, but the people thereabouts did not hear of them, our recommendations here, was from Lady Ann Talbot to Mrs. Wills, whose husband being abroad, she invited us to tea where we found 2 gentlemen, of whom & some acquaintance I picked up, we learn'd that those Seven Churches are not looked upon as great antiques, but that the oldest and most curious ones are those of Glandalough, so that we are glad, that the accounts agree so well. We are here at an inn, where I shall make as little stay as possible, & hope to go to morrow. For Mount Murray; we are inking our drawings …

The doors of the seven churches particularly of the Cathedrall are carved & somewhat in the taste of the Abbey of Cong, the other, doors are round & plastered to make them even, the plaster is another sign of modern work as in the old buildings it is all destroyed by time, in Harris's translation of Ware, they are pretty well represented, also the crosses which since that time are much wore, children throwing stones at them & the figures blunted, & just the form seen the plan of Do is pretty correct, I have marked on it the buildings which have been destroyed since, & the one which is roofed & mended serving for a Parish Church.

I hope you excuse the hurry of this letter, as I am imployed in drawing, & want to finish to day to have done at the inn & go off to morrow.

I have the honour to be with respect

Sir

Your most obt and most humble servant

Gabl Beranger

P.S. Bigary presents his respects to you. Mr. Talbot got our spring mended with clips, which with the iron fork which suports it will bring us to Dublin he would not tell the expences attending it, so it cost us nothing.

Fig. 195 (far left)
Bigari gives the impression that Temple Finghin at Clonmacnois, Co. Offaly, is a tall church by making his two male figures very small by comparison in this original unsigned view on p. 28 of 2122 TX(3) in the National Library.

Fig. 196 (left)
Though the side walls have suffered somewhat in the meantime, the Romanesque chancel arch and round tower of Temple Finghin at Clonmacnois, Co. Offaly, have remained virtually unchanged since Bigari sketched them 223 years ago (*Fig. 195*).

After this amount of text about Clonmacnois, it is sad to have to record that the marked plan no longer survives and that the only full view we have is one by Bigari showing Temple Finghin, which is now p. 28 of 2122 TX(3) in the National Library (*Fig. 195* — compare also *Fig. 196*). Curiously, neither it nor any of the other drawings done of Clonmacnois on this tour were engraved in Grose's *Antiquities*, which, surprisingly, illustrates nothing from 'The King's County'.

But we do have a number of detailed drawings by Beranger, one original in the Royal Irish Academy and the others copies by Cooper and Turner in the National Library, as follows.

(i)   Royal Irish Academy, MS 3.D.4 (10/53), a Beranger original, unsigned but bearing the original Beranger drawing number 53 in the top right-hand corner, and showing the left-hand half of the west doorway of the Cathedral, a cross-section through the upright part of it, and details of two of the capitals (*Fig. 197*). The doorway has undergone an amount of restoration in the intervening years (*Fig. 198*).

(ii)   National Library of Ireland, 2122 TX(4), p. 37, a copy of the above Beranger original, signed A(ustin) C(ooper), Oct(ober) 1799.

(iii) National Library of Ireland, 2122 TX(4), p. 38, a copy by J.T. (presumably Joseph Turner) of a lost Beranger original showing the left-hand half of the north doorway of the Cathedral (*Fig.*

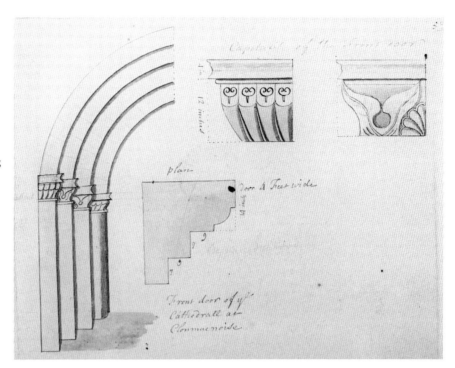

Fig. 197
MS 3.D.4 (10/53) in the Royal Irish Academy is a drawing with Beranger's original captions illustrating details of the doorway inserted perhaps shortly after 1200 into the west wall of the Cathedral at Clonmacnois, Co. Offaly. The arches above the capitals on the left may represent later repairs.

199), together with a cross-section (called a 'plan') and two varied rope-mouldings (*Fig. 200*).

(iv)   National Library of Ireland, 2122 TX(4), p. 39 (*Fig. 201*), a copy by A(ustin) C(ooper) dated October 1799, after an original by Beranger, showing the left-hand half of the chancel arch of Temple Finghin, as well as a cross-section and a sample of its decoration (*Fig. 202*), together with the two inscriptions (in the Cathedral and Temple Doolin — or Dowling — respectively) mentioned in the letter cited above.

(v)   National Library of Ireland 2122 TX(4), p. 40, a copy by A(ustin) C(ooper) of October 1799, probably after Beranger originals, showing the doors of the round tower, of the entrance to the tower in Temple Finghin and, apparently, of the Cathedral sacristy, together with a window in the chancel of the Cathedral and the exterior of the south window in its sacristy (*Fig. 203*).

One unexpected item to have survived from the visit to Clonmacnois is a sheet with an Irish text, presumably ripped from a book because, as Elizabeth Kirwan of the National Library noticed with her keen eye, traces of gold can be seen at the edges. It forms part of the Cooper Collection and is registered as Acc. 4841, Folder 18, in the Manuscript Department of the National Library (*Fig. 204*). Written by the interpreter Terrence McGuire, it tells of folk traditions of Clonmacnois found nowhere else to my knowledge, which makes a transcription of the full text desirable here along with an English translation, both kindly prepared by Pádraig O Macháin of the Dublin Institute for Advanced Studies, to whom I would like to express my deepest gratitude:

Fig. 198 (far left)
The capitals now on the north side of the Cathedral doorway at Clonmacnois, Co. Offaly, are similar to those shown on the south side in Beranger's drawing of 1779 (*Fig. 197*).

Fig. 199 (left)
Looking through the north doorway of the Cathedral at Clonmacnois to the western portal seen in the background.

Aig so cuntas no tuarasgbhail air chuid do mhiorbhuile na seacht tteampuill bheanuidhe chluain mhic cnois a gondae an righ do reir ghnátchchuimhne sheanduthchasaidh na criche angar dhóibh timchioll ocht míle do bhaile athluain

Ta se bhuaidhe air na teampuill reamhraite ud do bheannuidhe an naomh oirdheirc Ciaran, nach bhfuil a[o]n mhadudh rachas air mire an sa bparaisde chluain mhic cnois nach nimeochuidhe gan mhuill chum na deampull agus rachaidh tri huaire timchioll agus tuition marbh an sin. Deirid fós dha mhiadh corp marbh dha thabhairt as an bparaisde cheadhna chum paraisde eile dha chur dha adhnacail, dha déidis angoire na seacht tteampull nach bhfuireachadh brígh no neart ionta leis a chorp iomchar nias sia, acht gur bhéigin dóibh adhnacail a ccluain mhicnóis.

Bhi Eiriceach áiridh na chomhnuidhe láimh le cluain mhic cnóis roimhráite agus chuir roimhe Cros do na Crosaibh beannuidhe bhi aig teampoll do na teampuill tharuing as a háit le neart damh, ach anuair abhídh na doimh réidh ionalta aige chum an ghniomh phaganta ud, do

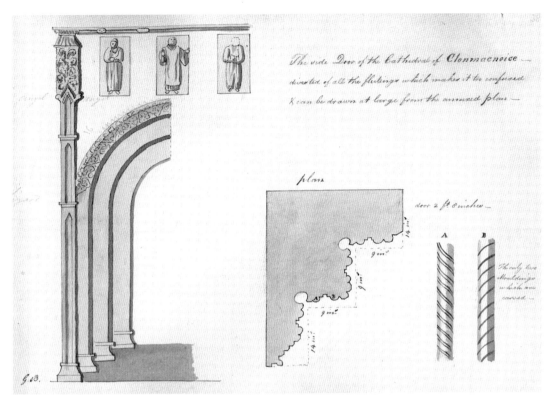

The side Door of the Cathedral of *Clonmacnoice* — divested of all the flutings which makes it too confused & can be drawn at large from the annexed plan —

plan

door 2 ft 8 inches —

A   B

The only two Mouldings which are carved.

Fig. 200
On p. 38 of 2122 TX(4) in the National Library we find a copy by J. T(urner) of a lost Beranger drawing illustrating half of the fifteenth-century north doorway in the Cathedral at Clonmacnois, Co. Offaly, along with a profile and details of its intricate mouldings.

thuitiodar na hainmhidhe marbh

Ta gnáchuimhne eile sa nait chéadhna air thochar na ttri Ndomhnall do thionsgain tri thochair no tri bhothar a dhéanamh thríd thri mhóinte chum sa seacht tteampoll chluain mhic cnóis, acht do sguireadhar don nobair an tra fiaffraidheadh dhiobh cread bádhbhar dhóibh leis na tochair [...].

Here is an account or a description of some of the miracles of the seven holy churches of Clonmacnois in the King's County according to the customary recollection of the old natives of the district near them about eight miles from Athlone.

One of the attributes of the aforementioned churches which the illustrious saint Ciarán blessed [is that] there is no dog who goes mad in the parish of Clonmacnois who will not go immediately to the churches and he will go round three times and then fall dead. They say also that if a corpse were being taken out of the same parish for burial or interment in another parish, if they were to pass close to the seven churches that they would not have the strength or energy to carry the corpse any farther but they would have to bury it in Clonmacnoise.

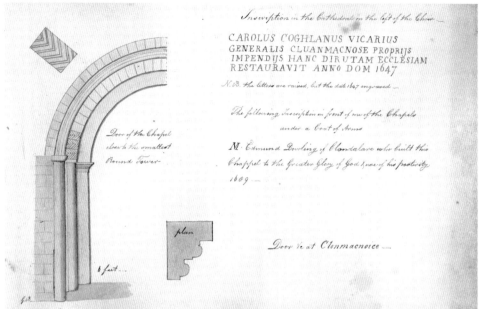

Fig. 201
In October 1799 Austin
Cooper initialled on the
bottom right the copy he
made of a lost Beranger
drawing of the chancel arch
of Temple Finghin at
Clonmacnois. The copy,
which also contains details
of inscriptions preserved on
site, is now p. 39 of 2122
TX(4) in the National
Library.

A certain heretic lived beside the aforementioned Clonmacnois and he proposed to pull one of the holy crosses which was in one of the churches from its place with the help of oxen, but when he had the oxen ready for that pagan act, the animals fell dead.

There is another customary memory in the same place regarding Tóchar na dTrí nDomhnall who began to make three paths or roads through three bogs to the seven churches of Clonmacnois, but they stopped their work when they were asked what reason had they for the paths [breaks off]

Before leaving Athlone, Beranger wrote into his Diary a last nostalgic valedictory farewell to the province where he and Bigari had spent the last two months and more:

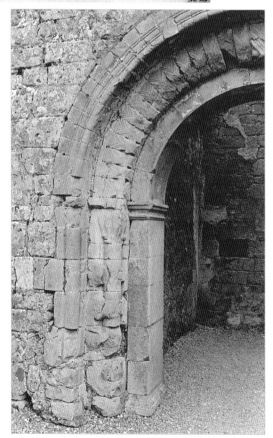

Fig. 202
The decoration on the chancel arch of Temple Finghin at Clonmacnois was simplified in Beranger's drawing (*Fig. 201*).

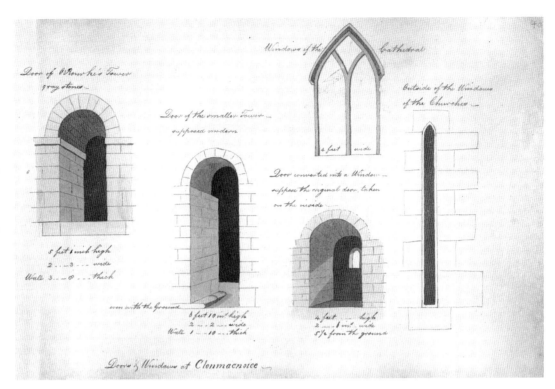

Fig. 203
Page 40 of 2122 TX(4) in
the National Library
presents initialled copies by
Austin Cooper of drawings
(presumably by Beranger)
of doorways and windows
in the round tower and the
Cathedral at Clonmacnois,
Co. Offaly.

Connaught province is in general very mountainous, and the least cultivated, but very thinly inhabited, and has a vast many boggs; it produces abundance of cattle, which makes the principal riches of it, which are disposed of at Ballinasloe, in the county of Roscommon, which has yearly the greatest fair of cattle and wool known in the three kingdoms; and though the cottagers have a poor appearance, I cannot say that I have seen here greater signs of poverty than I have seen four or five miles from Dublin, in the hilly parts of Wicklow.

August 14th, staid at home all day working at our sketches, and now and then looking at the crowd under our windows, it being market day, and the market held before the inn; we also packed up our baggage, and settled everything for our journey on the next day. Athlone is a borough town of the county of Westmeath, situated on the river Shannon, which divides it in two parts, the west side of the river being in the county of Roscommon, province of Conaught, and the eastern part in the province of Leinster, by which it communicates by a stone bridge, which serves for mall in the evening, when both sexes make it their walk, it was here that General Ginkel passed the Shannon in sight of the Irish army (who were intrenched on the opposite shore), in 1691. There is a barrack for four companies of foot, and two troop of horse. It returns two members of Parliament, and is situated almost in the centre of the kingdom; its look is but poor, but the river makes it pleasing.

Being now on the point of quitting Connaught and taking our leave of it, by crossing the bridge, I think it my duty to do justice to its inhabitants, on whom a late tour writer bestowed

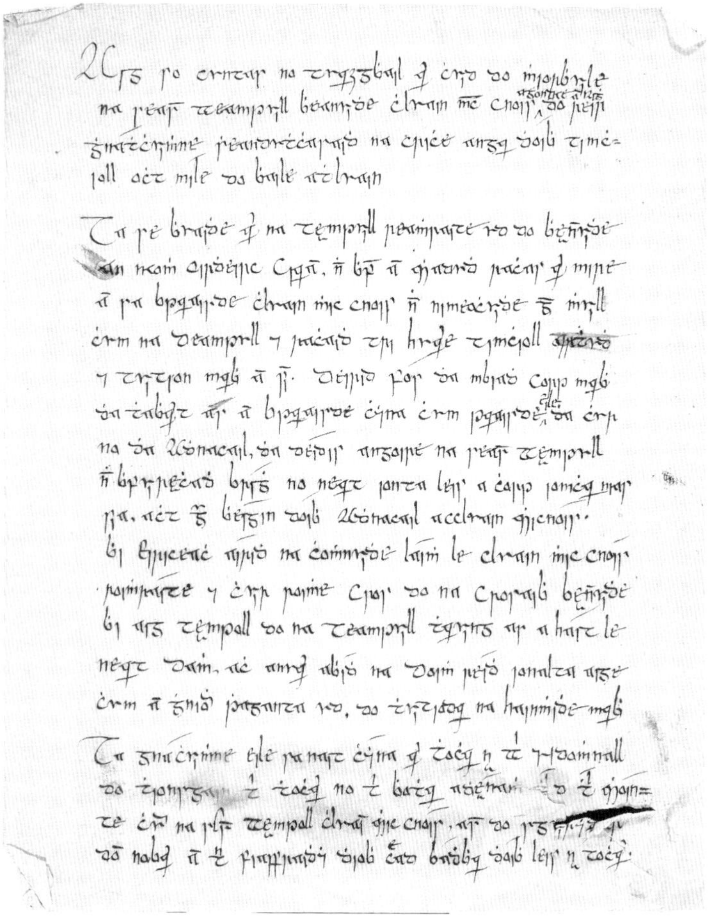

Fig. 204
One of the unexpected
treasures among the papers
of the Cooper Collection
was this single page,
apparently torn out of a
Gaelic manuscript book
written probably by the
expedition's interpreter,
Terrence McGuire, and
recounting some traditions
of Clonmacnois not
recorded elsewhere. It is
now in Folder 18 of Acc.
4841 in the Manuscript
Department of the
National Library of Ireland.

the name of savages, and asserted that there were no roads, on a bare hearsay; since he confesses that that prevented him from visiting this province. I declare then solemnly, that the roads are so excellent and firm, that during our tour through the province (in the hottest summer that the oldest men ever felt), we have not seen an atom of dust; and that in all the course of my life I never found more politeness and hospitality than we experienced from the inhabitants, both high and low. Mr. Bigari, who not able to converse in English, and of course could not enjoy the conversation, but in places where Italian and French was spoke, confesses that we can nowhere be better located than we have been in this province, and feels as well as myself a reluctance to quit it [Wilde, 87].

One down for Twiss, one up for Beranger!

Wilde's book on Beranger has nothing to report for the last four days of the tour, and for the details we have to rely on other sources. One of these is the end of the original articles which the book omitted, but which is found in vol. XI of the *Journal of the Royal Historical and Archaeological*

Association of Ireland, where, on p. 259, we find a transcript of Beranger's Diary for 15 August:

> Set out from Athlone; had not travelled half a mile on the turnpike road, but were all covered in clouds of dust, a thing quite new to us; passed through Ballymore, a village eleven miles from Athlone, where we baited; set forward through Rathcondra, another village, six miles from Ballimore, and arrived at Mount Murray, the seat of Alexander Murray, Esq., situated on Lough Hooyl, county of Westmeath, about five miles from Mullingar, and six miles from Rathcondra. Captain Murray, being abroad, had left orders to receive us. Eat two roasted ducks for our dinner; and Mr. Bigari, having the headache, went to bed at 8. I waited for Mr. Murray, who came home at 9, drank a bottle of claret, and went to bed at 11, having settled our journey for next day.

Tristernagh Abbey

Captain Murray accompanied them the following day to Tristernagh Abbey, the seat of Sir Pigot Piers, Bart., and thought to have been the model for Maria Edgeworth's *Castle Rackrent*. Situated close to Lough Iron, this once-rich priory of the Augustinian canons, founded around 1200 by Geoffrey de Costentin, was described on p. 29 of the National Library's MS 4162 as follows:

Fig. 205 (right)
A great octagonal tower was the most striking feature of Tristernagh Abbey, Co. Westmeath, in the original Bigari view preserved on p. 29 of 2122 TX(3) in the National Library.

Fig. 206 (far right)
The engraving of Tristernagh Abbey, Co. Westmeath, on plate 108 of vol. 2 of Grose's *Antiquities of Ireland* follows closely the original by Bigari (*Fig. 205*).

Fig. 207
In his drawing engraved as plate 107 of vol. 2 of Grose's *Antiquities,* Bigari omitted the unsightly blocking-up of the arches of Tristernagh Abbey, Co. Westmeath, in order to show it as it *ought* to have been. What it really looked like we shall never know, as almost the entire building was demolished by its owner, Sir Pigot Piers, only four years after Bigari sketched it.

Fig. 208
Bigari's original drawing of the imposing abbey at Tristernagh, Co. Westmeath, now preserved as p. 30 of 2122 TX(3) in the National Library, shows a social gathering on the right, including what may have been a Cake Dance of the kind he had experienced in County Leitrim earlier in the tour.

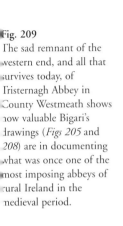

Fig. 209
The sad remnant of the western end, and all that survives today, of Tristernagh Abbey in County Westmeath shows how valuable Bigari's drawings (*Figs 205* and *208*) are in documenting what was once one of the most imposing abbeys of rural Ireland in the medieval period.

Augt 16th. This Abby was magnificent, and formerly larger; part of the entrance compose at present a portion of the dwelling of Sr Pigot Piers Bart and some parts are offices, we restored in the drawg its primitive state as much as possible, opening the arches, which were closed with masonry. it is of good workmanship, of blackish stone, the steeple is uncommon being an octogone on the top of a square and tho mutilated, is still 74 feet high; it is suported by a grand arch like those of Boyle and Ballintober which is at present 39 feet high, and was undoubtedly higher as the ground is raised so as to cover the bases of the colums, part of this arch serves for Deary and part a stable, nothing of the windows remain but their apertures, the colums are octogone and their capitals plain. See plan etc. No 54.

This description is valuable because it tells us that what we see on Bigari's two surviving original drawings — pp 29 and 30 respectively of 2122 TX(3) in the National Library (*Figs 205* and *208*) — is not actually what the buildings looked like when he drew his slightly restored version. The two drawings were engraved as plates 108 and 107 (*Figs 206–207*) respectively of the second volume of Grose's *Antiquities*. The fact that the letterpress attached to the Grose engravings informs us that the church was made into a total ruin by its proprietor in 1783, only four years after the artists' visit, makes description and drawings all the more valuable, because they record a building that has largely

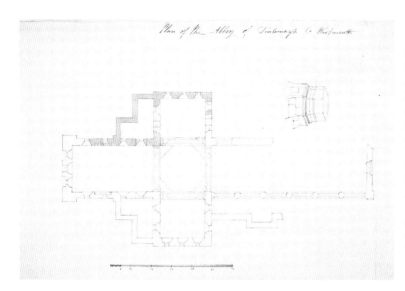

Fig. 210
MS 671 in the Manuscripts
department of the National
Library contains a drawing
of the plan and a detail of a
capital of the abbey church
at Tristernagh, Co.
Westmeath, which was put
forward as a potential
illustration for Grose's
Antiquities but never used.
The significance of the
darkened area is no longer
clear, as that part of the
building does not survive.

disappeared but yet had the most interesting-looking tower of any Irish medieval abbey. All that remains today of the church is the western gable and parts of two adjoining arches, seen on the right near where a number of figures are shown in the eighteenth-century representations dancing around a central raised figure holding a pole with something attached — better seen in detail in Bigari's original drawing than in the engraving. As Elizabeth Hickey suggested in the journal *Ríocht na Midhe* for 1980–1, this was a game with a cake tied on to the pole as a prize — making it look suspiciously like Bigari illustrating the game that he and Beranger had experienced at Glencar with Col. Irwin on 20 June (see above, p. 41), though also played in County Westmeath a century earlier, according to Hickey.

To judge from Beranger's description, the abbey buildings must have looked an awful mess, converted to a house, offices, dairy and stable, but the demolition of most of the complex is one of the greatest losses of all the structures visited by our pair on their tour, leaving behind today (*Fig. 209*) a sorry remnant of what was once a 'magnificent' church, to use Beranger's chosen adjective. Even before Sir Pigot or his family had done their conversions, it would appear that the area just inside the west doorway had been fortified and made into a kind of tower-house — probably shortly after the monastery had been dissolved and its riches appropriated in 1539. The plan of the abbey, to which Beranger referred at the end of his description quoted above, is preserved in a copy in the National Library's folder numbered MS 671, which came originally from the Burton Conyngham collection (*Fig. 210*). It shows us, in addition, a detail of part of one of the octagonal columns and its moulded capital, but what is puzzling about this plan is the area of the south transept and north part of the choir, and the angular wall that joins them, which have been marked with a darker wash. There is no sign that this part of the church survives today (or even survived the demolition of 1783), while that part of the western end of the church which still stands is not specially marked at all. Nor do the darkened areas correspond in location to the surviving part of a domestic red-brick building which probably formed part of a house built by Sir Pigot or his son John after the demolition of the older structure.

Multyfarnham Abbey

By a curious quirk of fate, Tristernagh has been owned, since about 1980, by the Franciscan friars of Multyfarnham, whose thirteenth-century friary there was the next — and last — site to have been visited on the tour. It was refurbished in 1976, mostly following the designs of the architect Wilfred Cantwell and Associates, but on p. 30 of the National Library's MS 4162 Beranger described it in the ruined condition in which he encountered it on 16 August 1779:

> This abby is sit. 4 miles from Mt Murry is very large and seems to be compleat in its plan. It is inferior to Tristernagh in workmanship but otherwise very good, of blackish stone, the form of the foundation of the cloysters are easily seen tho the cloysters are not extant, the east window is also entire but very plain, nothing remarkable about the doors & other windows, as plain finishing seems to have been observed thro' the whole. The steeple abt 60 feet high, has ofsets between the stories & stands on a small arch. See Drawings No 55.

Bigari's original view, surviving as p. 31 of 2122 TX(3) in the National Library (*Fig. 211*) and still bearing the original Beranger number 55 on the top right, was engraved as plate 121 in the first volume of Grose's *Antiquities* (*Fig. 212*) after the watercolour on p. 49 of the Royal Irish Academy's MS 3.C.29 (*Pl. 23*). Both show a slightly different picture to that seen today (*Fig. 213*), in that the thirteenth-century east window has now been restored, the tower completed to the top, and the buttresses at the south-western corner removed — perhaps already in an earlier restoration carried out in 1827. The foundations of the cloister, mentioned in Beranger's description quoted above but now no longer visible, were clearly marked on a plan surviving in a copy by Austin Cooper of 1799 after a lost original by Bigari, and bearing the accession number 2122 TX(96) in the National Library (*Fig. 214*). The paper on which it was drawn has suffered some damage, but the plan can be seen in its entirety in the engraving forming plate 121 in the first volume of Grose's *Antiquities*. This 'small thatched convent of the Franciscans', as Beranger's Diary described Multyfarnham, was to be the last monument our artists visited on their tour, and the Diary reports a suitable finale as follows:

> The Rev. Fathers came out, and invited us to refresh ourselves; went in, drank some bottles of good claret with them, found them learned gentlemen, well versed in antiquities, returned to Mount Murray, where we arrived about 9: discharged our interpreter.

It was intended that not Multyfarnham but Fore in County Westmeath should be the final stop on the antiquarian sketching tour, but financial business — and, one might suppose, some incipient fatigue — was to determine otherwise, as Beranger's final letter to William Burton Conyngham indicates:

The Abbey of Multifarnam, Co. of Westmeath

Fig. 211
The Franciscan friary at Multyfarnham, Co. Westmeath, was the last monument which Bigari sketched on the tour. His view, preserved as 2122 TX(3), p. 31, in the National Library, shows a building with tall gables pierced by large windows designed to let plenty of light into the church interior.

Vol. I.   Pl. 121.

MULTIFERNAM ABBEY, Co. Westmeath.

Fig. 212
Despite its roofless condition, the abbey at Multyfarnham, Co. Westmeath, illustrated here from the engraving published as plate 121 of the first volume of Grose's *Antiquities*, was peopled by learned and hospitable Franciscans who invited Bigari and Beranger to join them in a bottle of claret — which suitably rounded off the great archaeological tour of Connacht in 1779.

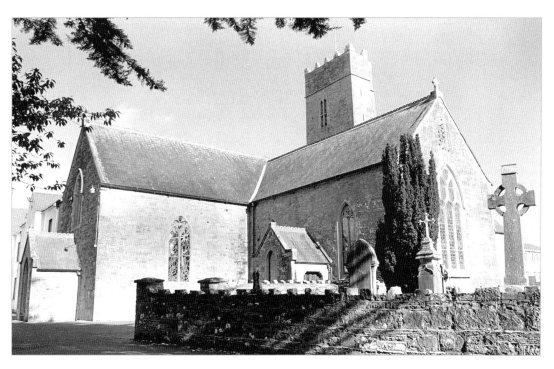

fig. 213
Since Bigari and Beranger's
visit in 1779,
Multyfarnham Abbey
underwent major
alterations in 1827 and
1976 to become the church
of the thriving Franciscan
community of today.

Sir

Having finished at Clonmacnois of which you have 3 general views & one particular one besides plan and parts etc., we left Athlone & sett out for Mountmurray, where we have drawn the Grand Abbey of Tristernagh, & the one at Multifernam, & were preparing after this to sett out for Fore 15 miles off, & follow the rout you have given us, when I received a letter from home which recalled me back to Dublin to settle my accounts with a Gentn for whom I have donne some agents business during 3 years & who has sold his house & effects & goes to reside in England, so that it is absolute necessity for me to be there & finish my accounts We sett out from Mountmurry this day. The bearer of this letter is Terrence McGuire, our honest interpretter, who has attended us through our tour, since the 17th of June, and which has behaved with all honesty and zeal, taking care of our horse and our self as much as in his power. He lives within four miles of Swanlinbar and hopes to be there in two days, if he finds out the roads readily, and is not led astray by miss informations. We told him that he should be paid by you. Our collection is swelled pretty well, and I flatter myself that the number will surprise you when you see it, and that you will be pleased with our exactness in ye views, plans and parts. Capn Murray presents his compts to you, and I have the honour to be

Sir

Your most obedt and most humble servant

Gl Beranger

Mount Murray, 17th August 1779

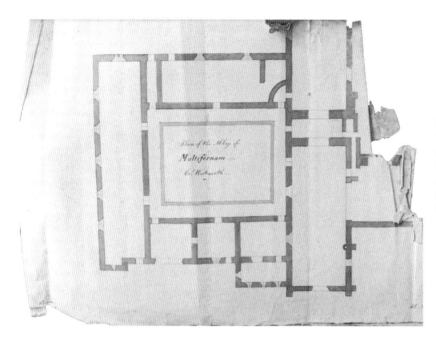

Fig. 214
The plan of Multyfarnham
Abbey that is 2122 TX(96)
in the National Library
gives valuable details of the
claustral buildings which
no longer survive.

This letter (Nat. Lib. MS 1415, pp 107–8) suggests that McGuire the interpreter went to Burton Conyngham for payment before returning home to Swanlinbar. His experience on the tour probably furthered his career, as we later hear of him as a scribe, writing a version of Geoffrey Keating's *Three Shafts of Death* (now University College Cork) in 1780, and contributing to a further manuscript in 1788 (MS 1185, pp 144–75, in the Royal Irish Academy). These works he signs with his Irish name Toirdhealbhach Mág Uidhir, which, as Pádraig O Macháin kindly informed me, he also appended to MS Advocates 72.3.2 in the National Library of Scotland and a Gaelic manuscript for Dr Donald Smith of Enniskillen in 1798, in which he describes himself as 'laimh le Florence Court'.

Concerning County Westmeath, Beranger wrote in his Diary

> This county is well cultivated, and the fields, meadows, &c., as well as the habitation on each side of the roads, have a clean and decent look. The same boggs are intermixed. Mullingar seems a pretty large town; the business of people and cars denotes some trade stirring there.
>
> We had received orders that, in case we met with a burial, and the cry of the Irish Pullulloe, to draw a representation of the ceremony and introduce it in the drawing of the antiquity of the quarter where it should happen, but in all our tour we met none.

Wilde reports that on 17 August the artists arrived in Kinnegad, 'famous for its cheeses', and from there set out for 'the New Inn', now known as Enfield, arriving back in Dublin on the following day, 18 August, doubtless weary but happy to get home after having been just over ten weeks (72 days) on the road.

In the flyleaf at the end of Beranger's Diary, Wilde (88) found the following notice, probably prepared by Burton Conyngham (see above, p. 13), which is a neat way of rounding off the account of the great antiquarian sketching tour of Connacht in 1779:

> Copy of my publication, after my tour in Connaught, in the Galway Paper:—Messrs. A.M. Bigari and Gabriel Beranger, having made the tour of Connaught by appointment of the Hibernian Antiquarian Society, under the direction of the Right Hon. William Burton, with a view to collect drawings of the antiquities of Ireland for publication, think it their duty to undeceive the public in regard to some aspersions thrown on that province by a late tour writer who, by his own confession, never visited that part of Ireland, and to assure them that they found the roads excellent; and that they cannot find words to express their gratitude to the inhabitants for the polite reception, hospitable entertainment, and friendly assistance they received in the prosecution of their design. In particular, they beg the following noblemen and gentlemen to accept this public proof of their sincere gratitude, viz.:—

Co. Monaghan	—	Rev. Mr. Ward, of Clones
Co. Fermanagh	—	Right Hon. Lord Enniskillen, Florence Court
Co. Sligo	—	L. F. Irwin, Tanrego, Esq.
	—	W. Ormsby, Willowbrook, Esq.
	—	John M'Donnough, of Heapstown, Esq.
	—	Rt. Hon. Jos. Cooper, Mercrea
	—	Capt. Jones, Tubberpatrick
	—	Robert Brown, Fortland, Esq.
Co. Mayo	—	— Jones, of Ardnaree, Esq.
	—	Right Hon. James Cuffe, of Newtown Gore
	—	Right Rev. Lord Bishop of Killala
	—	Right Hon. Earl of Altamont, Westport
	—	— Garby, of Murrisk, Esq.
	—	J. Gallagher, Ballinrobe, Esq.
	—	— Ireland, of Cong, Esq.
	—	Sir John Brown, The Neal, Bart.
Co. Roscommon	—	Right Hon. Earl of Kingston, Boyle
	—	Charles O'Connor, of Belinegar, Esq.
	—	Denis O'Connor, of Belinegar Esq.
	—	Arthur French, of French Park, Esq.
	—	Rev. John O'Connor, D.D., Roscommon
	—	William Talbot, of Mount Talbot, Esq.
	—	William J. Talbot, of Mount Talbot, Esq.
	—	Nehem. Sandys, of Sandfield, Esq.

Co. Galway	—	Ralph Ousley, of Dunmore, Esq.
Co. Westmeath	—	Denis Kelly, of Castle Kelly, Esq.
	—	Alexander Murray, of Mount Murray, Esq.
	—	Sir Pigot Piers, of Tristernaght, Bart.

10 . EPILOGUE

After their return to Dublin, the two artists presumably handed over their drawings, their 'treasure of antiquities', to Burton Conyngham, the man who had commissioned them to undertake the tour on behalf of the Hibernian Antiquarian Society. The description of each site visited contained in MS 4162 in the National Library is likely to have been a copy of a description and list of illustrations prepared not long after the completion of the tour, even though the manuscript itself was not completed until October 1780 at the earliest.

Having received the illustrations and text, Burton Conyngham seriously pursued the question of having the drawings engraved in London. He had obviously asked Lord Carlow (see above, p. 1) to get an estimate of costings for a volume of engravings of Irish monuments from Paul Sandby, the well-known English painter and engraver who had used some of Lord Carlow's drawings in his *Virtuosi's Museum*, bearing the date 1778 on the title page. This we can glean from what is probably the sole surviving letter of a correspondence between Burton Conyngham (the Col. Burton of the letter), Lord Carlow (the 'your Lordship' of the letter) and Paul Sandby. It was written by Paul Sandby to Lord Carlow, dated London, 15 March 1780, now preserved as pp 175–7 of MS 1415 in the National Library, and is as follows:

My Lord

I had the honour of your Lordship's letter last week but deferred writing till I had seen Mr. Kinsman — the drawings — and Mr. Kearsley. After a consultation with the latter and making an estimate of the expence of the engraving, printing etc., woud come to, it appears there must be a certain sale of 400 copies to defray the expences. The profits increase considerably in case 800 or a thousands were sold; we imagine the price to have the plates well engraved one with another woud cost 12 Guineas, allowing beside to me 3 Guineas each for making or correcting the drawings and superintending the engravers, for they want a good deal looking after. I suppose Col. Burton is aware the best mode of publishing his work woud be in Numbers 4 Plates each and to be sold for 5 shillings. The estemate was made for that, allowing the usual profit to the trade.

If it should prove agreeable to Col. Burton to risk one number for trial, and deposite an adequate sum of money in bankers ward in London and allow me to draw it out to pay the engravers and when they have done their work I will do him all the justice in my power. I am sorry I have no money myself to spare from other engagements to risk on this work, or I woud readily do it, as I think it must answer. The drawings the Col. has sent me over are in general fine subjects but too slight, except Weatleys and Barralets, for the engravers to work after, — they are a set of Gentry must have ev'ry thing fully and clearly made out. It is pitty the drawings were not at first made all of the size fix'd on for the plates. Those sent me run very unequal. Those done by Bigari, have a good share of taste but too slight for the Engraver. Beranger's stones etc. will do very well — the Abbey at Tristernagh has a very singular beautiful Tower. The inside view of the Abbey Ballintober in a stile of building uncommonly fine, and Cormack Chappel is charming. If Ireland abounds with such fine ruins, I am afraid our English publication will look small after they become known here. I hope your Lordship will employ your pencil next summer amongst them for surely they must have irresistible charms for a lover of virtu. I shall return the drawings safe in a few days to Mr. Kinsman, and shall be much obliged to your Lordship if you woud do me the honour to acquaint the Col. with my opinion and that I shoud be very happy to be engaged with him in the publication, a person of his rank and connections surely must … demands sure from 500 or a thousand people. I woud be well content to take half the profit for my trouble, be it what it may.

I have not heard from Mr. Weatley a long time. I thought to have had the drawing before this, the plate is ready for it. I beg your Lordship's pardon for not taking more pains in writing to you but hope you know, I would sooner make a drawing than write a letter, altho I shall ever think it my duty to do both for one who has done me so many kindness's, and which will ever be gratefully remembered by your Lordship's most obedient servant
Paul Sandby

This letter, presumably passed on by its addressee, Lord Carlow, to Burton Conyngham, whom we have to thank for its preservation, is revealing for a number of reasons. Firstly, it supports the notion expressed in an earlier chapter (pp 1–2) that Sandby's *Virtuosi's Museum* of 1778 was one of Burton Conyngham's models for his intended book of engravings, and it is interesting to note that Sandby thought that engravings of fine Irish ruins might dwarf his English publication (another volume of his, incorporating the Irish drawings in *Virtuosi's Museum,* was to appear in 1781). Secondly, it shows how Burton Conyngham was planning to have Sandby as the man in charge of producing and issuing a volume of Irish engravings in London. Thirdly, it demonstrates that the material destined for that volume was intended to cover various parts of Ireland, the three places mentioned in the letter — Tristernagh, Ballintubber and Cormac's Chapel — being in the provinces of Leinster, Connacht and Munster respectively. Fourthly, Sandby praises the Wheatleys and Barralets that were sent to him (some of which I published in *The Irish Arts Review* for 2000) but, while finding satisfaction in 'Beranger's stones etc.' (presumably the prehistoric tombs), it is surprising to find him criticising Bigari's drawings as being too slight, despite having 'a good share of taste'. Herein may lie one reason why the projected book of engravings of Irish ruins never saw the light of day — namely that the London engravers (or perhaps even the London public) considered the material 'too slight', which was perhaps why Sandby was not prepared to risk investing money in it.

Whether Burton Conyngham was put off by Sandby's comments, or was daunted by the prospect of re-doing many of the illustrations so that they would fit the size of the plates, or simply felt that he might not be able to sell the required 400 copies to break even, we shall probably never know. What we do know, however, is that what could have been a fine volume of engravings revealing the glorious buildings of Ireland's past was never realised by Burton Conyngham himself. The demise of the project must have saddened him and weakened the resolve of the Hibernian Antiquarian Society, which finally came to virtual collapse in 1783 after unpleasant internal wrangling between two of its members, Vallancey and Ledwich. But the portfolio of drawings amassed over a number of years by Burton Conyngham did not go to waste, and it was Edward Ledwich who was finally to reap the benefit by using many of them in Grose's *Antiquities of Ireland,* which he managed and produced almost from the very start after Grose had died when plans for it were still in their infancy. Ledwich brought out Grose between 1791 and 1796 (despite the date of 1791 on the title pages of both of the volumes), and formally dedicated the second volume to Burton Conyngham. The Preface to the first volume, dated 1 January 1794, acknowledges the debt to the Right Honourable William Conyngham 'who, with unexampled munificence, generosity and patriotism, bestowed his noble collection of drawings for the use of this work' and for whom the beautiful views illustrated in it 'are the truest panegyric on his taste and love of the arts'. The Grose volume was doubtless for Burton Conyngham the nearest thing to the fulfilment of his own original dreams and intentions, and it was through his involvement that so many of the Bigari illustrations from the 1779 tour finally came to be engraved — and reproduced here in this volume along with the originals. Ledwich did use some of the Beranger drawings — MacDermott's Island (*Fig. 64*) and many of the plans — but did not have the courtesy to acknowledge their authorship.

Burton Conyngham died in 1796, but his portfolio of drawings is likely to have remained intact, at least for a while. After his death, it was clearly placed at the disposal of the Cooper family, whose members copied much original material (now partially lost) during the month of October 1799. In handwritten notes in the Cooper family copy of Wilde's *Memoir of Beranger,* Austin Damer Cooper (1831–1900) states that his grandfather, Austin Cooper, the antiquary, 'purchased all Colonel Conyngham's drawings, Books and works of art' in the year 1810, and, after his decease in 1830, the 'entire valuable and extensive Library' 'was disposed of by his son who, unlike his father, was devoid of all literary taste'. It was perhaps while the collection of drawings (which the family had retained) were in the possession of that son, the Rev. Austin Cooper (1804–71), that some of the original drawings were dissipated, and we only know of their former existence through the copies made by members of the Cooper family in the 1790s which have managed better to survive the ravages of time. However, there is always the hope that some of this lost material may yet come to light. Given the span of 223 years since Burton Conyngham first added all the Connacht artwork to his portfolio, we should consider ourselves fortunate that so much of it has survived through the Cooper Collection, thereby making possible this pictorial and literary reconstruction of what was undoubtedly the most extensive and best-documented archaeological survey carried out in eighteenth-century Ireland.

BIBLIOGRAPHY

Abbreviations

JGAHS *Journal of the Galway Archaeological and Historical Society*
JRSAI *Journal of the Royal Society of Antiquaries of Ireland* (including the earlier *Journal of the Royal Historical and Archaeological Association of Ireland*)
PRIA *Proceedings of the Royal Irish Academy*
UJA *Ulster Journal of Archaeology*

Works germane to the text

William Camden, *Britannica, or a chorographical description of Great Britain and Ireland, together with the adjacent islands* (London, 1722).

Anne Crookshank and the Knight of Glin, *Watercolours of Ireland. Works on paper in pencil, pastel and paint c. 1600–1914* (London, 1994).

Anne Crookshank, the Knight of Glin and William Laffan, *Masterpieces by Irish artists 1660–1860* (London, 2000).

(?) Richard Downings, *The County of Mayo* by Mr. Downing. National Library of Ireland, MS 5628, pp 60–75.

P. Froggatt, 'Sir William Wilde, 1815–1876', *PRIA* 77C (1977), 261–78.

D.C. Grose, 'Ancient sculpture over the door of Ballymote church, County Sligo', *The Irish Penny Magazine* (5 February 1842), 47.

Francis Grose (ed. Edward Ledwich), *The antiquities of Ireland*, 2 vols (London, 1791 (but actually 1794–6)).

Peter Harbison, 'Clonmacnois by Beranger 1779' (with notes by N.W. English), *Journal of the Old Athlone Society* 1 (3) (1972–3), 195–6.

Peter Harbison, *Beranger's Views of Ireland* (Dublin, 1991).

Peter Harbison, *Beranger's Antique Buildings of Ireland* (Dublin, 1998).

Peter Harbison, *Cooper's Ireland. Drawings and notes from an eighteenth-century gentleman* (Dublin, 2000).

Peter Harbison, ' "Irish artists on Irish subjects". The Cooper Collection in the National Library', *Irish Arts Review Yearbook* 17 (2001), 61–9.

Britta Kalkreuter, *Boyle Abbey and the School of the West* (Bray, 2001).

Lord Killanin and Michael Duignan, *The Shell Guide to Ireland* (2nd edn, London, 1967).

William Laffan (ed.), *The sublime and the beautiful. Irish art 1700–1830* (London, 2001).

Harold Leask, *Irish churches and monastic buildings*, 3 vols (Dundalk, 1955–60).

Edward Ledwich, *Antiquities of Ireland* (Dublin, 1790; 2nd edn 1804).

Walter D. Love, 'The Hibernian Antiquarian Society. A forgotten predecessor to the Royal Irish Academy', *Studies* 51 (Autumn 1962), 419–31.

Hugh MacCurtain, *The elements of the Irish language, grammatically explained in English* (Louvain, 1728).

Philip McEvansoneya, 'A colourful spectacle restored. The State Coach of the Lord Mayor of Dublin', *Irish Arts Review Yearbook* **17** (2001), 80–7.

Dubhaltach MacFhirbisigh, *Leabhar Genealach an Dubhaltaigh Mhec Fhirbisigh* ('Book of Genealogies'). University College Dublin Add. Ir. MS 14. (An edition by Nollaig Ó Muraíle is forthcoming.)

John McTernan, *In Sligo long ago* (Sligo, 1998).

A.N.L. Munby (introd.), *The Phillipps Manuscripts* (2001).

Monica Nevin, 'General Charles Vallancey, 1725–1812,' *JRSAI* **123** (1993), 19–58.

Diarmaid Ó Catháin, 'Charles O'Conor of Belanagare: antiquary and Irish scholar', *JRSAI* **119** (1989), 136–63.

Charles O'Conor, *Dissertations on the history of Ireland to which is subjoined a dissertation on the Irish colonies established in Britain, with some remarks on Mr. MacPherson's Translation of Fingal and Temora* (Dublin, 1766).

Sylvester O'Halloran, *An introduction to the study of the history and antiquities of Ireland, in which the assertions of Mr. Hume and other writers are occasionally considered* (Dublin, 1772).

Philip O'Sullivan Beare, *Historiae Catholicae Iberniae Compendium* (Lisbon, 1621).

Liam Price (ed.), *An eighteenth century antiquary. The sketches, notes and diaries of Austin Cooper (1759–1830)* (Dublin, 1942).

Sybil Rosenfeld and Edward Croft-Murray, 'A checklist of scene painters working in Great Britain and Ireland in the 18th century', *Theatre Notebook* **19**, Number 1 (Autumn 1964), 6–20 (part. 10–11).

Paul Sandby, *The Virtuosi's Museum* (London, 1778).

Roger Stalley, *The Cistercian monasteries of Ireland* (London/New Haven, 1987).

Ann M. Stewart, *Irish art loan exhibitions 1765–1927*, 3 vols (Dublin, 1990).

Walter G. Strickland, *A dictionary of Irish artists*, 2 vols (Dublin/London, 1913).

Walter G. Strickland, 'The State Coach of the Lord Mayor of the City of Dublin and the State Coach of the Earl of Clare, Lord Chancellor of Ireland', *JRSAI* **51** (1921), 49–67.

C.E.F. Trench, 'William Burton Conyngham (1733–1796)', *JRSAI* **115** (1985), 40–63.

Charles Vallancey, *Collectanea de rebus Hibernicis*, 7 vols (Dublin, 1770–86).

Charles Vallancey, *A grammar of the Iberno-Celtic, or Irish language* (Dublin, 1782).

Charles Vallancey, *A vindication of the ancient history of Ireland* (Dublin, 1786).

Sir James Ware (ed. Walter Harris), *Works … concerning Ireland*, 3 vols (2nd edn, Dublin, 1764).

Sir William R. Wilde, *Lough Corrib, its shores and islands: with notices of Lough Mask* (Dublin, 1867; reprinted Headford, 2002).

Sir W.R. Wilde, 'Memoir of Gabriel Beranger, and his labours in the cause of Irish art, literature, and antiquities, from 1760 to 1780', *JRSAI* **11** (1870), 33–64, 121–52 and 236–60; **12** (1872–3), 445–85; and **14** (1876–8), 111–56 (with an introduction by Lady Wilde).

Sir William Wilde, *Memoir of Gabriel Beranger, and his labours in the cause of Irish art and antiquities from 1760 to 1780* (Dublin, 1880).

W.G. Wood-Martin, *Rude stone monuments of Ireland (Co. Sligo and the island of Achill)* (Dublin, 1888).

Works pertinent to the sites visited on the tour

General background

Anon., *Archaeology in County Sligo* (Sligo (Fás), 1998).

T.B. Barry, *The archaeology of medieval Ireland* (London, 1987; reprinted 1994 and 1999).

Philip A. Crowl, *The intelligent traveller's guide to historic Ireland* (Chicago, 1990).

Peter Harbison, *Guide to the national and historic monuments of Ireland* (Dublin, 1992).

Lord Killanin and Michael Duignan, *The Shell Guide to Ireland* (2nd edn, London, 1967).

Damien Noonan, *The Daily Telegraph Castles and Ancient Monuments of Ireland* (London, 2001).

Jacqueline O'Brien and Peter Harbison, *Ancient Ireland from prehistory to the Middle Ages* (London, 1996).

Megalithic tombs

GENERAL

Stefan Bergh, *Landscape of the monuments. A study of the passage tombs in the Cúil Irra region.* Arkeologiska undersökningar, Skriften nr 6 (Stockholm, 1995).

Michael Herity, *Irish passage graves* (Dublin, 1974). (The map of Carrowmore is not in Beranger's hand.)

Seán Ó Nualláin, *Survey of the megalithic tombs of Ireland. Vol. V — County Sligo* (Dublin, 1989).

W.G. Wood-Martin, *Rude stone monuments of Ireland (Co. Sligo and the island of Achill)* (Dublin, 1888).

INDIVIDUAL SITES

Carrowmore, Co. Sligo

Göran Burenhult, *The archaeological excavation at Carrowmore, Co. Sligo, Ireland. Excavation seasons 1977–79.* Theses and Papers in North-European Archaeology 9 (Stockholm, 1980).

Göran Burenhult, *The megalithic cemetery of Carrowmore, Co. Sligo* (Tjörnarp, 1995).

F.T. Kitchin, 'The Carrowmore megalithic cemetery, Co. Sligo', *Proceedings of the Prehistoric Society* **49**, (1983), 151–75.

Clog Glass, Co. Sligo

See Ó Nualláin above, 48, no. 75 (Tanrego West).

CuChullin's Tomb, Co. Sligo

See Wood-Martin above, 192.

Ennishowen 'Druid's Monument', Co. Mayo

Sir William R. Wilde, *Lough Corrib: its shores and islands: with notices of Lough Mask* (Dublin, 1867), 227–8 (reprinted 2002).

Finn mac Cool's Griddle, Co. Sligo
See Ó Nualláin above, 37, no. 55, 'Caltragh' — not 'Tawnatruffaun', no. 56.

Heapstown, Co. Sligo
See Herity, Ó Nualláin and Wood-Martin above.

Misgaun Mewe
See all of the general works quoted above.

Westport, Co. Mayo
See Herity above, 279.

Earthworks

INDIVIDUAL SITES

Rathcroghan, Co. Roscommon
John Waddell, 'Rathcroghan — a royal site in Connacht', *Journal of Irish Archaeology* 1 (1983), 21–46.
Michael Herity, 'A survey of the royal site of Cruachain in Connacht', *JRSAI* **113** (1983), 121–42; **114** (1984), 125–38; **117** (1987), 125–41; **118** (1988), 67–84.
John Waddell, 'Excavation at "Dathi's Mound", Rathcroghan, Co. Roscommon', *Journal of Irish Archaeology* 4 (1987/8), 23–36.
Emania 5 (1988).
Gerry Kennedy, *Heritage Guide to Rathcroghan, Co. Roscommon* (Killala, 1989).
Michael Herity, *Rathcroghan and Carnfree* (Dublin, 1991).

Rathmulcah, Co. Sligo
Michael Herity, 'Rathmulcah, Ware and MacFirbisigh. The earliest antiquarian description and illustration of a profane Irish field monument', *UJA* **33** (1970), 49–53.
Francis John Byrne, 'Rathmulcah: an historical note', *JRSAI* **102** (1972), 73–6.
Nollaig Ó Muraíle, *The celebrated antiquary Dubhaltach Mac Fhirbisigh (c. 1600–1671). His lineage, life and learning* (Maynooth, 1996).

Round towers

GENERAL

Lennox Barrow, *The round towers of Ireland* (Dublin, 1979).
Brian Lalor, *The Irish round tower. Origins and architecture explored* (Cork, 1999).
Roger Stalley, *Irish round towers* (Dublin, 2000).

INDIVIDUAL SITES

Drumcliffe, Co. Sligo
Peter Harbison, *The high crosses of Ireland*, vol. 1 (Bonn, 1992), 70–4.

Killala, Co. Mayo
Thomas McDonnell, *The diocese of Killala from its institution to the end of the Penal Times* (Ballina, 1976).

Turlough, Co. Mayo
Martin J. Blake, 'Notes on the place names mentioned in Browne's map of Mayo, 1584', *JGAHS* **8** (1913–14), 39–40.

Monasteries, churches, abbeys and religious orders

GENERAL

Olive Alcock, Kathy de hÓra and Paul Gosling, *Archaeological inventory of County Galway. Volume II — North Galway* (Dublin, 1999).
Patrick Conlon, *Franciscan Ireland* (Cork, 1978).
Brian De Breffny and George Mott, *The churches and abbeys of Ireland* (London, 1976).
Aubrey Gwynn and R.N. Hadcock, *Medieval religious houses: Ireland* (London, 1970).
Britta Kalkreuter, *Boyle Abbey and the School of the West* (Bray, 2001).
Harold G. Leask, *Irish churches and monastic buildings*, 3 vols (Dundalk, 1955–60).
F.X. Martin, 'The Augustinian friaries in pre-Reformation Ireland 1282–1500', *Augustiniana* (Louvain) **6** (1956), 346–84.
Canice Mooney, 'Franciscan architecture in pre-Reformation Ireland', *JRSAI* **85** (1955), 133–73; **86** (1956), 125–69; **87** (1957), 1–38 and 103–24.
Daphne D.C. Pochin Mould, *The Irish Dominicans: the Friars Preachers in the history of Catholic Ireland* (Dublin, 1957).
Seán D. O'Reilly, *Irish churches and monasteries. An historical and architectural guide* (Cork, 1997).
R.A. Stalley, *Architecture and sculpture in Ireland 1150–1350* (Dublin, 1971).
Roger Stalley, 'A Romanesque sculptor in Connaught', *Country Life* (21 June 1973), 1826–30.
Roger Stalley, *The Cistercian monasteries of Ireland* (London/New Haven, 1987).

INDIVIDUAL SITES

Abbeyknockmoy, Co. Galway
Martin Blake, 'Knockmoy Abbey, otherwise called the Monastery of the "Hill of Victory" ', *JGAHS* **1** (1900–1), 65–84.
J.A. Glynn, 'Knockmoy abbey, County Galway', *JRSAI* **34** (1904), 239–43.
Robert Cochrane, 'Abbey Knockmoy, County Galway: notes on the buildings and "frescoes" ', *JRSAI* **34** (1904), 244–53.

J. Brenan, 'A note on Abbey Knockmoy, Co. Galway', *JRSAI* **35** (1905), 420–1.

Henry S. Crawford, 'The mural paintings and inscriptions at Knockmoy Abbey', *JRSAI* **49** (1919), 25–34.

Roger Stalley, *Irish Cistercian monasteries* (London/New Haven, 1987).

P. David Sweetman, 'Archaeological excavations at Abbeyknockmoy, Co. Galway', *PRIA* **87**C (1987), 1–12.

Athenry Abbey, Co. Galway

Martin J. Blake, 'The abbey of Athenry', *JGAHS* **2** (1902), 65–90.

R.A.S. Macalister, 'The Dominican church at Athenry', *JGAHS* **10** (1917–18), 139–55.

Ann Healy, *Athenry. A brief history and guide* (Athenry?, 1989).

Etienne Rynne, 'Athenry', in Anngret Simms and J. H. Andrews (eds), *More Irish country towns* (Cork, 1995), 106–18.

Ballindoon Abbey, Co. Sligo

Bernard Curran, *Ballindoon Abbey, being fragments collected by the Rev. Bernard Curran, O.P., of Holy Cross Sligo, 1970–71* (privately circulated, 1971).

Ballintubber Abbey, Co. Mayo

M.J. Blake, 'Ballintubber Abbey, Co. Mayo: notes on its history', *JGAHS* **2** (2) (1903–4), 65–88.

Thomas A. Egan, 'Ireland's unique abbey. The Abbey that refused to die', *Capuchin Annual* (1963), 215–34.

Thomas A. Egan, *The story of Ballintubber Abbey* (Ballintubber, 1967).

Michael Viney, '750 years of Ballintubber Abbey', *Ireland of the Welcomes* **15** (3) (September/October 1966), 10–14.

Ballymote church, Co. Sligo

James C. McDonagh, *History of Ballymote and the parish of Emlaghfad* (Dublin, 1936).

Nuala Rogers, *Ballymote. Aspects through time* (Ballymote, 1993).

Ballysadare church, Co. Sligo

W.F. Wakeman, 'Notice of the architectural peculiarities of some ancient churches in the County of Sligo', *JRSAI* **17** (1885), 43–54.

T. O'Rorke, *History, antiquities and present state of the parishes of Ballysadare and Kilvarnet, in the County of Sligo* (Dublin, 1878).

Banada/Bennada Abbey, Co. Sligo

Katherine Butler, *The story of Beneda* (c. 1983).

C.J. Lynn, 'Some 13th-century castle sites in the west of Ireland: note on a preliminary reconnaissance', *JGAHS* **40** (1985–6), 95–8.

Máire McDonnell-Garvey, 'Benada Abbey, a short history', *The Corran Herald* **32** (1999/2000), 9–12.

Boyle Abbey, Co. Roscommon

G.M. Hills, *Boyle Abbey and the architecture of the Cistercian abbeys of Ireland* (no date).

P.A. Sharkey, *The heart of Ireland* (Boyle, no date), 104–40.

H.A. Wheeler, *Boyle Abbey, Boyle, Co. Roscommon. A short descriptive and historical account* (no date).

Roger Stalley, *The Cistercian monasteries of Ireland* (London/New Haven, 1987).

Roger Stalley, 'Saint Bernard, his views on architecture and the Irish dimension', *Arte Medievale* II Serie, **VIII** (1), tomo 2 (1994), 13–19.

Britta Kalkreuter, *Boyle Abbey and the School of the West* (Bray, 2001).

Burrishoole Abbey, Co. Mayo

M. O Donnell, *Burrishoole Abbey* (Dublin, 1929).

Pádraig Ó Moráin, *Annála Beaga pharáiste Bhuiréis Umhaill: a short account of the history of Burrishoole parish* (1957).

Christiaan Corlett, *Antiquities of west Mayo* (Bray, 2001), 81 and 88.

Church Island, Lough Gill, Co. Sligo

John O'Donovan, *Annals of the Kingdom of Ireland by the Four Masters* (2nd edn), vol. IV (Dublin, 1856), 828–9, s.a. 1417.

Clones, Co. Monaghan

W.F. Wakeman, 'On the ecclesiastical antiquities of Cluain Eois, now Clones, County Monaghan', *JRSAI* **13** (1874/5), 327–40.

Peter Harbison, *The high crosses of Ireland*, vol. 1 (Bonn, 1992), 47.

Clonmacnois, Co. Offaly

John Ryan, *Clonmacnois. A historical summary* (Dublin, 1873).

John Corkery, *Cluan Chiaráin — the city of Ciaran* (Longford, *c.* 1979).

Conleth Manning, *Clonmacnoise* (Dublin, 1994).

Annette Kehnel, *Clonmacnois — the church and lands of St Ciaran. Change and continuity in an Irish monastic foundation (6th to 16th century)*. Vita Regularis 8 (Münster, Westphalia, 1997).

Heather A. King (ed.), *Clonmacnoise Studies, Vol. 1. Seminar Papers 1994* (Dublin, 1998).

Cong Abbey, Co. Mayo

Dr Healy, 'Two royal abbeys by the western lakes — Cong and Inismaine', *JRSAI* **35** (1905), 1–20.

John Neary, *Notes on Cong and the Neale* (Dundalk, 1938).

H.G. Leask, 'The Augustinian Abbey of St Mary the Virgin, Cong, Co. Mayo', *JGAHS* **19** (1941), 107–17.

J.A. Fahy, *The glory of Cong* (Cong, 1960).

Devenish, Co. Fermanagh

W.F. Wakeman, 'The antiquities of Devenish', *JRSAI* **12** (1872–3), 59–94.

J.E. McKenna, *Devenish (Lough Erne): its history and antiquities* (*c.* 1931).

C.A.R. Radford, 'Devenish', *UJA* **33** (1970), 55–62.

Ann Hamlin, *Devenish*. Guide Card (Belfast, 1979).

Alistair Rowan, *North-west Ulster*. The Buildings of Ireland (Harmondsworth, 1979), 232–5.

A. Hamlin, 'Devenish', in A. Hamlin and C. Lynn (eds), *Pieces of the past* (Belfast, 1988), 52–4.

E.G. Elliott, *The parish of Devenish and Boho* (Belfast, 1990).
Colm J. Donnelly, *Living places* (Belfast, 1997), 53–6.

Dromahair, Co. Leitrim — Abbey and O'Rourke's Hall
J.E. MacKenna, 'The Franciscan friary of Creevelea, in the Barony of Breffny, Co. Leitrim', *UJA*, 2nd ser., **V** (1899), 190–201.
Henry S. Crawford, 'Carvings in the cloisters of Creevelea Abbey, Co. Leitrim', *JRSAI* **46** (1916), 177–9.
Anon., *Creevelea Abbey, Co. Leitrim*. Official guide book (Dublin, no date).
Rosemary Kerrigan and Jack Kerrigan, *A signposted walking tour of Dromahaire* (Dromahaire, 1990).
Proinnsíos O Duigneáin, *Dromahaire. Story and pictures* (Manorhamilton, 1990).

Dunmore, Co. Galway
J. Neary, 'On the history and antiquities of the parish of Dunmore', *JGAHS* **8** (1913–14), 100–1.

Ennismacreeny or Ennismacreedy/Church Island, Lough Key, Co. Roscommon
Heather King, 'Church Island, Lough Key', in Isabel Bennett (ed.), *Excavations 2000: summary accounts of archaeological excavations in Ireland* (Bray, 2002), 294, no. 860.

Inishmaine/Killemanain, Co. Mayo
Dr Healy, 'Two royal abbeys by the western lakes — Cong and Inismaine', *JRSAI* **35** (1905), 1–20.

Inishmurray, Co. Sligo
W.F. Wakeman, *A survey of the antiquarian remains on the island of Inishmurray* (London/Edinburgh, 1893).
Catríona MacLeod, 'Some mediaeval wooden figure sculptures in Ireland. Statues of Irish saints', *JRSAI* **76** (1946), particularly pp 158–61.
Patrick Heraughty, *Inismurray: ancient monastic island* (Dublin, 1982; reprinted 1996).
Fergus O'Farrell, 'The Inishmurray statue of St Molaise: a re-assessment', in Etienne Rynne (ed.), *Figures from the past. Studies on figurative art in Christian Ireland* (Dun Laoghaire, 1987), 205–8.
Denis Molaise Meehan, *Molaise of Inismurray* (Tralee, 1989).
Charles James Roy, *Islands of storm — Eileán annraidh: Inishmurray, Iona, Inishkea North* (Dublin, 1991).
Joe McGowan, *Inishmurray, gale, stone and fire. Portrait of a fabled island* (Sligo, 1998).
Jerry O'Sullivan, Niamh Connolly, Don Cotton and Marie Heraughty, *Innismurray. An island off Sligo.* Heritage Guide No. 18. Supplement to *Archaeology Ireland* **16** (2) (Summer 2002).

Kells, Co. Meath
Helen M. Roe, *The high crosses of Kells* (Dublin, 1958).
J.H. Andrews and Anngret Simms, *Kells*. Irish Historic Towns Atlas No. 4 (Dublin, 1990).
Leo Swan, 'The Market Cross, Kells, Co. Meath', *Ríocht na Midhe* **9** (4) (1998), 49–55.

Kilconnell, Co. Galway
Sir Thomas N. Deane, 'Report on Kilconnel Abbey', *47th Annual Report of the Commissioners of Public Works in Ireland* (Dublin, 1879).

Francis Joseph Bigger, 'The Franciscan friary of Kilconnell', *JGAHS* **1** (1900–1), 145–67; **2** (1902), 3–20; **3** (1903–4), 11–15.
Tadhg MacLochlainn, *The parish of Aughrim and Kilconnell* (1980).

Moyne Abbey, Co. Mayo
Canice Mooney, 'The Franciscans in County Mayo', *JGAHS* **28** (1858), 43–52.

Multyfarnham, Co. Westmeath
Harold G. Leask, 'The Abbey buildings in medieval times', *Franciscan College Annual, Multyfarnham* (June 1950), 6–15.
Pádraig O Gibealláin, *Multyfarnham Abbey. Monuments and memories* (Multyfarnham, 1984).
Pádraig O Gibealláin, *Multyfarnham. The Abbey restored* (Multyfarnham, *c.* 1980).
Richard Hurley and Wilfrid Cantwell, *Contemporary Irish church architecture* (Dublin, 1985), 98–9.
Peter Wallace, *Multyfarnham parish history* (Multyfarnham, 1987).

Murrisk Abbey, Co. Mayo
H.G. Leask, 'Murrisk Abbey, Co. Mayo', *JRSAI* **73** (1943), 137–41 (see also **74** (1944), 87).
Pádraig O'Moráin, *500 years in the history of Murrisk Abbey, 1457–1957.* Reprinted from *Mayo News*, 7 and 14 September 1957 (National Library copy annotated).

Roscommon Abbey, Co. Roscommon
Anon., 'Roscommon', *JRSAI* **37** (1907), 341–6.
Henry S. Crawford, 'The O'Connor tomb in Roscommon Abbey', *JRSAI* **54** (1924), 89–90.
John Hunt, *Irish medieval figure sculpture*, vol. 1 (London, 1974), 216–18.

Rosserk Abbey, Co. Mayo
Canice Mooney, 'The Franciscans in County Mayo', *JGAHS* **28** (1958), 59–60.

Sligo Abbey, Co. Sligo
Henry S. Crawford, 'The carved altar and mural monuments in Sligo Abbey', *JRSAI* **51** (1925), 17–31.
Anon., *Mainistir Shligigh. Sligo Abbey. Historical and descriptive notes on the Dominican friary of Sligo* (Dublin, *c.* 1968).

Strade Abbey, Co. Mayo
Canice Mooney, 'The Franciscans in County Mayo', *JGAHS* **28** (1958–9), 42–3.
John Hunt, *Irish medieval figure sculpture*, vol. 1 (London, 1974), 201–2.

Tristernagh Abbey, Co. Westmeath
Maud V. Clarke, *Registrum cartarum monasterii B.V. Mariae de Tristernagh. Registry of the Priory of the Blessed Virgin Mary at Tristernagh* (Dublin, 1941).
Elizabeth Hickey, 'Some notes on Kilbixy, Tristernagh and Temple Cross, and the family of Piers who lived in the Abbey of Tristernagh in Westmeath', *Ríocht na Midhe* 7 (1980–1), 52–75.

228 OUR TREASURE OF ANTIQUITIES

Tulsk Abbey, Co. Roscommon

Kieran O'Conor, Mark Keegan and Padraig Tiernan, 'Tulsk Abbey', *Co. Roscommon Historical and Archaeological Journal* **6** (1996), 67–9.

Maurice Craig and Michael Craig, *Mausolea Hibernica* (Dublin, 1999).

Castles

GENERAL

Brian De Breffny, *Castles of Ireland* (London, 1977).

Plantagenet Somerset Fry, *Castles of Britain and Ireland* (Newtown Abbot, 1996).

H.G. Leask, *Irish castles and castellated houses* (Dundalk, 1941).

C.J. Lynn, 'Some 13th-century castle sites in the west of Ireland: note on a preliminary reconnaissance', *JGAHS* **40** (1985–6), 90–113.

Tom McNeill, *Castles in Ireland. Feudal power in a Gaelic world* (London, 1997).

Wolfgang Metternich, *Burgen in Irland. Herrschaftsarchitektur im Hochmittelalter* (Darmstadt, 1999).

Mike Salter, *Castles and stronghouses of Ireland* (Malvern, 1993).

Terence Reeves-Smyth, *Irish castles* (Belfast, 1995).

David Sweetman, *The medieval castles of Ireland* (Cork, 1999).

INDIVIDUAL SITES

Athenry (Birmingham) Castle, Co. Galway

H.T. Knox, 'The Bermingham family and Athenry', *JGAHS* **10** (1917–18), 139–55.

H.T. Knox *et al.,* 'Notes on the Burgus of Athenry. Its first defences and its town walls', *JGAHS* **11** (1920–1), 1–26 (see also **14** (1928–9), 77–9).

Ann Healy, *Athenry. A brief history and guide* ((?) Athenry, 1989).

Cliona Papazian, 'Excavations at Athenry Castle, Co. Galway', *JGAHS* **43** (1991), 1–45.

Avril Thomas, *The walled towns of Ireland,* vol. 2 (Blackrock, 1992), 8–13.

Etienne Rynne, 'Athenry', in Anngret Simms and J.H. Andrews (eds), *More Irish country towns* (Cork 1995), 106–18.

Conleth Manning, 'Low-level roofs in Irish great towers', *Château-Gaillard* **20** (forthcoming).

Ballinafad Castle, Co. Sligo

D.M. Waterman, 'Some Irish seventeenth-century houses and their architectural ancestry', in E.M. Jope (ed.), *Studies in building history. Essays in recognition of the work of B.H. St. J. ONeil* (London, 1961), 270–2.

Paul M. Kerrigan, 'Seventeenth century fortifications, forts and garrisons in Ireland: a preliminary list', *The Irish Sword* **14** (1980), 147.

Paul Kerrigan, *Castles and fortifications in Ireland 1485–1945* (Cork, 1995), 64.

Ballintober Castle, Co. Roscommon

The Right Hon. O'Conor Don, 'Ballintubber Castle, County Roscommon', *JRSAI* **19** (1889), 24–30.

Robert Percy McDonnell, *Ballintubber Castle* (reprint from *The Roscommon Messenger, c.* 1913).

John A. Claffey, 'Ballintubber Castle, Co. Roscommon', *Journal of the Old Athlone Society* 1 (3) (1972–3), 143–6.

Ballymote Castle, Co. Sligo

J.E. FitzPatrick, 'Ballymote Castle', *JRSAI* 57 (1927), 81–99.

James C. MacDonagh, *History of Ballymote and the parish of Emlaghfad* (Dublin, 1936).

P.D. Sweetman, 'Archaeological excavations at Ballymote Castle, Co. Sligo', *JGAHS* 40 (1985–6), 114–24.

Nuala Rogers, *Balllymote. Aspects through time* (Ballymote, 1993).

Claddagh Castle, Co. Galway

Olive Alcock, Kathy de hÓra and Paul Gosling, *Archaeological inventory of County Galway. Volume II — North Galway* (Dublin, 1999), 403, no. 3928.

Enniskillen Castle, Co. Fermanagh

Alistair Rowan, *North-west Ulster.* The Buildings of Ireland (Harmondsworth, 1979), 279–80.

Hugh Dixon and John Johnston, *Enniskillen Castle, County Fermanagh.* Guide Card (Belfast, 1980).

Rinndoon, Co. Roscommon

J.E. Fitzpatrick, 'Rinndown Castle, County Roscommon: with a comparison of the systems of fortification used in Ireland in the 12th and 13th centuries', *JRSAI* 65 (1935), 177–90.

John A. Claffey, 'Medieval Rindoon', *Journal of the Old Athlone Society* 2 (5) (1978), 11–14.

Sheelagh Harbison, 'Rindown Castle: a royal fortress in Co. Roscommon', *JGAHS* 47 (1995), 138–48.

Roscommon Castle, Co. Roscommon

Denis Murphy, 'The castle of Roscommon', *JRSAI* 21 (1891), 546–56.

Anon., 'Roscommon', *JRSAI* 37 (1907), 341–6.

Robert Percy McDonnell, *Roscommon Castle* (reprinted from *The Roscommon Messenger c.* 1913).

HOUSES

Mark Bence-Jones, *Burke's Guide to Country Houses. Volume 1. Ireland* (London, 1978).

The Marquess of Sligo, *Westport House and the Brownes* (Ashbourne, Derbyshire, 1981).

INDEX